INSTRUCTIONAL MESSAGE DESIGN
Principles from the Behavioral Sciences

instructional message design

principles from the behavioral sciences

malcolm fleming and w. howard levie
INDIANA UNIVERSITY

EDUCATIONAL TECHNOLOGY PUBLICATIONS
ENGLEWOOD CLIFFS, NEW JERSEY 07632

Library of Congress Cataloging in Publication Data

Fleming, Malcolm L
    Instructional message design.

    Bibliography: p.
    Includes index.
    1. Lesson planning. I. Levie, W. Howard, joint
author. II. Title.
LB1027.F584   371.3   77-26089
ISBN 0-87778-104-4

Library of Congress Catalog Card Number:
77-26089.

International Standard Book Number:
0-87778-104-4.

First Printing: February, 1978.

DEDICATION:

TO

R & D

PREFACE

Our purpose in this book is to narrow the gap between research and practice in instructional message design.

The research we are talking about is not research that has dealt with message design per se. Very little such research has been done. We are talking about research from selected areas in the behavioral sciences; in particular, the areas of perception, memory, concept formation, and attitude change. We have attempted to maximize the usefulness of this research by offering sets of generalizations stated as principles. The principles are: (1) based upon empirical evidence, (2) selected for their relevance to practical message design problems, and (3) expressed in non-technical language. Further, numerous examples for practice are offered.

We do not treat the step-by-step process of instructional message design. We do, however, assume the reader has a basic familiarity with procedures for analyzing learners and subject matter, stating objectives, evaluating outcomes, and other techniques involved in the scientific design of instruction. We believe that these systematic and self-correcting processes are necessary. But they are not sufficient. Analysis of a problem is a necessary but not sufficient basis for synthesis of a remedy. Given that the dimensions of an instructional problem have been defined and analyzed, what do you do next? That is the arena of our concern! Moving from well-defined problems to effective solutions through the application of research-based principles.

There is no necessary order in which this book should be read. A practicing professional can access relevant principles by first deciding which cognitive process is primarily involved in the instructional problem: perception, memory, concept formation, or attitude change. Then reference to the appropriate sub-heading within each chapter should produce pertinent information. Other users may find a straight-through reading better.

We believe that the book will be useful to practitioners and students who (1) work in a particular medium such as television, photography, graphics, or print; (2) are involved in designing messages in a variety of media; or (3) are broadly concerned with instructional design—instructional developers and classroom teachers as examples.

Consistent with the design process we espouse, all users are urged to send evaluative feedback regarding the design and utility of this book to the authors. Fleming is basically responsible for the chapters on perception, memory, and concept formation. Levie is responsible for the chapter on attitude change.

The authors acknowledge their debt to the large number of investigators and smaller number of reviewers from whose findings and generalizations we have selected the substance upon which the principles are based. They are the discoverers and summarizers, we are the translators and disseminators. We acknowledge as well our debt to the reviewers of an early draft of Chapter 1 (R.N. Haber, J.E. Kemp, S.M. Markle, and R.W. Wagner) and to the generations of university students in our design course who have provided constructive feedback to make the following chapters more readable and relevant.

Malcolm Fleming
W. Howard Levie

Bloomington, Indiana
March, 1977

INTRODUCTION

Glaser suggests the nature of the problem that gave rise to this book:

> The experimental psychology of learning and cognition has been almost exclusively a theoretical endeavor, with little effort devoted to application and the design of practical techniques for assisting in the conduct of human affairs (1976, p.11).

In this brief introduction we hope to provide a gestalt of the arena of human affairs with which we are concerned, and to suggest ways in which the principles we offer can be applied to this arena.

What Is Instructional Message Design?

A "message" is a pattern of signs (words and pictures) produced for the purpose of modifying the cognitive, affective, or psychomotor behavior of one or more persons. The term does not imply any particular medium or vehicle of communication.

"Design" refers to a deliberate process of analysis and synthesis that begins with a communications problem and concludes with a plan for an operational solution. The process of design is separate from the execution process. That is, message design is conceptually distinct from the eventual act or event of communication or instruction.

However, message design can occur contemporaneously with the act of instruction. Gagné (1965) distinguishes between predesign and extemporaneous design. Teachers typically do both, that is, they plan instruction ahead of time (predesign) and they also modify it during execution (extemporaneous design). Research on instruction has examined both kinds of designs, e.g., programmed instruction (PI) variables (predesign) and alternative teacher moves and strategies (extemporaneous design). Principles from both lines of inquiry are included in this book so long as they are not specific to one mediator (PI or teacher). However, the book is written primarily in the spirit of predesign, for predesign permits more careful consideraton of more factors at the time of decision and permits pre-testing, evaluation, and re-design.

"Instruction," as used here, will refer not only to relatively formal classroom contexts in which the acquisition of particular skills and concepts is central, but also will include much of what the term "communication" implies, including informal contexts of diverse types, typically self-selected, in which attitudes and emotions may be strongly implicated. This broadening of the definition of instruction is partly for convenience and partly to suggest that many of the concerns of communication scholars are pertinent to the classroom, especially where instruction is being individualized and open classrooms are being developed.

"Instruction" is a function performed by teachers, materials, and other mediators, while "learning" is done by students (we shall optimistically call them "learners"). The functioning designer is frequently outside the final interaction that takes place between mediator and learner. She/he can influence it only indirectly. While instruction is intended to provide the *conditions* for learning, it never provides learning. This is made explicit in the following excerpt from Engelmann (1969).

> ... the teacher changes the learner only through the manipulation of environmental variables. He presents stimuli. He talks, he praises, he shows things to the learner, he requires responses. Only through the manipulation of environmental variables can he produce change ... we must express learning in such a way that we can produce it. This means that the focus is on what we do—how we manipulate the environmental variables to produce desired changes (pp. 7-8).

Thus, what a designer can do is limited to the manipulation of environmental variables, or as we have conceived it, the manipulation (choice and arrangement) of message variables.

Accordingly, "Instructional Message Design" refers to the process of manipulating, or planning for the manipulation of, a pattern of signs and symbols that may provide the conditions for learning. Our assumption is that practitioners in this domain can be more effective if they make use of appropriate generalized research findings from the behavioral sciences. These generalizations are expressed in this book as "principles."

How Can Behavioral Science Principles Be Applied to Instructional Message Design?

How can abstract principles be applied to concrete instructional problems? One means of facilitating this transfer is to state both propositions (both the principle and the problem) in parallel forms. This form can be generalized as: What *conditions* lead to what *results*?

Most principles in this book are stated in this form. For example, a well-known principle is, "Where reinforcing stimuli are presented (the condition), the preceding response will tend to be repeated or learned (the result)." Another useful principle is, "Novelty (a condition of instructional stimuli) attracts attention (a result)." Such principles summarize the outcomes of research which has examined the relation between experimental stimuli (conditions) and responses (results). As summaries of numerous controlled "experiences," such principles are likely to be more reliable than one designer's experience.

Most design questions can also be stated in this form: What instruction (conditions) will lead to the desired learning (result)? For example, the objective, "The learner will be able to distinguish experiments from non-experiments," translates into the design question, "Which instructional conditions will teach the learner to distinguish experiments from non-experiments?"

Answers to this question are contingent upon answers to a series of other questions, such as the following:

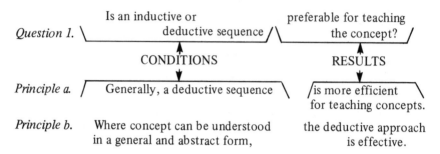

Question 1.
Is an inductive or deductive sequence
CONDITIONS
preferable for teaching the concept?
RESULTS

Principle a. Generally, a deductive sequence   is more efficient for teaching concepts.

Principle b. Where concept can be understood   the deductive approach
in a general and abstract form,   is effective.

NOTE: The answer to question #1 is a decision based on matching relevant principles, e.g., a and b.

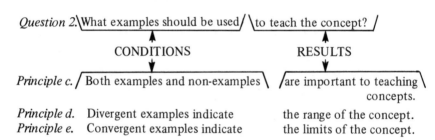

Question 2. What examples should be used to teach the concept?
CONDITIONS   RESULTS

Principle c. Both examples and non-examples   are important to teaching concepts.

Principle d. Divergent examples indicate   the range of the concept.
Principle e. Convergent examples indicate   the limits of the concept.

NOTE: Answers to question #2 are based on matching relevant principles, e.g., c-e.

Some words of caution are necessary at this point. Despite the utility of research-based principles matched in form to design questions, the reader will frequently not find clear-cut or easy answers to design problems. The complexity of practical instructional problems is far greater than can be adequately encompassed by present-day research-based principles of human behavior, and many of the instructional designer's problems have not been investigated scientifically. Adherence to the procedures and principles offered in this book will not automatically result in better learning, and these ideas are not offered as substitutes for experience and creativity. It is hoped, however, that this information may guide the insightful designer to analyze problems from more than one point of view, and may suggest effective solutions which might otherwise have been overlooked. The message designer who has a richer understanding of the diversity of factors which influence human behavior should, at minimum, be less prone to unjustified confidence in his/her ability to communicate with unerring fidelity, and at best, be able to avoid some communication errors.

Thus, because of the uncertainties implicit in the application of research and because of the inadequate scope of present research, the authors strongly recommend that every application suggested or inspired by these principles be tested and validated with reference to the constraints of each situation. This is entirely consistent with contemporary models of the design process, which include formative evaluation during design and development and summative evaluation of the final product (material, method, medium). Quite probably, the designer will learn more from the field evaluations of his/her product than from our principles, but the principles may at least provide a conceptual framework within which she/he can better examine, interpret, and remember the results of each design experience.

Finally, lest the reader think science has, in our opinion, replaced artistry and intuition in message design, we must make it amply clear that while our principles can inform the creativity of designer/teachers, they do not replace or lessen the need for innovation in instruction.

References

Engelmann, S., *Conceptual Learning.* San Rafael, California: Dimensions Publishing Co., 1969.

Gagné, R.M., *The Conditions of Learning.* New York: Holt, Rinehart, and Winson, Inc., 1965.

Glaser, R. Components of a psychology of instruction: Toward a science of design. *Review of Educational Research,* 1976, *46,* 1-24.

TABLE OF CONTENTS

INSTRUCTIONAL MESSAGE DESIGN
Principles from the Behavioral Sciences

Chapter 1
PERCEPTION PRINCIPLES

The study of perception deals with the ways in which we sense or become immediately aware of our environment. Perception is a complex process by which we receive or extract information from this environment. It is considered to be a stage in cognition, along with others, such as learning, concept formation, problem solving, and thinking. Being one of the earliest stages in cognition, perception has an important influence on the others. Reciprocally, the other cognitive processes markedly influence perception. For example, prior learning influences how we perceive.

Fundamentally, perception principles are pertinent because the learner, in the reception of instruction, perceives before s/he learns; and, in the view of this chapter, those perceptions set important limits and conditions on what s/he learns. There is little merit in applying learning principles to what has not been accurately selected out of the stimulus array nor given adequate perceptual processing.

Although the study of perception includes a variety of senses, such as touch, taste, smell, sense of balance, and muscle sense, the following will dwell almost entirely on vision and audition, the two senses of greatest interest to the instructional message designer.

There are several reasons for the designer to know and apply perceptual principles:

1. In general, the better an object or person, event, or

relationship is perceived, the better it can be remembered (Berelson and Steiner, 1964).

2. It is important in instruction to avoid misperceptions. If a student misperceives the intent or content of a paragraph or film sequence, s/he may also misunderstand it or may learn something false or irrelevant.

3. Where it is desirable in instruction to replace the real world with some substitute or surrogate, such as a photograph or drawing, it is important to know how to represent that reality adequately for perceptual purposes (Hochberg, 1966).

This chapter begins with a discussion of five basic principles which appear to underly many of the numerous additional principles in later sections. Following this are a series of three sections dealing sequentially with the perception process, from initial attention to the detection of visual and auditory elements, and finally to the perceptual construction of figures (objects, words, pictures). Then a section examines principles of perceptual capacity, single and two-channel. Finally, several sections consider the perceptual antecedents of concept learning and the specific problems of perceiving size, distance, space, time, and motion. In all sections are numerous suggestions for applying the principles to the design of instruction.

Basic Principles*

While it is frequently impossible to predict reliably what an individual will perceive in a given situation, it is possible to consider some of the major ways in which perceptions will vary and some of the conditions under which they will vary. Knowing

*The Perception Chapter is an extensively revised and updated version of a report, *Perceptual Principles for the Design of Instructional Materials,* written by Malcolm Fleming under a grant from U.S. Office of Education, Bureau of Research, Project 9-E-001. Final report (1970) available as ERIC Document # Ed 037 093.

some of the regularities of perception, the message designer can arrange conditions of stimulation that are consistent with the perceiver's general tendencies. This is another way of asserting a basic assumption of the book. The more a communicator knows about an audience, the more effective s/he is apt to be with that audience.

What follows in this section is a rather sketchy portrait of the human perceiver. It is simply an outline drawing intended to reveal several general aspects. Subsequent sections will add some of the fascinating details as well as expose some of the remaining puzzles.

1.1. *Perception is relative rather than absolute, aotbe.* *

When estimating size, brightness, or loudness, we are not scientific instruments. A piece of paper perceived as "white" in sunlight will also be perceived as "white" in moonlight. Although its absolute brightness is vastly different, it reflects the same percent of the available light. That is, its *relative* brightness, which is the same in both cases, is what is perceived. Size judgments are relative to the perceived distance between object and observer. The perceived loudness of a chord in a music track will be relative to the just-preceding level of sound.

We cannot estimate reliably the number of pounds an unfamiliar object weighs nor the exact speed of a passing car, but we can very well judge the *relative* weights of a number of objects and the *relative* speeds of cars. One object will tend to become a standard and the others rated as lighter, much heavier, or about the same as the standard; faster, slower, or about the same speed as the standard.

*Aotbe means all other things being equal. It means that the preceding statement holds under controlled research conditions but may well vary in applied situations, i.e., other factors may reduce or nullify its effect. Though "aotbe" holds for every numbered guideline in this book, it will appear only at the first of each chapter as a reminder to the reader.

    1.1a.   *Perceived levels of stimulation are relative to concurrent experience or to immediate past experience which serves as an anchor or reference point in judging subsequent stimulation.*

A familiar example is the perceived scene-to-scene brightness of a film or the brightness of successive slides. The first few scenes or slides, whether light or dark, set a reference point for judging succeeding scenes or slides as relatively light or dark. Thus, the absolute brightness of the series, within limits, becomes less important than the scene-to-scene uniformity.

    1.1b.   *Where immediate past experience is at a high level, new stimulation may be underestimated; where immediate past experience is at a low level, new stimulation may be overestimated.*

This is another way of saying that the initial impact of a change in stimulation level is greater than shortly thereafter. We squint when the lights go on after a projection; we shiver on first entering the swimming pool.

This phenomenon is well known in the communication realm. The dramatic pause heightens the effect of the first words to follow; a large white space may add punch to a small figure in the corner of an advertisement.

The very principle of perceptual relativity can be used by the designer to control or increase the predictability of the audience's perceptions. For example, the perceptions of the reader of a book or the viewer of television are relative to the just finished part of the book or program. Because the designer knows a great deal about these immediate past perceptions, s/he can design the next page or scene accordingly. The writer of self-instructional programs is even better informed, for s/he knows in detail the sequence of prior perceptions as reflected in prior responses. Hence, s/he can more reliably predict the readiness of the learner to correctly perceive the next frame.

There are many other relativities in perception—how one feels, what one is seeking, what other people think. The notion of perceptual relativity is pervasive and will be encountered again in what follows.

However, the designer should not leave this section with the view that it implies either that our perceptions are unreliable or that they are so changeable as to be unpredictable. The fact is that, in spite of a very large number of studies that demonstrate the relativity of perception, our senses, aided by our past experiences, prove in practice to be highly reliable and serviceable to our needs.

> *1.2. Perception is very selective. We attend to only a few of the sights, sounds, and smells available to us in our environment at any one time.*

It follows that the designer who can predict what the audience will selectively perceive in a message will be the most successful. S/he will know what aspects of the message will need to be accentuated to gain attention and which will need to be removed or de-emphasized to prevent distraction.

> *1.2a. Selective perception is in part dynamic, i.e., it depends on what we have learned about a situation, what we at any moment want or feel an interest in, and what our general perceptual tendencies are.*

The poet's perception of cloud formations differs from the meteorologist's. Each selects the attributes of clouds that are familiar, that are seen as relevant to interests and needs. Perceptual selectivity is of two types, exposure and awareness, and the designer will deal differently with each.

Directing the gaze, inclining the ear, extending the finger tips involves choice—a choice to attend to some aspects of the environment and not to attend to others. This has been called "selective *exposure.*" The designer's audience may selectively expose itself to other messages, such as a fellow student's conversation, instead of to the available instruction. Outside the classroom the competition is still keener between available messages looking for an audience, especially messages from those with ideas, goods, and services to sell. There will be more about the designer's struggle for the attention of an audience in the next section.

After a perceiver has chosen to be exposed to a message, s/he may only become aware of a small portion of it, at least at any one time. This is "selective *awareness.*" Of the many words on this page which are imaged on the viewer's retina, only a very few are in awareness at any time. Concurrently, other senses are receiving stimulation: the weight and feel of the book, the temperature of the room, perhaps a distant radio. Awareness thus involves selection both within and between senses. The designer's message may even be in competition with itself, for there may be more information in the message than the audience can attend to and process in the available time or interest span. That is, our perceptual processes have limited capacities.

> *1.2b.   Selective perception is in part physical, i.e., each input channel has load limits, and the total information processing capacity from all inputs is limited. The stimulus potential of the environment is great, but the perceiver can attend to only a limited amount at a time.*

It can thus be said that we do not so much decide to be selective as that we are physically incapable of doing otherwise, i.e., of attending to more than a fraction of the information available to us at any one moment. It is a common experience of people who walk the same street each day that they still find objects and details of objects which they never noticed before.

The limitation in the amount of information we can process at one time is usually not serious so long as there is time to examine more aspects of the situation. Over time many sights and sounds along that street become familiar and require only a passing glance, i.e., minimum information processing.

The lessons for the designer are double edged; s/he must not exceed the perceptual capacities of the audience, but neither can s/he allow those capacities to be so underemployed that a more stimulating message will be selected.

The problem of channel capacity is very complex and still being intensively investigated. The capacity problem is particularly acute in fixed-paced (designer-paced) messages such as television, film, and audio recordings. In contrast, books and programmed materials permit the learner to keep input well within channel and processing capacities. Capacity problems are given more attention in the section on Perceptual Capacity.

It is important for the designer to remember that the problem of controlling perceptual selectivity includes both that of controlling attention *within* a channel, e.g., between visual elements, and that of controlling attention *between* channels, e.g., between visual and auditory stimuli. The options also influence overall perceptual capacity, as we shall see in that section.

> *1.3.   Perception is organized. We do not generally perceive chaotic arrays of different brightnesses, colors, temperatures, and noises. Rather, we perceptually construct relationships, groupings, objects, events, words, and people.*

Without organized perceptions, we could scarcely cope with the environment. Organized perceptions provide the stability, order, pattern, and predictability necessary to normal functioning.

Organization is in part determined by the characteristics of the given stimulus and in part by what the perceiver chooses to impose upon or construct out of the stimulus. We shall consider the stimulus determined part here.

1.3a.   The organization (spatial or temporal) of a stimulus markedly influences the speed and accuracy of perception.

The designer needs to know how different kinds of stimulus organization affect the perception of the audience. For this purpose the Gestalt "laws" of perceptual organization, though quite general, will provide some clues. Two of these laws follow; some of the others will be considered in later sections.

1.3b.   The first and perhaps the simplest perceptual organization is that of "figure and ground."

Within a fraction of a second, the visual system organizes the field into one or more figures which appear to stand out against a background or ground. Similarly, sounds are divided into figure and ground, e.g., concert music as figure and sound of air conditioner as ground.

Good figures are readily perceived, hence the designer will want the important elements in messages to be perceived as figures, whether they be visual or auditory, pictorial or verbal* (see Figure 1.1). Some of the characteristics of good figures are considered in the section on Perceiving Figures: Objects, Pictures, and Words.

1.3c.   Stimulus figures that are incomplete may be completed by the perceiver. This is called "closure," for the perceiver closes or completes what are objectively open or incomplete figures.

This, is further evidence of the perceiver's need for organized perceptions. In the final analysis any organization is preferable to none.

*The term "verbal," as used here, refers to printed as well as spoken words. We can communicate verbally and nonverbally in both sensory modalities.

Studying Noun Clauses

You have learned that a dependent clause may be used as an *adjective* or as an *adverb*. Dependent clauses may also be used as *nouns*. A dependent clause that is used as a noun is called a **noun clause.**

The second sentence in each of the pairs of sentences below illustrates how noun clauses may be used in a sentence. Study the examples silently. Be prepared to discuss them with your teacher and your fellow students.

Noun Clause as a Subject

1. The committee *reports* were fascinating.
2. *What the committees reported* was fascinating.

Noun Clause as a Predicate Nominative

1. One committee suggestion was a *panel discussion.*
2. One committee suggestion was *that the class hold a panel*

Figure 1.1. Each paragraph and each italicized word is a "good figure." Both facilitate selection and organization by the perceiver. Titles give a "set" for what follows; the second paragraph gives a set for studying the examples. (From Wolfe, Josephine B., and Ryan, Thomas A., *English Your Language, Book 8,* Copyright © 1964 Allyn and Bacon, Inc. Reprinted by permission of Allyn and Bacon, Inc.)

In a way, this simplifies the designer's task. S/he can leave figures incomplete, just sketches or outline drawings, and the audience will close or complete them. There is certainly abundant evidence that the barest of figural representations are accurately perceived. Cases in point are the road signs for a turn or winding road, or stick figures for people and their actions. Also, verbal statements can imply, suggest, or outline rather than state in full.

However, there are risks in the above as a general strategy, especially where the situation is unfamiliar or ambiguous, for perceivers may then impose their own organization on the situation, "improving," simplifying, or reorganizing as desired. The result may be a misperception of the designer's intent.

The designer's choices are simple: organize the message, or realize that each perceiver will impose his/her own organization upon the message. (S/he may anyway.)

Other principles dealing with the stimulus control of perceptual organization are treated in subsequent sections.

1.3d. *Perceptual organization is affected not only by the stimulus but by the perceiver's past experiences, present interests, and needs.*

There may be many situations where the designer should permit or encourage a diversity of perceptual organizations. An example would be where inquiry methods of instruction were being employed.

The designer otherwise is responsible for arranging conditions which facilitate the desired perceptual organization. In the case of a lengthy message or a connected series of messages, s/he has some influence over the perceiver's immediate past experience as well as the perceiver's present interests and needs. Hence, s/he has some additional means of influencing organization.

1.4. *Perception is strongly affected by what we expect or are "set" to perceive. This influences both what we select and how we organize and interpret it.*

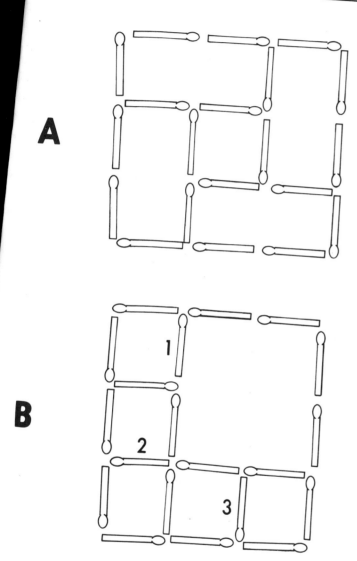

Figure 1.2. *Match puzzle (A).* Change 4 rectangles and 1 square to 6 squares by moving only 3 matches. *Solution (B).* Matches 1, 2, and 3 have been moved.

The influence of set is pervasive in the perceptual process, i.e., it can determine what in the environment is sought, what is selected, how it is organized, and how it is categorized or interpreted (see Figure 1.1).

Message designers who can control the set of their audience are more likely to achieve their purpose. A set to perceive in a certain way can be induced by instructions given the perceiver and by characteristics of the stimulus (Murch, 1973). For example, when the first chapter of a book begins with a brief synopsis and ends with a series of questions, one expects the subsequent chapters to be similarly patterned. A film that begins with a crisis or problem is expected to deal thereafter with the causes, the consequences, the resolution, or all three. What is stated in a caption or narration for a filmstrip provides a very strong set for interpreting the accompanying picture. The TV teacher's instructions provide a set as to what to look for and also a set for liking or disliking what follows.

1.4a. ***The presence and strength of a set (or sets) can influence the number of alternative interpretations which are likely, and can encourage either convergent or divergent thinking.***

It can be very useful to think of the design process as one of controlling the amount and kind of information available, or more particularly, of exercising some control of the number of alternative ways an audience may perceive a message.

The designer can structure the situation highly by the selection and arrangement of message elements, or s/he can permit or plan for conditions that are less structured and which allow the perceiver a variety of interpretations. Which alternative to pursue is not a trivial matter. The designer would not ordinarily make such decisions independently, but once they are made s/he has the problem of arranging stimulus conditions favoring the chosen alternative.

The designer asks, "In what different ways will my audience be apt to perceive and interpret this message? S/he can armchair guess, or better, s/he can seek the estimate of a teacher having extensive experience with the audience, or ideally, s/he can try the message out on a sample of the audience. Based on such estimates and depending on the instructional objectives, the designer can attempt to modify the message so as to either reduce or increase the overall number of interpretations. In either case, designers' use of set may determine their success.

For example, simply asking a question, posing a problem, or presenting a puzzle may readily induce a set to direct attention a certain way. Set can also influence how perceived information is processed. For example, a set to do any of the following will induce different perception and processing of information: to make a speech about it, to criticize it, to pass a true-false test over it, or to perform some procedure given in it. Clearly, set enhances or facilitates perception and learning of a particular kind, but at the same time it reduces or limits other kinds that the audience is not set to deal with.

Where materials are to involve the audience in the process of inquiry or of open discussion, it will be very important for the activity to be introduced so as to avoid a restrictive set. Otherwise, the students will sense which answers and responses are preferred and will assuredly provide them. So powerful is the effect of set that it is in fact very difficult to control. For example, such effects have been found even in highly controlled research experiments, where they are supposedly inoperative. The set of experimenters to see their hypotheses confirmed has at times resulted in experimenters' unwarranted perception of confirming evidence or failure to perceive disconfirming evidence.

1.4b. *In cases where sensory data are ambiguous or unfamiliar, expectations and motives play a large role in governing interpretation.*

It is well-known that puzzles and p[...] difficult because of our expectations. [...] puzzle, for example, begins with a symmetr[...] four rectangles around a central small sq[...] Three matches are to be moved so that si[...] expectation is that the squares should all b[...] the one in the beginning figure, whereas t[...] five small squares and one four-times larg[...] Though normal expectations may be misle[...] situations, they are apt to be accurate in n[...] Expectations, being built up or learned from[...] are apt to be functional in comparable situatio[...]

Culturally determined expectations as to [...] event will be perceived are obviously very[...] designer of messages for people of the par[...] applies as well to sub-cultures whether th[...] ghettos or in exclusive suburban ghettos.

1.5.   *The perceptions of one individual [...] vary markedly from those of a[...] same situation.*

This chapter is frankly selective in its coverage[...] literature, and one of the omitted areas is t[...] differences in perception, particularly those a[...] factors as personality, attitude, and motivati[...] omitted is the developmental area, the chang[...] attributable to maturation or to perceptual learn[...] to perceive.

Summary of Basic Principles of Perception

Our perceptions are relative, selective, and org[...] these characteristics provides some general gui[...] designer. Some examples of how they might a[...] given; others follow.

I. *Perception is relative rather than absolute.*
  A. Provide anchors or reference points to which perception can be related.
     1. The size of an unknown object should be compared to a known one. The height of the Empire State Building can, for example, be expressed as equal to the height of 215 adults.
     2. The lengths of different lines, as in a bar graph or time line, can compare relative costs, relative populations, etc.
  B. Pace the message relatively.
     1. An interesting message will be perceived as relatively short.
     2. Divide difficult concepts into small, relatively easy steps.
II. *Perception is selective.*
  A. Limit the range of aspects presented.
     1. A map used to teach physical features need not include numerous political features.
     2. A complex process can be dealt with a step at a time.
  B. Use pointers.
     1. Words can direct the audience to select the relevant aspects of a television demonstration.
III. *Perception is organized.*
  A. Make apparent the organization of messages.
     1. Simply numbering the steps in a series of events gives organization to perception and memory.
     2. Verbal clues give order: before-after, greater-lesser, either-or, superset-subset, another, next, in contrast.
  B. Choose organizations consistent with concepts or subject matter.
     1. A circular figure may be consistent with the representation of cyclic events such as the seasons, life cycles, business cycles.
     2. A question-raising message can be seen as consistent with the inquiry processes of science.

IV. *Perception is influenced by set.*
  A. Use set to converge or control perception.
      1. Instructions to notice, or appreciate, or find an answer in an illustration can strongly influence how the perceiver responds to it.
      2. A topic sentence can provide a set for interpreting in a particular way the paragraph which follows.
  B. Use set to diverge or free perception.
      1. Ask open-ended questions (Why do you suppose this happened? What do you think this might be? Guess.)

Attention and Preattention

One of the message designer's first problems is to gain the attention of the audience, and thereafter s/he has the continuing problem of holding that attention. Though a certain amount of audience attention can be expected in a classroom, it is far from guaranteed. Further, a generalized attending is often insufficient, for attention must be directed narrowly and precisely to critical aspects of the subject matter.

In this section, several principles of attention, as a perceptual phenomenon, will be noted, and ways for the designer to make use of them will be explored.

The most apparent indices of attention are the movements of the eyes and head which aim the eyes toward chosen sources of interest and information. We are well aware that looking somebody in the eyes is a way of communicating such things as: I want to talk to you, I'm listening to what you're saying, etc. Teachers use students' eye movements to judge what they are attending to; the perception researcher does the same.

Thus, a general consideration of eye movements is important to the designer's understanding of attention. For example, how do we achieve stable perceptions when our eyes are so frequently "swish panning" from point to point in the scene like motion picture or TV cameras, doing so an "impossible" three or so times a second? How are images from the two "cameras" (eyes) superimposed without apparent blur or distortion? There are numerous such fascinating problems in visual perception, many of which have not been settled to the satisfaction of either investigators or practitioners.

For present purposes it should be sufficient to clarify a few probable misconceptions relevant to the way we attend to, or give attention to, our visual world. The analogy between camera and eye is misleading in many ways, though it may be of limited use here. The retina of the eye (see Figure 1.3) may be conceived as a very strange film in which the sensitivity varies from color in the center to black-and-white at the edges. Still stranger, if the film were 4 x 5 inches, the fine-grained portion of it would be limited to a central area no greater than 1/4 inch across, and the film would rapidly become coarse-grained toward the edges. The result is a dual system (Figure 1.3) in which the edges of the film, the coarse-grained* peripheral vision area, serve to detect the points in the environment to which the small central fine-grained area, the fovea, will be next directed.

Such a visual system obviously has had great utility for survival. Peripheral vision is especially sensitive to changes in movement and brightness, both highly relevant to the detection of approaching danger, be it from prehistoric enemy or modern automobile (Gregory, 1973). Following this alert, the head and eyes are moved to center the threatening object on the fine-grained fovea, where it can be critically examined and identified. This kind of interaction between peripheral and foveal inputs typifies much of visual perception.

---

*The reader should realize that grain, either coarse or fine, is a characteristic of photographic film. The intended analogy is to the cells in the retina, which are very tiny and very numerous and tightly packed in the fovea but become thicker and much more widely spaced toward the periphery; hence the difference in acuity or sharpness between foveal and peripheral vision (Graham, 1965).

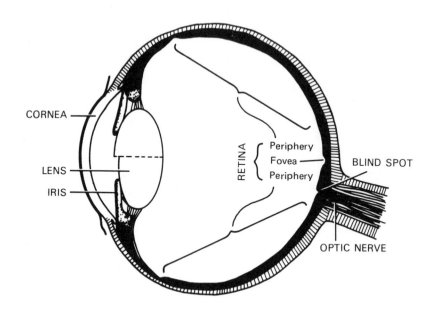

Figure 1.3. Principal parts of the eye, showing the light-sensitive retina divided into fovea and periphery.

> *1.6.   Vision includes both preattentive and attentive aspects. Preattentive vision is largely peripheral and is wide angle. It provides a global, holistic view of the visual field in which figures are separated from each other and located with reference to each other. Attentive vision is largely foveal and is narrow angle. It builds from the elemental to the complex in a process of analysis and synthesis in which figures are "constructed" in full detail, color, and shape.*

It should be clear that peripheral and foveal vision are intimately related and highly interdependent. One's awareness readily shifts back and forth between them. As we need to orient to a new situation, we shift awareness to the holistic and global condition. Within this field or context, and as we need more detailed information, we shift awareness to the foveal condition and direct the tiny central portion of the retina to each selected feature. Even while so narrowly attentive, however, we quickly become aware of changes in brightness and movement at the far edges of the field.

It is also presumed that auditory perception includes a preattentive phase, which detects changes in level or direction of auditory input and serves to alert the selective and attentive phases of audition (Neisser, 1967).

Thus, the designer needs to know how to globally get attention and how to specifically direct it. Principles relative to both follow.

> *1.7*   *One form of global stimulus control of visual attention is by a change in preattention, i.e., by the changes to which peripheral vision is most sensitive: brightness changes, movement. Similarly, auditory attention could be controlled by changes in volume, pitch, or direction.*

A loud sound or an intermittent one may be noticed where sounds have been relatively low or steady. Wind is noticeable on a quiet day; a lull, on a windy day. Record rainfalls and heat waves attract attention, while normal weather does not.

Thus, if the screen is dark, gain attention by brightening it; if it is static, gain attention by adding movement. "Popping on" of overprint titles directs attention to them and what they label. Similarly, the teacher can get attention by moving rapidly or suddenly or by changing the level or quality of his/her voice.

However, while such global changes in the environment are generally attended to spontaneously, the details of the stimuli (especially where numerous) will not ordinarily receive full attention (Rock, 1975). Consequently, in instruction, it is frequently necessary to *direct* attention to relevant details. How is this done?

*1.8.   Specifically, attention is drawn to what is novel,
to whatever stands in contrast to immediate past
experience or to life-long experience.*

While appearing to say very little, this is in fact saying
something that is quite fundamental to human behavior. Question:
How do I direct the attention of my audience? Answer, two other
questions: What is your audience attending to now? What can you
present them that is different? If they are looking at a series of
black and white pictures, a color picture may attract their
attention.

If a person is reading a book, what s/he has not yet read may be
relatively novel as compared to what s/he has, and thus may
command his/her attention. Similarly, a story in film or TV form
which continues to develop in a novel or not too predictable way
may hold an audience's attention.

In sum, attention is not necessarily drawn to the excessively
loud, bright, or extraordinary, only to what is quantitatively or
qualitatively different from what has been attended to previously.

The kinds of stimulus novelty that have been shown to direct
attention include color and shape. In visual displays containing
several figures of one color or shape, a figure of different color or
shape attracts attention.

The designer can readily provide numerous kinds of stimulus
novelty. Make the key words red or underline them. Exaggerate
the features (shape) of a known person or object, as in caricature
or cartoons, to draw attention to the whole figure or to particular
relevant features of it. However, such novelty can be overdone.
Supporting evidence comes from Navy training films in which the
introduction of mermaids kept the trainees awake and attentive
but to something other than operating ships.

*1.9.   Attention is drawn and held by complexity,
providing the complexity does not exceed the
perceivers' cognitive capacities.*

For example, given a choice, people have been found to look at:

a. figures having more numerous elements rather than fewer (see Figure 1.4).

b. displays having an irregular arrangement of elements; or

c. elements in a group which differ in structure as opposed to being homogeneous.

It is important that complexity be neither too much nor too little. The designer would certainly be ill-advised to add complexity to messages just for the sake of gaining attention. Yet, a learner will not pay much attention to material that is too simple in content, pace, or treatment.

It would thus appear that complexity is a difficult factor for the designer to use wisely. Optimum levels would depend on the age and sophistication of the learners, their interest in the subject matter, their level of aspiration, etc.

Here the programmer would have a distinct advantage. S/he could arrange for the more sophisticated to skip the beginning material entirely by correctly answering critical questions. Further, at subsequent stages in the program s/he would know a great deal about what degree of complexity might then attract attention.

The several principles above deal with very dynamic sets of relationships, because what seemed novel or complex a few seconds ago is so no longer. Attention is thus fickle and fleeting, at least to the extent that it is subject to the sometimes kaleidoscopic changes in the environment. However, we are clearly not at the mercy of our environment; we can direct our attention.

1.10. *People direct their attention where they will, i.e., where their interests, experiences, and needs suggest.*

And where is that? Obviously, if one is interested in football, s/he directs attention to the sports part of news broadcasts. If one has lost a credit card, s/he is very attentive to any object that

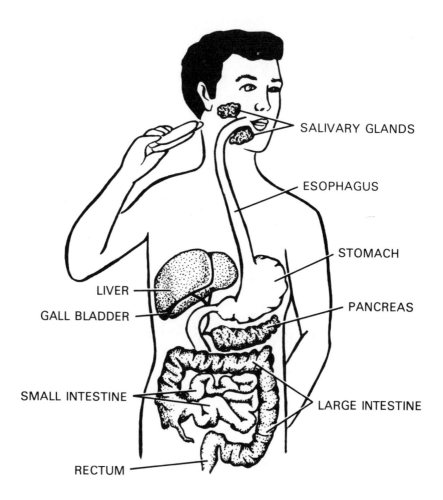

SALIVARY GLANDS

ESOPHAGUS

STOMACH

LIVER

PANCREAS

GALL BLADDER

SMALL INTESTINE

LARGE INTESTINE

RECTUM

The Digestive System

Figure 1.4. Relative complexity of the organs in the digestive system may draw attention to them and away from less relevant areas. (Based on illustration from Jacobson *et al.*, *Broadening Worlds of Science*, Copyright © 1964 American Book Co.)

looks like one. If one is hungry, s/he is interested in anything remindful of food, such as odors, vending machines, clocks striking twelve, rattling dishes, store signs. Thus, we may consistently attend to some things (sports), occasionally attend to others (lost things), and at regular intervals attend to still others (food).

In order to make use of this principle, the designer would need to know a great deal about the audience. Otherwise, s/he is left with gross generalizations such as: boys are interested in (will give attention to) sports and mechanical things. Even this is of some use, for concepts dealing with percentage can be taught to boys with reference to batting averages, and types of levers can be taught with reference to claw hammers and pliers.

Of greater utility would be a design strategy for directly influencing attention. This is usually done verbally: "On the map, notice which states border the Mississippi River. As you read this paragraph, pay attention to . . ." Such instructions have been shown to markedly influence what learners attend to and what they learn (Kahneman, 1973).

> *1.10a.* *In directing our attention, we seek a balance between novelty and familiarity, between complexity and simplicity, between uncertainty and certainty.*

Familiarity in excess produces boredom, while novelty in excess produces anxiety, and both lead to escape from the situation physically and/or perceptually.

However, there is evidence that an equilibrium is *not* instructionally desirable.

> *1.10b.* *A moderate degree of uncertainty or anxiety is a strong incentive to act, i.e., to attend carefully, to learn, to resolve the problem.*

Thus, the designers' problem can be seen as maintaining some optimum mix between familiarity and novelty, simplicity and complexity, and certainty and uncertainty in messages. When increased attention and learning are desired, the mix should be weighted toward novelty, complexity, and uncertainty.

Summary of Principles of Attention and Preattention

A number of stimulus characteristics can influence attention: brightness changes, movement, novelty (changes in color and shape), complexity (relatively more elements, more variety in their structure and arrangement).

It would appear that these are examples of a more pervasive principle, namely change. Attention is drawn to changes in stimulation, changes from immediate-past experience, and changes from long-term experience. In a sense, the more that new stimulation differs from the prevailing, the more distinctive or attention-getting it is.

For the designer, the findings point to the need for change, innovation, and creativity. But these are not for the purpose of finding the one best kind of message which will thereafter be used repeatedly. A more desirable consequence would be the frequent introduction of change into the otherwise repetitive (dull) stream of instruction.

One word of caution: change or novelty should *direct attention to the most relevant ideas* in a message rather than the marginal or superficial.

Attention is strongly related to the individual's interests, experiences, and needs. Regardless, attention can be appealed to directly through the use of verbal imperatives (look, listen, notice) as well as by asking questions and posing problems. The evidence is clear that messages will be attended to very differently, depending on the suggestions or directions which precede them: observe, be ready to discuss, enjoy, etc. Such guides to learner attention are particularly useful in increasing the effectiveness of instructional illustrations and are relatively simple for designers to use.

Perceptual Elements and Processing

This section will deal with that part of the perceptual process which in general follows attention. It deals with stimulus elements (brightness, color, line, area) which are familiar to the designer. Such sensory data are processed or modified at a number of points in the perceptual system, and this may influence what stimulus elements the designer provides.

Information is not simply transferred intact from the environment or from other humans to the perceiver's mind. It is transduced, translated, transformed into something else that stands for it, i.e., it is coded. This internal coding is in neural terms, which constitute the code or language of the brain, i.e., chains and patterns of electrical impulses. These internal chains and patterns somehow represent the external objects, people, and events. There is no internal picture in the brain of what is seen, no projected image nor TV-like image (Gregory, 1973).*

Considerable visual coding occurs at the retinal level; and additional coding occurs at successively higher levels of the nervous system.** There appears to be a hierarchical sequence in which groups or patterns of lower level signals are represented by (recoded into) fewer signals at a higher level; and groups or patterns of signals at this level are represented by (recoded into) still fewer signals at a still higher level.

From the designer's viewpoint, the more appropriate the design of the message, the more rapidly and accurately it will be perceived, for coding transformations involve time, are subject to error, and consume some of the capacity of the perceiver.

*However, there is a fairly precise point-for-point relation between retina and visual cortex, such that the spatial relations of neural elements in the retina are generally preserved in the cortex (Bishop and Henry, 1971).

**For example, at the retinal level visual input is coded almost immediately into three kinds of signals: red-green, yellow-blue, and white-black (Boynton, 1968).

Perceiving Brightness and Color

Brightness* and color are basic attributes of a message that are under the control of the designer. There follow some principles of perception that deal with such attributes.

> *1.11.   A change in stimulation is necessary for sustained sensitivity and normal functioning.*

An absolutely unchanging and homogeneous sensory field, be it overall light or dark, or colored, becomes perceptually the same as nothing at all. Persons confined to such undifferentiated environments have difficulty sustaining perception, become disoriented, and tend increasingly to hallucinate.

Further, any particular level of sensitivity will decrease over time if the level of stimulation remains constant (Triesman, 1974). That is to say, our sensory apparatus satiates, i.e., it becomes fatigued under unchanging stimulus conditions.**

In the realm of instruction there are severe constraints placed upon changes in stimulation. Change for its own sake can readily become distracting and is not desirable so long as change can be introduced into the central flow of the message. Ideally, as a message develops, the page-to-page or frame-to-frame change in sensory stimulation is one-to-one with the changing flow of pertinent information.

---

*A change in intensity of stimulation is represented (coded) as a change in the frequency with which a nerve cell fires and a change in the number of cells firing.

**This has been demonstrated most dramatically with special apparatus by which a visual image has been "locked" or stabilized on one precise area of the retina. The perception of that image remains intact for only a few seconds. Thereafter, it fades and restores piecemeal, i.e., unified features of the image (such as lines and angles) reappear momentarily (Murch, 1973). Of course, under normal conditions, the continuous movements of the eyes serve to constantly shift the position of an image on the retina and thus to avoid noticeable fading.

It should be noted in passing that the dynamic qualities of sensitivity noted above influence the prospects for subliminal communication. The limen is the threshold or minimum level of energy that can be detected. Thus, the fact that the limen varies, between individuals and from time to time for any individual, makes the study and practice of subliminal (below limen) perception very difficult to control. Consequently, its use in advertising or instruction to "plant" ideas without the observer's awareness is apt to be quite unreliable, particularly in mass or group situations (Murch, 1973).

Human sensitivity varies widely with the conditions of stimulation. Sensitivity is lowest where stimulation is highest in intensity (as with a very loud sound), and sensitivity is highest where stimulation is lowest (as at night where the eyes are fully dark-adapted). In effect, sensitivity is as great or as little as the conditions require. This is consistent with the principle of perceptual relativity noted earlier.

Variation in sensitivity follws one of the basic laws of perception, the Weber-Fechner Law.

1.12. The amount of change in energy necessary to effect a just-noticeable difference varies directly with the initial amount of energy present. *

That is to say, the lighter the initial shade of gray the greater the change in illumination will need to be in order for the change to be detectable. Or again, the louder the sound track level the greater the gain in level necessary for it to be distinguished from the initial level.

*This law is generally consistent with visual and auditory data, but begins to fail toward lowest detectable levels of stimulation (Kling and Riggs, 1971). Thus, differences in intensity are more difficult to detect at *both* the high and very low levels.

Thus, differences in shades of gray are more noticeable in the low to middle range of grays than in the upper (brighter) range and (because of the failure of the Weber-Fechner Law) in the very lowest (darkest) range. The same holds for low to middle levels of sound as compared to very low or high. This is important to the artist or photographer interested in separating various gray areas, details, or objects, and to the audio person interested in separating various sounds.

Where a considerable spread of intensities (light or sound) is to be distinguished in a message, the spread should be placed somewhere other than at the upper or lowest limits of the available range of intensities. However, there may be obvious reasons for doing otherwise in some situations, for example, where high levels of light or sound are necessary for a mood.

The kinds of changes just noted are changes in intensity such as brightness or loudness. Our visual and auditory receptors are also sensitive to changes in frequency, i.e., to changes in color and in pitch.

Color perception, in spite of the large quantity of research, is still only partially understood. The once-accepted theory of three primary colors (red, green, and blue) is being challenged by the opponent-color theory, which assumes that yellow is also a basic color, making four altogether plus black and white.* About 350,000 different hues can be distinguished (Forgus, 1966).

---

*A current resolution of this controversy includes both color systems. Presumably, color receptors in the retina (cones) are relatively selectively sensitive to red or green or blue. However, the output of these three types is complexly recoded (also in the retina) so that red signals oppose green and blue signals oppose yellow. This outcome is consistent with our sensation of color in that the opponent colors cannot be simultaneously experienced, i.e., either red or green is experienced and either blue or yellow is experienced. Combinations are experienced between pairs of opponent colors, e.g., red plus blue, but *not within* pairs, e.g., not red plus green. Presumably, the brightness detection system is separate from the color detection system (Kling and Riggs, 1971).

> *1.13. In general, the most highly preferred surface colors for adults appear to be red and blue. Green is also ranked high. Generally ranked lowest are violet, orange, and yellow.*

These ratings were generally based on a *small* range (typically six) of *saturated* colors, and hence should be applied with caution to the much larger universe of colors. Further, the status of yellow and orange appears somewhat equivocal.* There is evidence that they are given high ratings by children, but most studies show a much lower rating by adults. However, there are exceptions to the latter. Differences based on sex or on culture were generally found to be minimal.

The above principle should not move the designer to excesses in the use of preferred colors. For one thing, it would become boring, and for another the evidence is that we have less sensitivity for saturated blues and reds (the two ends of the visible spectrum) than we do for greens and yellows (middle of the visible spectrum).

> *1.14. The most visible colors are white, yellow, green, and the least visible are red and blue, i.e., where colors of equal intensity (physical energy) are compared (see Principle 1.20).*

This might influence a designer's choice of colors, especially where materials are to be used under low light conditions. Of course, under conditions of use which do not stretch visibility constraints (projection situations using large figures and bright colors) most colors are quite adequately read.

*The color preference principle is based both on an older comparison of 27 studies (Eysenck, 1941) and on a more recent summary (Plack and Shick, 1974). However, recent work with larger samples of colors (different hues and saturations) indicates a reversal of the status of yellow and orange, at least for the art students tested. Both were ranked high (along with reds and blues), and a maize-yellow was the most preferred of all. Pinks were rated lowest (Gotz and Gotz 1975).

1.15.   Though explanations vary, people tend to associ-
ate colors with moods or emotions. The red and
yellow end of the spectrum is said to be "warm"
and is felt to be exciting and happy. The green
to blue is said to be "cool" and is felt to be
controlled, peaceful, comfortable.

These relations are generally assumed to be learned and hence
somewhat culture-specific. There is also evidence that red may be
perceived as closer and blue as farther than they really are (Plack
and Shick, 1974).

1.16.   Apparent brightness and color are influenced by
adjacent brightness and color, and this adjacency
can be either side-by-side in space or one-after-
the-other in time.

A piece of gray paper looks lighter on a black surface and
darker on a white surface (see Figure 1.5). This effect of enhanced
contrast appears greatest along the contours or borders between
the adjacent light and dark areas. A contrast effect also occurs
between adjacent colors, especially between complementary colors
(red and blue-green, green and magenta, blue and yellow), i.e.,
each appears more saturated beside its complement than beside
other colors or gray. Also, a gray patch placed beside a saturated
color will appear slightly colored in a complementary hue. These
effects can influence the choice and arrangement of grays and
colors by the graphics designer.

These can be seen as specific examples of the principle of
perceptual relativity. Insofar as the apparent differences between
adjacent brightnesses and colors are accentuated, the phenomenon
is related to a more general tendency for perceived differences
between objects, people, and events to be accentuated. This
principle will be discussed in a later section, on Perceptual
Distinguishing, Grouping, and Organizing.

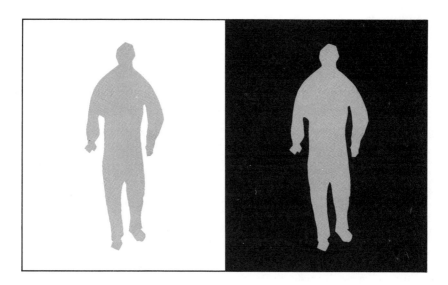

Figure 1.5. Apparent brightness of identical figures is relative to the adjacent brightnesses, white ground or black ground.

However, familiar objects are perceived as having their known brightness and color over a wide range of given brightnesses and colors. This is called brightness and color constancy. Its positive effect is to relieve the designer of the necessity of representing known objects (known to the learner) with precise brightness and color fidelity.

Perceiving Elemental Features

Stimulus features or attributes are the physical characteristics of stimuli. They are the brightness, color, texture, form, and size characteristics which designers select and manipulate as they construct message materials. A very large number of types and degrees of such features are available to the designer. S/he must select those which are judged to be relevant to the objectives of the communication and then arrange them appropriately in time and space.

The search for basic elements and units of visual perception has a long history and continues today. It was once thought that knowledge of each of the presumed elements of visual perception (points of energy such as of brightness, hue, and saturation) could by addition explain our everyday experience of the combinations of these elements in our images of objects and events. But the whole was found to be greater than or different from the sum of its parts. Consequently, research interest has diminished with reference to points of energy as basic elements, and grown with reference to larger configurations called stimulus features. These are the lines, edges, angles, contours, and movements of the retinal image to which particular brain cells (feature detectors) respond differentially (Hochberg, 1966). Such stimulus features are potentially of great interest and importance to the message designer, for they appear to be some of the elements with which graphic artists and photographers work.

1.17. *Certain kinds of visual stimulus features, such as contours, are accentuated in perception, while others, such as uniform areas, are not.*

For example, physiological evidence suggests that contours and edges are some of the most "exciting" visual phenomena we encounter. That is, a given cell in the visual cortex of the brain will have a certain receptive field (area of light sensitive cells) in the retina. These receptive fields are of different shapes, as shown (greatly magnified) in Figure 1.6. Images on the retina which correspond to the shape of a receptive field will evoke maximum firing of the associated brain cell.

Note that a stimulus consisting of a light spot in a dark field would correspond to receptive field "a" and would thus, if imaged on such an area, cause the associated brain cell to respond

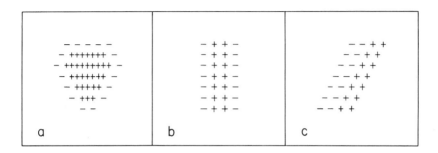

Figure 1.6. Receptive fields, i.e., regions of the retina which influence the firing of a brain cell. Light on + areas increases the firing. (After Hubel, D.H., and Wiesel, T.N. Receptive fields, binocular interaction, and functional architecture in the cat's visual cortex. In R.N. Haber (Ed.), *Contemporary Theory and Research in Visual Perception*. New York: Holt, Rinehart, and Winston, 1968.)

maximally. Similarly, a vertical white line or bar would match field "b," and a diagonal edge (dark above and light below) would match field "c." The movement of the appropriate line or edge through the appropriate field (b or c) would be a still more "exciting" stimulus feature. The uniform illumination of such fields causes only minimal firing of the respective brain cells.

In some such ways, stimulus elements or features which are imaged on the retina become recoded into the firing of single brain cells. Another type of brain cell has been found which is not so localized in its sensitivity. It will fire selectively and maximally whenever a particular type of contour (size, shape, or orientation) is presented anywhere within a relatively large area of the retina (Robson, 1975).

This fascinating new area of research is just beginning to probe more deeply the mysteries of visual form perception and may correspond to the shape of a receptive field will evoke maximum firing of the associated brain cell.

eventually yield basic guidelines for message designers. For now it serves mainly to re-emphasize the marked changes that sensory input undergoes in the human nervous system.

> *1.18.* *Horizontals and verticals are perceptually "special," i.e., in contrast to oblique orientations of line and pattern, they are more "intense" (evoke more activity in the visual cortex of the brain), are more readily compared (similarities and differences more apparent) and more accurately judged for spatial orientation.*

Horizontal and vertical lines appear to be more readily perceived than slanting lines, or at least they provide more stable and reliable anchor points. Deviations from horizontal or vertical lines are more readily detected than deviations from a line at 30 degrees from vertical, for example.

This idea would seem to be consistent with artists' conceptions that a horizontal or vertical line feels stable while a diagonal line feels more dynamic or active.

> *1.19.* *Lines seem to carry information by way of the following: location of the point of origin, curvature (if any), direction, length, point of change (angle or arc), or terminus.*

Contrariwise, a line continuing in the same direction or on the same arc is relatively low in information until it changes in some way. For a mathematician, a line is adequately defined by the locus of the beginning point and end point. All points in between are predictable, redundant, and unnecessary.

There is evidence, too, that a straight line is very quickly perceived as compared to a less regular and less predictable line. As suggested earlier, we seem to have feature detectors in our perceptual system which quickly respond to the presence of such regularities. This oversimplifies the matter, for an artist knows that a line has other very important characteristics, such as width, color, and quality, e.g., feathered with a brush (see Figure 1.7).

Lines are, of course, very fundamental to the graphic artist; and contours separating light and dark or variously colored areas are fundamental to lighting and camera personnel. Lines and contours establish the borders of objects; they separate areas; they contribute to the feeling or affective tone of an image.

Dark lines constitute handwriting and print. Lines are used to enclose important paragraphs and to underline important words. Light strips or areas between rows of print serve to separate, space, and aid legibility.

While such spatial dimensions are critical in vision, temporal dimensions are critical in audition. Examples of sounds which are of most relevance to instruction are speech and music.

In general, we are sensitive to sounds ranging in pitch (frequency) from approximately 20 cycles per second* (Hz) to approximately 20,000 Hz. (Our vision is sensitive to light between wavelengths of approximately 400 millimicrons [mu] to 70 mu.)

> *1.20.* *Sensitivity varies with the frequency (color or pitch) of the stimulus, being greatest in the middle range and falling off at higher and lower frequencies. For color the region of greatest sensitivity is a yellowish green (approximately*

---

*Sound waves (variations in air pressure) become translated into waves (variations in liquid pressure) in the inner ear, which become translated into the electric impulses of the auditory nervous system. There appear to be systematic relations between the audio frequency of the stimulus and the resulting firing frequencies of certain auditory nerves. At low auditory frequencies there occurs a volley of nerve impulses for each cycle of the stimulus, whereas for higher auditory frequencies a nerve fiber may fire every second or third cycle (Kling and Riggs, 1971). Nerve cells in the auditory cortex of the brain have been found to have a characteristic frequency (pitch) to which they selectively respond (Raab, 1971).

Figure 1.7. Suggestions of the range of information (affective and cognitive, figural and textural) which lines and contours (edges of areas) can provide.

> *555 mu), and sensitivity decreases markedly*
> *toward the red and blue ends of the spectrum.*
> *For sound the region of greatest sensitivity is*
> *three to four octaves above middle C (approxi-*
> *mately 3,000 Hz) at the top of the piano*
> *keyboard, falling off toward higher and lower*
> *pitches. The decrease is moderate to middle C*
> *but more rapid toward lower pitches.*

To apply this principle the designer doesn't need instrumentation to measure frequencies (hue and pitch), rather, his own eyes and ears will suggest that certain stimuli are difficult to perceive, i.e., are those to which the eye or ear has low sensitivity. For example, saturated blue (under bright light) may appear black on a dimly lit hallway bulletin board (more stimulus energy needed because of our low sensitivity to blue). Audio systems are frequently designed to compensate for our reduced sensitivity to low and very high frequencies (pitches) by reproducing them at greater levels of intensity so as to match the apparent levels of the middle range of frequencies. (This boosting of high or low frequencies is also intended to compensate for intrinsic losses in recording-reproducing systems, e.g., film sound track.)

There is a kind of spatial summation of visual input over time and a kind of temporal summation of audio input whereby the stimulus elements and features we have been sensing become the objects, words, music, people, and events of perception.

Perceiving Figures: Objects, Pictures, and Words

Out of the elements or features discussed in the last section, the perceiver constructs figures, e.g., objects, pictures, and words. The perceptual principles related to this construction process will be considered in this section. Because words and pictures are of primary interest to the designer, particular emphasis will be given them.

The perceiver does not take snapshots of the whole visual scene. Rather, a process of analysis and synthesis "constructs" figures (objects, pictures, words) out of stimulus features.

This process is complex and has been called analysis-by-synthesis to suggest the essentially constructive character of the process (Neisser, 1967). Objects and pictures are visually perceived by being rapidly constructed in increasing detail from numbers of foveal inputs, all within the holistic field, which includes peripheral vision. Similarly, words, phrases, and sentences are constructed from the temporal sequence of auditory features. Importantly, the products, while correlated in important ways with the auditory and visual stimuli, are markedly different from them. The products are in neural codes.

During this analysis-by-synthesis process, the figure becomes clearly differentiated from the ground; and detail within the figure is revealed or built up (Neisser, 1967).

> *1.21. The figural portion of a stimulus—such as a person or object—is given more attention, is perceived as solid and well-defined, and appears to be in front of the ground. The common contour between figure and ground belongs to the figure. In contrast, the ground attracts less attention, is perceived as amorphous and less definitely defined, and appears to be behind the figure.*

The perception of a figure and a ground appears to be a rapid and spontaneous initial part of the analysis-by-synthesis process.

It follows that a designer will want to make the most important message elements figural. Elements perceived as figures will typically be not only bounded, but boundaries will be well-defined, and there will be an apparent internal unity and solidity. However, in many pictures the figure-ground relationship is not so clearcut. There may be multiple figures competing for attention, and the ground may (contrary to expectations) appear to approach closer than the figure. Also, it is clearly the case that as we visually explore a scene, one aspect of it after another becomes figural, in the sense that it comes to dominate our attention for a while.

It is also worth noting that while in some cases the ground may be nothing but the undifferentiated white paper on which a word is printed or a drawing is made, it may in other cases be very informative. Particularly where the figure is somewhat ambiguous, the ground may determine categorization. For example, a man with unshaven face, long hair, old clothes, and shoulder pack may in a street setting (ground) be classified as "hippie," while in a desolate wilderness be classified as "prospector."

> *1.22. Perception of a stimulus (figure) is determined not only by the characteristics of the main stimulus but also by those of the surrounding context (ground). Perception of brightness, color, size, shape, pattern, and movement have all been shown to be influenced by contextual variables.*

Context can be temporal as well as spatial. For example, studies have shown that the meaning of a neutral scene (expressionless face) can be markedly influenced by immediately preceding or succeeding scenes (pretty girl, automobile accident, food) (Isenhour, 1975).

Clearly, the so-called figure-ground relationship is not limited to pictorial stimuli. The printed word can be a figure on a page ground, and the spoken word can be a figure on a ground of car engine noise. A melody can be perceived as a figure on a ground of accompaniment. A sound may be figural because of its volume, pitch, rhythm, or greater interest for the perceiver. In the jumble of conversations at a party, one can selectively tune in (make figural) a particular voice over all the others (ground).

Words are surprisingly dependent on context or ground for interpretation. A word depends on its sentence context, a sentence on its paragraph context, and a paragraph on its chapter or book or subject-matter context. Much of this dependence is not apparent because we so seldom encounter words out of some context, be it verbal, situational, interpersonal, or other. The logical necessity for a context for words can readily be seen in a dictionary, which supposedly establishes meaning. But does it? Words typically have multiple rather than unitary meanings, so some context is necessary in order for accurate meanings to be selected. And the problem becomes acute for the 500 most common non-technical English words used by adults, for these have about 14,000 dictionary definitions, or an average of 28 each (Fabun, 1965). Included are such words as run, cut, go, come, tell, man, dog, air, aid, and table.

> *1.23. A given contour can belong to only one of the two areas it bounds and shapes, and whichever side it shapes will be perceived as figure.* The most definitive characteristic of a visual figure is its boundedness. "Good figures"** are closed; they exhibit a continuous contour. And of the closed areas in a field, the smaller and the more symmetrical will be more likely to be perceived as figures.*

This principle provides the designer with some hints as to what constitutes a "good figure" and thereby suggests desirable characteristics for the important objects, places, and events in his messages (see Figure 1.8).

*Reversible figures lack sufficient cues as to which side of a counter is figure and which is ground, hence the vacillation. A message designer will typically deal with closed figures within which may be added other features, thus assuring unambiguous delineation into figure and ground (see Figure 1.8).

**Good, as used here, is not a value (good vs. bad or evil) but a quality of simplicity, regularity, and stability.

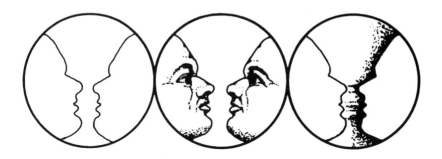

Figure 1.8. Effects of various degrees and kinds of designer control over what will be perceived as figure.

The organization of perception into figure and ground is a basic example of the general principle of perceptual organization. More complex types of perceptual organization will be dealt with in subsequent sections.

> *1.24.* *Where lines or contours are overlapping or competing with each other, the emerging figure will tend to be the one with good continuation, i.e., having more continuous and uninterrupted straight lines or smoothly-curved contours (see Figure 1.9).*

Such regular contours are more readily perceived in the sense that they appear to require fewer and shorter fixations (the pauses between eye movements) and thus apparently to provide information which takes less time to process (Mackworth and Morandi, 1967).

Carried to its extreme, this principle might influence the designer to use only straight lines, regular curves, or symmetrical

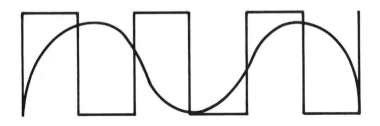

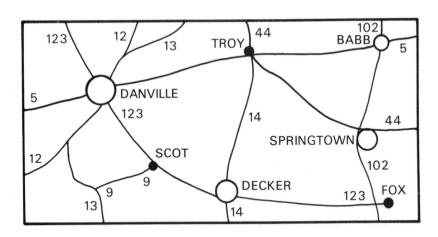

Figure 1.9. Abstract example (above) shows good continuation of the curving line despite the rectangular line. In map, some routes exhibit good continuation, some do not.

figures. Processing of such information would be rapid, but interest would probably be brief. Perhaps this principle interacts with familiarity-novelty factors as follows: If the object is new to the audience, use representations which are easily processed (straight lines or regular curves); while if the object is quite familiar, use representations which are more irregular or unusual.

> *1.25. Where alternative figures can be constructed by a perceiver, the most likely will be the simplest and most symmetrical figure which the available stimuli allow.*

This idea has been referred to as the Minimum Principle in the sense that differences and complexities are minimized (Hochberg, 1966). The idea is remindful of the Law of Parsimony in science whereby the most economical or least complex explanation for a phenomenon is preferred.

When the available stimulus is a traffic sign, it should allow only one unambiguous percept; but where the stimulus is a painting, it may be appropriate to allow a variety of interpretations, each "economical" to particular observers.

In fact the Minimum Principle may be anathema to creative artists, for they seem to prefer asymmetry. It, for them, creates tension and uncertainty. Just the opposite usually characterizes the programmer's intent, i.e., where there is uncertainty in how the audience will perceive or respond, then re-program or redesign so as to reduce uncertainty and increase the probability of a correct response.

Probably the products of instructional message designers should generally be situated between the traffic sign and the painting. The most economical perception of their work should be something relevant to the instructional objective intended, but perhaps there should be enough asymmetry in their work to make the act or product of perception interesting. The puzzle is in deciding just where in a display or figure to introduce asymmetry or complexity or uncertainty.

It may be that the point of greatest (within limits) relative asymmetry and complexity in a display should coincide with the point of greatest relevance to the objectives. For example, a globe may be pictured on a tilt, not just because it appears more dynamic that way, but also because the asymmetry may call attention to a phenomenon important to the understanding of seasons in the northern and southern hemispheres.

Signs vs. Modalities

Implicit in much of the previous discussion has been the distinction between the channel or sensory modality (vision, audition) the perceiver employs to receive information and the form or code (verbal, pictorial) in which the information is transmitted. The latter is called a sign in that it stands for or refers to something. Both the word "apple" and the picture of an apple are signs for, refer to, a particular fruit.

Although concrete objects such as rock specimens and green plants are commonly employed in instruction, most instructional materials are composed of signs in that they *stand for* some object, event, or relation. Iconic signs* include pictures, globes, maps, diagrams, and geometric figures, while digital signs* include words, numbers, and the like. Signs are not instructionally important in themselves (except in spelling and writing, photography and drawing) but only in what they represent or refer to, i.e., their referents. Digital signs, such as words, do not resemble their referents, while iconic signs, such as pictures and diagrams, do resemble, at least to some degree, their referents (Knowlton, 1966).

Signs are frequently confused with perceptual modalities. The

---

*Technically, one should distinguish between a sign vehicle (the physical object such as a photo or a printed word) and a sign (that upon which meaning is conferred by the viewer or interpreter of such a physical object) (Knowlton, 1966). However, for present purposes this distinction will be overlooked.

designer should be clear in making distinctions between them. Words—digital signs—may be perceived in either visual or auditory modality, while most iconic signs are perceived visually. It seems appropriate to refer to some auditory signs, such as "moo" and "bang," as iconic because they "resemble" or are the characteristic sounds of that to which they refer. Perhaps even the voice quality of a particular speaker in a sense "resembles" or is characteristic of the person and is thus iconic.

One of the perennial problems of the message designer is that of choosing between modalities (audition or vision) and between signs (digital or iconic).* Principles related to such problems will be considered next.

Modalities

> *1.26.*   *Vision is specialized for making spatial distinctions but relatively poor for temporal. Audition is specialized for making temporal distinctions but relatively poor for spatial.*

These two senses can thus be understood as complementary. Each compensates for inadequacies of the other. Each makes a unique contribution to informational input. However, there is some interchangeability. Audition is to a degree spatial, for one can fairly well identify the direction of the source of sounds. Vision can generally distinguish between successive events, but successive pictures in a motion picture are seen as one, i.e., they exceed the capability of vision to temporally distinguish rapid successive events.

---

*Message researchers and designers frequently conceive of "visual" as synonymous with "iconic," though in fact vision encompasses both verbal signs (print) and iconic signs. Psychological researchers frequently conceive of "visual" as synonymous with printed words (and audition as spoken words) thus ignoring visual iconic signs. Hence, the word "visual" can be quite misleading. We will use it to refer to the visual modality, thus including the perception of both pictures and words (print).

The above principle provides the designer some initial hints for modality decisions.

> *1.26a.* *If a concept is basically spatial, like mountain, mile, cube, anatomy, leaf shape, Big Dipper, or Venus de Milo, then vision is appropriate. Also, where it is desirable to hold a message in the perceptual field of an audience for some time, then vision is appropriate. Auditory sensations fade rapidly and for critical examination must be presented repeatedly.*

> *1.26b.* *If a concept is basically temporal—like rhythm or time or sequence or frequency, or like poetry or music or speech—then audition is appropriate.*

Because temporal events are transitory, they frequently are translated (coded) into spatial form. Speeches are put into print, clocks represent time in a spatial manner, musical scores are represented in space (simultaneous events spaced above and below, sequential events spaced left to right). Extended periods of time can be represented spatially. The seasons, years, eons are frequently depicted left-to-right on time lines. These translations of time to space involve conventions (codes) which must be learned. Designers who use these must either teach the code or be sure the audience knows it.

Signs: Words and Pictures

In an earlier section there was a discussion of the coding of information in neural terms within the perceptual processing system. The notion of coding is also applied to external codes invented by humans for communication purposes. Examples include not only the Morse Code but all languages and even drawings, models, etc. Useful conceptions for the designer are those of encoder and decoder, the designer being the encoder and the audience the decoder. The merit of the conception lies in its reminding the designer that information must be encoded (put into some code, e.g., words or pictures) before it can be transmitted, and further, the receiving audience must be able to decode (take the information out of code). The process is indirect, and involves transformation and "noise" that may distort the designer's intent. Communication is highly dependent on some commonality between encoder and decoder, at the very least a common knowledge of the code or language used. The designer's problem is to so encode the message that the audience can (will) decode it with maximum fidelity.

In this section we have chosen to use the word "sign" instead of the word "code" to refer to that which the designer uses to represent or stand for or refer to the intended ideas.

The choice between sign types, digital or iconic, has only recently had the benefit of some substantial research. Most earlier studies were media comparisons: TV versus live teacher, film versus textbook, etc. Few of these provide clearcut comparisons either between modalities or between signs. Further, the status of the digital sign for study and teaching purposes has often been held to be well above that of the iconic sign. Exceptions are those academic areas committed to the iconic (such as fine arts, TV, audio-visual) and those dealing with spatial concepts (geography, geology, physics). The designer has proceeded intuitively or has just preferred words over pictures or vice versa. The choice has been further weighted by institutional commitments toward one or the other, i.e., publishing houses, film companies.

In what follows, words and pictures will be compared from a perceptual viewpoint. While printed words appear to have some perceptual advantage over speech and pictures, the learning research (next chapter) clearly favors pictures over words.

The utility of each sign type is in part determined by the perceptual modalities each employs.

1.27. Digital messages (words, numbers) can be per-

> *ceived through either auditory or visual modal-*
> *ities or both. Iconic messages can only be*
> *perceived through vision.*

Thus, a designer employing digital signs can capitalize on either their spatial characteristics (print) or their temporal characteristics (speech), for verbal messages can appeal to either modality.

A designer employing iconic signs is constrained for the most part to spatial characteristics and visual modality. However, as noted earlier, the sequence and duration of iconic presentations provide a temporal dimension to vision.

The relative utility of each sign type is also determined in part by the effective duration of initial percepts, as the following principles suggest.

> *1.28.*   *Sign types differ in regard to initial apprehen-*
> *sion. Speech apprehension is limited by the*
> *typical brevity of the stimulus (generally no*
> *repetition nor going back). Print and picture*
> *apprehension is typically more depend-*
> *able, for the stimulus can generally be repeated-*
> *ly viewed and studied.*

This difference is basically attributable to the temporal (fleeting) nature of auditory perception as compared to visual. As a consequence, speech communication requires particular care (choice of words, rate of word delivery, technical audio quality). These will be discussed further later.

> *1.28a.* *Sign types differ in regard to opportunity for*
> *covert rehearsal and for reporting and recording.*
> *speech and print effectiveness can both be*
> *extended by covert rehearsal (talking to one-*
> *self). Both can be readily reported (speech)*
> *and recorded (writing) by a perceiver. Pic-*

tures can be extended by imaginal rehearsal (mental imagery) but cannot be readily and directly reported (except verbally) or recorded unless the perceiver can draw well or has a camera at hand.

In the above analyses, print appears to have the perceptual advantage, for it has both the apprehension advantage of vision and the reporting and recording advantage of words. However, analysis of other factors appears to lead to what is essentially a standoff. This is because of the further processing that can occur following exposure to either pictures or words.

1.28b. The eventual effect of information processing is not necessarily limited by the sign type of the stimulus. Pictorial stimuli can be (frequently are) recoded into mental words, and verbal stimuli can be recoded into mental images.

Consequently, in a sense, a picture often functions as a multi-sign stimulus, arousing both imagery and verbal processes in the perceiver. Similarly, words can arouse imagery in the mind of a reader, and as noted in the next chapter, imagery can markedly improve memory for words (Paivio, 1971).

Choice of words or pictures thus depends on the particulars of the instructional situation. The above principles provide a basis for choice, and certain memory principles provide additional bases. Further influencing the choice are the subject-matter, the objectives, the characteristics of the audience, etc.

Because digital signs have been studied more extensively than iconic, some additional aspects of perception can be noted with reference to them.

Extensive searches for the basic features or units in verbal perception have revealed that there are several kinds of stimulus features instead of one. A person can listen or look for letters, syllables, words, or phrases depending on the situation. It is apparent that we recognize words in reading without identifying all letters. Some of the features used are the redundancy of spelling patterns and the overall shape of words (letters extending above and below the line, overall length). It is also apparent that good readers do not identify every word in reading. They read too fast for that, making only about three to four fixation pauses per line of reading and consuming about one second in doing so (Neisser, 1967). Further, foveal vision would permit no more than one five-letter word to be in maximum sharpness for each fixation (Taylor, 1963). Language redundancy accounts for part of the success in skipping words, for words can often be removed from print or speech without seriously impairing meaning. Also, the context of words within phrases and sentences permits accurate guesses or hypotheses about the meaning which are based on only partial perception.

The auditory perception of speech (whether live or recorded) presents some different problems. Words and phrases must be constructed from the temporal sequence of auditory features. This process requires extensive short-term memory, because the exact meaning of a sentence strung out in time may not be apparent until the end. Meanwhile, all the rest of the sentence must be held in memory.

The difficulty of this process is influenced by phrasing (the grouping of a string of spoken words preceded and followed by pauses), for the longer the phrase the greater the memory load. Spoken phrases (independent of grammatical ones) should be kept short enough for auditory analysis and synthesis (Hoops, 1969). There is generally no difficulty in spoken phrase length where speech is impromptu, but where we read a speech or narration our phrase length may exceed the perceptual capacity of our audience.

Some of the cues useful in the perceptual construction of speech are frequently occurring function words (the, in, we, and, after), common endings of words (-ly, -s, -ing, -tion), rhythmic patterns of speech, and word orders (noun before verb).

Summary of Perceiving Figures: Objects, Words, and Pictures

This section first dealt with the perceptual process by which figures (objects, words, and pictures) are constructed from the stimulus elements or features discussed in the previous section.

The concepts of figure and ground were introduced, and considerable attention was given to the attributes of a "good" figure which a designer could employ. Among these were boundedness, closed area, continuous lines or contours, symmetry, and simplicity. Briefly considered were the rival demands for figural symmetry (good figure, readily perceived and coded) and asymmetry (creates interest, tension).

The last part of the section endeavored to make three distinctions which are basic to the designer: that between sensory modality or channel and sign, between auditory and visual channels, and between digital and iconic signs.

The visual channel was reported to be especially appropriate for representing spatial concepts such as "immigrate," the auditory channel for representing temporal concepts such as "poetic meter." Exceptions to these relationships were noted.

The comparative perceptual advantages of verbal vs. pictorial signs were discussed, including their modality differences, their ease of apprehension, reporting, and recording (writing vs. drawing), and their recoding (words into mental images and pictures into mental words).

Perceptual Capacity

Once designers have gained and directed the attention of their audience, they have the problem of maintaining an optimum level of stimulation, not too much and not too little. But how much is too much and how little is too little?

1.29.   Since the human information processing system is limited in capacity, the amount of energy

> *devoted to encoding a stimulus places limits*
> *upon other information processing.*

The implications for designers are obvious. The more codable a message the less the perceptual demands it makes upon the processing system. Thus, intelligent use of the codability factors, discussed in several sections, will in effect permit the designer to present more information in a given time.

Interestingly, there is some evidence that well organized, readily coded material can be presented too slowly for perceptual and learning purposes, allowing students to perform unnecessary or erroneous coding operations (Neisser, 1967).

> **1.30.** *The amount of information processed depends*
> *both on the number of discrete objects or*
> *events processed and the depth to which each*
> *is processed.*

Apparently, several types of information can be processed superficially, e.g., gross brightness, color, or form differences, in the same time required to process one type in greater depth, e.g., naming the color or assessing its beauty or fidelity. The designer can exert some control over both factors, by regulating the number of objects presented per unit time and by the set or directions or task given for processing each one.

More specifically, how much can a person perceive at one time?

> **1.31.** *We can perceive at a glance up to about seven*
> *items.* That is, for familiar objects one can*
> *report some attributes about them: number,*
> *name. Similarly, we can store in immediate*
> *memory up to about seven familiar items.*

*The so-called "magic number" of 7 +/- 2 has been found across a wide variety of stimuli and across modalities: vision, audition. It appears to be a reliable measure of human capacity (Miller, 1968).

Of course, the designer cannot continue to bombard an audience with seven unrelated items every second, but the principle does provide a very useful point of reference. A more dependable ball-park figure for regular design use would be five items.

One of the difficulties in applying this principle is that of defining an item, for it can vary greatly in size. It may be a single digit or letter, a five-letter word, or a well-known phrase. An item must be a meaningful unit. For example, for a beginning science student VELOCITY might initially be eight items (letters) which could soon become four (VE-LOC-I-TY). Later, when velocity, distance, and time become meaningful concepts, each will be an item. Eventually, all could become one item, V = d/t.

Thus, for each phase or step in such instruction, the designer should choose an appropriate size of item, the maximum size being the largest or most inclusive unit which has been encountered and used enough to be meaningful.

1.32. Perceivers partition the available information into as large or as appropriate an item size as the stimulus and their experience and intention allow. They are said to chunk or cluster or group.

Faced with the task of checking a complex instrument panel, the operator may group various instruments so that 20 instruments become five groups. Much research has gone into the problem of designing the layout, scaling, and size of such instrument arrays so as to maximize the amount that can be perceived at once.

Similarly, the student who must learn 16 new words may, initially at least, seek ways of grouping them: alphabetically by first letters, by related meanings, or by spatial arrays such as columns or lines. The groups may be imposed by the student, and their use would depend on the student's prior associations or prior success with alternative grouping strategies.

Grouping can also be facilitated by the character of the stimulus. As a consequence of the order (patterns, groupings) inherent in a situation, less order needs to be imposed upon it by the observer, and perceptual information is more readily processed, categorized, and acted upon.

> ***1.33.   The better organized or patterned a message is perceived to be, the more information we can receive (and process) at one time (see Figure 1.10).***

For example, a string of nine digits is more difficult to perceive than three strings (groups) of three digits, as the telephone company knows full well. Here the ingenuity of the designer is important. By such devices as the appropriate spatial arrangement or temporal ordering of message elements, the designer can facilitate perceptual grouping and hence reduce processing demands. Particular techniques and examples were introduced in the first section of this chapter and more will be considered in the next section.

> ***1.34.   The more familiar the message to its audience, the more readily it is perceived.***

Reading rates vary directly with the familiarity of words and relations in the passage. Unfamiliar material takes longer and involves more re-reading.

The designer can thus minimize perceptual demands and facilitate learning by using familiar examples, digital or iconic, and by referring back to previous learning.

Programmers and those who design large units of instruction can make most effective use of this principle, for they know what aspects of the subject have at any point become meaningful and familiar. More particularly, they can systematically arrange for those very aspects to become familiar which will be needed for

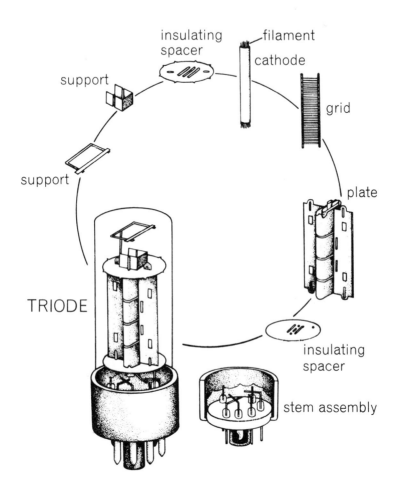

Figure 1.10. Example of a large amount of information made "readable" by organization. The tube is shown piece-by-piece from top to bottom, the pieces being organized accordingly in a clockwise direction. (From Navarra, John G., and Garone, John E., *Today's Basic Science: The Atom and the Earth,* Copyright © 1965 Harper and Row. Reprinted by permission of Harper and Row, Publishers, Inc.)

understanding the next concept. Thus, capacity is not exceeded at any point.

Next to be considered are the capacity problems associated with single and multiple channels. Some instructional materials involve one channel or modality such as vision, while others require two or more channels or modalities.

Single Channel Capacity

As already indicated in this chapter, our perceptual capacities are quantitatively limited, but the types and consequences of the limitation remain under active investigation.

Pictorial capacity has been investigated recently in a variety of studies and found to be remarkably large. For example, after a self-paced look through a group of 612 different pictures, subjects in one study were able to recognize a sample of the pictures with a median accuracy of 98.5 percent. Exposure to the pictures (mainly magazine illustrations) was for an average of only six seconds each (Shepard, 1967). Of course *recognizing* the pictures is not as demanding a memory task as would be the *recall* of numerous details in the pictures. Nevertheless, the above feat is remarkable and is superior to the recognition of words.

An aspect of verbal single-channel capacity having importance to designers is that of redundancy. Everyday speech is generally so redundant that considerable amounts of it can be clipped out without much loss in intelligibility. The clipping can be done electronically with sound recordings so that a fraction of the recording is removed every fraction of a second, the result being called compressed speech. Studies show that speech can be compressed to 50 percent of its original length while remaining over 90 percent intelligible (Foulke, 1966). The effect is to increase the number of words transmitted per minute, thus functionally increasing single-channel capacity. Redundancy can also be controlled by the writer or speaker. Instructional film narrations, being under severe time limitations, are usually written and re-written so as to eliminate most redundancy, most repetition. However well *perceived* such compressed or non-redundant material may be, the effect on *learning* may be serious, for much learning depends on repetition (see the Memory chapter).

> *1.35.*   *For verbal materials in a single channel situation, the more difficult or complex the verbal material, the greater the perceptual advantage of the visual channel (printed) over the auditory (spoken).*

It is important for the message designer to remember, as the above principle implies, that verbal auditory information presents special perceptual problems. For one thing, it is strung out in time and usually allows the learner only one opportunity to perceive, and minimal opportunity for rehearsal. If a reader misses a word, s/he can stop and look again; but a listener has no such option unless s/he can stop the person who is speaking or reverse the tape recorder. The problem of auditory selection may be particularly difficult in instructional situations. For example, it may be impossible to follow the teacher's speech under classroom conditions which inhibit the normal adaptive process of moving closer to the selected speaker and farther from too-talkative neighbors.

Recorded speech (television, film, tape, disc) may be difficult to perceive where the recording includes even a moderate level of noise or competing conversations. The problem is that such recordings do not permit the directional localization of sounds. Normally, we can turn attention to sounds from one direction and thus effectively reduce noise or competing conversations from other directions. However, this selectivity by way of localization is not possible when all sounds, desirable and undesirable, are coming from the same direction—the audio-speaker system. It follows that audio recordings of speech for instructional purposes must be exceptionally well controlled if the full capacity of this channel is to be realized.

Two-Channel Capacity

The two-channel research which has been most controversial for message designers is that by Travers. On the basis of an extensive series of studies, he states the implications for designers as follows:

> The evidence indicates that multiple sensory modality inputs are likely to be of value only when the rate of input of information is very slow ... The silent film with alternation of picture and print would appear to find much theoretical support as a teaching device (Travers, 1966, p. 14).

Though the above statements do not follow directly from the studies reported,* the indication that multiple modal materials (TV, film, sound filmstrip) are frequently overloaded with information does seem highly probable. The condition becomes most acute where presentation is at a fixed pace. This condition is least characteristic of programmed materials, in which information is more carefully rationed, and the learners are expected to perceive and learn a certain portion of it at a time and at their own pace.

Another point is that though a sound film may be overloaded, it has been shown in several instances to produce more learning than either the sound or picture separately (Levie and Dickie, 1973). This finding suggests that the two-channel aspect of such instructional films is not necessarily a deterrent to perception and learning.

> *1.36.   Where an audio-visual presentation is too rapid, the perceiver must choose between the two channels. S/he will report separate strings of auditory information from one channel or visual*

*The multiple-modality studies were limited to the case where there was redundant information in visual and aural channels. Typically, the same words were presented to both modalities. Under these conditions no difference was found for perceiving meaningful words whether they were presented simultaneously to both modalities or separately to either. However, at very high presentation rates (faster than 300 words/minute) the two modality (audio-visual) condition was superior (Travers, 1966).

information from the other channel. Only at
slower rates can s/he interrelate information
from both channels.

1.37. *When information is received simultaneously*
from several sources, one source can degrade,
accentuate, or bias other sources. There is an
interaction.

How these principles speak to the problem of designing
multimodal instructional materials is not obvious. There seem to
be two problems which are basic to multi-channel processing. The
one has to do with overall capacity of the perceptual system,
which was considered in the preceding sections. The other has to
do with the interrelationships between the separate channels, i.e.,
whether they act in parallel (no interaction) or interactively
(facilitation or interference). Following are some principles and
some hunches on the problem of interrelations between perceptual
modalities.

1.38. *Capacity appears to be larger where two modali-*
ties are utilized (audition and vision) rather than
one. Two tasks involving the visual modality, for
instance, will interfere more than where one
involves the visual and one the auditory modal-
ity.

Further evidence of the somewhat separate processing of
auditory and visual information is that of the specialization of the
two cerebral hemispheres (for right-handed people). The left
hemisphere appears specialized for serial information, especially
languages (speech), and the right hemisphere for simultaneous
information, especially spatial stimuli (pictures) (Posner, 1973).
Also, the spatial character of vision permits parallel (simultaneous) processing in different parts of the field, thus increasing the

capacity for pictorial information. In contrast, the serial character of speech constrains auditory processing to a separate, one-at-a-time basis, thus limiting capacity for auditory verbal information.

It seems probable that research to date, being focused narrowly on the one- or two-channel issue, has failed to take adequate account of the type of relationship between information in each channel: redundant or non-redundant, meaningfully related or unrelated. Such relationships are considered in the following analysis.

    a. Multi-channel communications which combine words with *related or relevant* illustrations will provide the greatest gain because of the summation of cues between channels.

    b. Multi-channel communications which combine words in two channels (words aurally and visually in print) will not result in significantly greater gain than single-channel communications since the added channel does not provide additional cues.

    c. Multi-channel communications which contain *unrelated* cues in two channels will cause interference between channels and result in less information gain than if one channel were presented alone.

    d. Single-channel communications will be superior to condition *c* (above), equal to condition *b,* and inferior to condition *a* . . . All of these predictions assume that testing for gain from the communications will be in the channel or channels of presentation . . . (Severin, 1967, p. 243) (*italics* added).

While the above are not all sufficiently well supported to be given the status of principles, they seem consistent with much of the research to date. The designer would be well advised to follow them at least until more definitive research has been done.

Parenthetically, the possibility that many instructional materials are already informationally overloaded raises some doubts about the further jamming of the perceptual channels through the use of multiple media, wrap-around screens, 3-D sound, and other

stepped-up rates of audio and visual delivery which are characteristic of our time. Perhaps these are appropriate where their intent
is not to inform in the usual moderate pedagogical sense but to
overwhelm, impress, exhilarate, or "send." Informational overload
may be an essential stimulus condition for such outcomes.

Summary of Perceptual Capacity

This section has related material from previous sections plus
new material to the problem of perceptual capacity. Usually, the
designer wants to communicate as much as possible per message or
per unit of time, but the capacity of the learner to perceive, code,
and store information sets very important limits.

The reciprocal relation between coding difficulty and perceptual capacity is crucial. The more difficult the message is to
perceive, code, and learn, the less the capacity remaining for
additional information processing. Much of what has been covered
under various headings concerning the facilitation of coding
applies here: stimulus chunking, clustering, or grouping; familiarity and meaningfulness; and appropriate use of signs and modalities.

Estimates of single-channel capacity are still tentative. For
words presented auditorially the estimates range up to 400 words
per minute for a prose passage (Travers, 1966). Much less is known
about pictorial capacity, though subjects can remember (recognize) with 90 percent accuracy over 2,500 pictures which have
been presented at the rate of one every ten seconds (Standing,
Conezio, and Haber, 1970).

The weaknesses of the auditory channel were noted, particularly
for difficult material. The lessons for the designer are clear:
shorter sentences for auditory material, more redundancy, and
excellent technical quality.

Multiple-channel capacity has been a recent source of controversy among researchers. The case for simultaneous processing of
information in two modalities or of two sign types is still to be
unequivocally demonstrated, though motion picture and TV

producers may be convinced that one can hear a track and see the action simultaneously. In fact, of all the possible combinations of modality and sign, the one that appears to be most compatible and to permit the highest information load is the auditory modality (verbal sign) in combination with the visual modality (iconic sign), i.e., the slide and tape presentation, the film and television, the teacher talking while showing an overhead transparency. Thus, employing separate modalities, each with differing signs, should permit the perceiver to select one or the other with minimum interference or, to a degree, simultaneously perceive both. We certainly come to such situations with a great deal of prior experience, for example, experience in simultaneously seeing a person and hearing his name.

It does appear that the message designer can act as if simultaneous processing occurs in the perception of multimodal and multisign media, for even if there is not much simultaneous processing, there is at least very rapid alternation between separate sequential processing.*

Perceptual Distinguishing, Grouping, and Organizing

The principle of perceptual organization was introduced in the first section, and in the preceding section perceptual capacity was related to stimulus organization. This section will amplify these principles and add others.

Our processes of perception and categorization are facilitated by the perceived regularities in the environment. Arranging for perception of these regularities is an essential part of the designer's task. This may involve accentuating the regularities to make them more apparent or more perceptually dominant.

---

*Recent evidence places switching time between auditory and visual channels at no more than 1/20 second (Swets and Kristofferson, 1970).

Environmental regularities are important for three reasons. First, perceived regularities make it possible for us to categorize and thus cope with the great quantity of sensory information bombarding us. Second, perceived regularities are the bases for much of knowledge: facts, concepts, opinions, attitudes. Finally, the organization of messages is one of the designer's prime means of influencing an audience's perception of those regularities.

A perceptual field is organized and regularities become apparent through a process of both analysis (distinguishing or separating) and synthesis (grouping or combining). Both will be considered in this section.

Distinguishing and Grouping

The process of distinguishing one figure or feature from another in the field is referred to as perceptual discrimination. Perceiving differences, i.e., making discriminations, is one of the most basic aspects of perceiving and learning.

> *1.39. Objects and events perceived as different, as standing in contrast along one or more dimensions, will tend to be distinguished from each other and be separately grouped in perception.*

The process of perceiving a difference or making a discrimination will obviously be aided by instructional materials in which the differences between objects, events, or ideas are made apparent (see Figure 1.11). More particularly, the differences shown should be relevant differences, i.e., those that define or provide the criterial evidence for the desired discrimination (Gibson, 1968).

Supporting evidence comes from studies of concept learning which suggest the importance of perceiving what are *not* examples (non-examples) of a concept as well as what are examples of it (Klausmeier, Ghatala, and Frayer, 1974). The concept "pine tree" is more reliably learned where several non-pine trees (fir, spruce) which are frequently confused with pines are shown as well.

Figure 1.11. Side-by-side arrangement of characteristics of Articles of Confederation and of Constitution facilitates perception of the differences. (From Wests' *Story of Our Country,* revised by Gardner, William E., Copyright © 1960, 1963 Allyn and Bacon, Inc. Reproduced by permission of Allyn and Bacon, Inc.)

Perceiving the distinctions between one group and another may be an essential part of perceiving the characteristics of each group.

Perceived difference or contrast is often employed in message design in order to separate or space. Chapter headings separate ideas or events in a book, frames separate the parts of a filmstrip or a self-instructional program, fades to black separate sequences in television, color separates countries on a map.

Perceived difference or contrast also serves to accentuate critical portions of a message or to cue responses to it. Speakers may raise or lower their voices to call attention to important words or phrases. Capital letters and italics stand in contrast. Artists and cameramen use emphatic devices: color, brightness, etc.

The process of determining which distinctions need to be made and in which context may be an essential part of the design task. For example, it seems probable in driver training that some discriminations are better learned from reading the state laws, others from trial and error in a simulator, and still others in a driver training car. A thorough task analysis of each aspect of driving should reveal the kinds of discriminations to be learned and suggest suitable conditions for perceiving and learning each.

As noted earlier, it is only by perceiving regularity amid all the diversity that we can learn to cope with the complexities of the world. To this end, the perception of similarity is essentially the counterpart of perceiving difference.

> *1.40. Objects and events perceived as similar, in any of a number of ways such as appearance, function, quantity, direction, change, and structure, will tend to be grouped or organized together in perception.*

Learning to recognize and label the important regularities of our world is certainly a primary objective of formal education. It underlies the formation of concepts, principles, and generalizations. Clearly, the more ways in which two things appear to exhibit common characteristics, the more likely they are to be perceived as related, as belonging to some common category. Thus, if the designer desires to communicate that two languages are of common origin, or that several widely dispersed land forms are of the same type, s/he can so select the conditions of perception as to emphasize common attributes and de-emphasize the different ones. See also the example in Figure 1.12.

One of the most apparent consequences of perceiving similarities is the act of grouping. Perceptual grouping or organization is facilitated by stimulus conditions in which relevant similarities are displayed and apparent differences are eliminated or made less apparent.

Of course, in practice the design task is never as simple as this would suggest. For one thing, people differ in their tendencies to select attributes that are alike, i.e., some are more analytically inclined and tend to perceive subtle differences instead of apparent similarities. Then too, as noted earlier, one's attention is

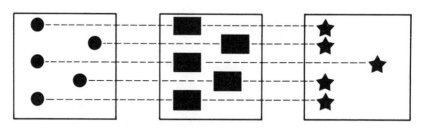

Five

Figure 1.12. The horizontal lines facilitate grouping by similarity (concept of five) instead of grouping by difference (circles, rectangles, stars). (From Brumfiel, Eicholz, and Shanks, *Introduction to Mathematics,* Copyright © 1963 Addison-Wesley.)

powerfully attracted to novelty in the environment, so that similarities that are obvious or quickly perceived may not sustain attention for long.

The similarity principle is consistent with research on concept teaching, which indicates that a variety of examples of a concept should be presented at once so that the similarities, the defining attributes, would be apparent (Klausmeier, Ghatala, Frayer, 1974). For example, the concept of isosceles triangle could be represented by an array of examples, all of which had two equal sides, but which otherwise differed systematically in various irrelevant ways, such as size, shape, and position. (More on this in the Concept Learning chapter.)

1.41. *Once a figure or pattern is fully distinguished from its ground and organized, the various elements within it tend to be perceived as more homogeneous than they in fact are. Further, distinctions between one figure and another may become accentuated.*

In essence, perceived similarities and differences may be greater than actually exist. The perceived difference between a figure and a ground may, once stabilized, be experienced as a greater contrast than actually exists in the relative energies of the stimulus. So, too, in social perception we tend to exaggerate the differences between those things we like and those we dislike. Differences between political parties are accentuated, while those within one's own party are minimized, are assimilated. Judgments of good and evil may be so contrasted that no relativities are distinguished. All shades of gray are distorted into black and white. Social organizations are seen as "good figures" in that individual members "belong" by way of their common qualities. Unfortunately, people of a certain race may be perceived as all alike, and people in certain groups (doctors, farmers, policemen) as being the same. (The illusion is aided in the latter case by the similarity of uniform.) Differences are minimized and assimilated.

This principle may be either an aid or an obstacle to the designer. Where distinctions and similarities are difficult to perceive, accentuation may be facilitative. However, where previously accentuated distinctions and similarities must be changed, the designer is faced with one of the most resistant-to-change behaviors s/he will encounter. Such attitude-change problems are discussed in a subsequent chapter.

> *1.42.* *Objects and events encountered in proximity*
> *with each other, i.e., close together in time or*
> *space or in the same context, will tend to be*
> *perceived as somehow related, e.g., ideationally,*
> *functionally, etc. Comparisons will be facili-*
> *tated, both similarities and differences becoming*
> *apparent.* *

Things appearing close together in either time or space are apt to be perceived as belonging in some common category or as functionally or causally related.

Temporal proximity is readily arranged and can produce strong perceptions of causality that may or may not be appropriate. A film maker can record a ball crashing through a window many days before and many miles away from where s/he records a baseball player hitting a ball, but causality will be strongly perceived where the two scenes are shown in the proper temporal relationship. However, a newsreel cameraman can inadvertently misrepresent the impact of a politician's speech by recording the chance expressions of members of the audience. A pained expression that really means "I ate too much," can by proximity to a critical part of the speech be interpreted as, "I don't like what you're saying."

*It is worth noting that similarity and proximity factors are typically difficult to separate in practice. If their effect is in a common direction, all is well. If not, it may be difficult if not impossible to predict in advance which effect will predominate. There is some evidence that whichever one is initially dominant will tend to persist even though the other is strengthened (Forgus, 1966).

Spatial proximity is also readily arranged by the message designer. For example, s/he can place two pictures or two sentences side-by-side on the same page or same slide. Such a message strongly invites comparisons, both of difference and of similarity (see Figure 1.11, p. 66).

This principle is particularly useful either where distinctions or similarities are subtle or where they involve a number of attributes. In the latter case, proximity functions to reduce memory load, i.e., with differences or similarities simultaneously apparent, the learner need not remember all details in the two examples, just the relevant parts. For example, the similarities and differences between two Presidents can more readily be perceived where their terms of office, parties, beliefs, actions are listed side-by-side, item-by-item, instead of on separate pages and mixed in with other information.

Proximity gains further significance because it is not only a stimulus condition for perception but also for learning, though under a different label, namely contiguity. Events that occur close together, i.e., that are contiguous, are considered likely to become associated or learned. Contiguity is one of the basic laws of learning (see the next chapter.)

In sum, objects and events perceived as similar in any dimension or as proximate may be grouped and given a label. Some groupings are of objects which are perceptually identical, such as manufactured products. Such groupings, a series of cups or pencils, for example, are very useful in teaching children to count or in teaching the concept of "set." Other groupings are formed, not only because of perceived similarities, but in spite of perceived differences. Such groupings are called concepts.

1.43. *Familiar objects maintain many of their perceived characteristics (brightness, size, shape, color) almost independently of changes in stimulus conditions. This phenomenon is called perceptual constancy.*

Each of the perceptual constancies (brightness, size, shape, color) can be considered a kind of concept in that it involves the perception of regularity or invariance across widely divergent conditions of stimulation (Forgus, 1966).

As noted earlier, a piece of paper will be perceived as "white" under extreme conditions of brightness ranging from daylight to moonlight (brightness constancy). A VW "bug" comes to be perceived as having invariant size and shape, though at different distances and angles its image on the retina will be radically different (size and shape constancies) (see Figure 1.13).

The phenomenon of perceptual constancy is generally a remarkable ally of the designer. Familiar objects, though minimally and variously represented, will tend to be perceived as having the known attributes of such objects. People can be

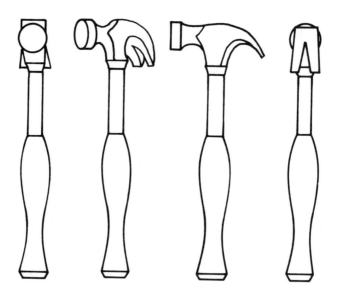

Figure 1.13. Familiar objects usually are perceived as having a constant shape despite markedly different appearing shapes.

represented as tiny as ants; grass, as gray; and table tops, as a line or square or any kind of parallelogram. However, the situation is quite different for representing new and unfamiliar objects. Here it may be necessary to introduce a scale for relative size, to display all sides and surfaces, and to render the object in accurate color.

Relating and Organizing

In addition to perceiving the regularities of difference and similarity, we also perceive regularities of relationship. In the following section several stimulus conditions for the perception of relationship will be noted.

The likelihood that certain things will be grouped in a common category varies with stimulus conditions. These are typically conditions of spatial or temporal relationship between things, and they lead to such fundamental types of perceptions as cause or effect, before or after, better or worse.

1.44.   Perception of relationships will be facilitated where objects and events are encountered as comprising or contributing to a common idea, pattern, rhythm, structure, or organization.

It is tautological to state that where stimuli are patterned perception will be patterned. It may also be erroneous to so state, for cognitive patterns may depart markedly from stimulus patterns. Nevertheless, there are many reasons for patterning in message design. At minimum, perception is more efficient where stimuli are pre-patterned, or where they are "good" and symmetrical.

Also, knowing that an audience will impose pattern or regularity where stimuli are ambiguous, the designer would logically pre-pattern stimuli in a way consistent with objectives.

One of the simplest temporal patterns is alternation, what in kindergarten is known as "taking turns." Many adult conversations are patterned the same way, and thereby become more readily perceived. However, such simplistic patterns can readily be overdone. Consider a film in which closeups alternate mechanically with long shots. The effect can be to induce boredom.

People can cope with much more complex patterns. They perceive, learn, and come to anticipate certain language patterns, for example. Nouns are preceded by adjectives, verbs by nouns. Capital letters begin sentences and periods end them. We are intrigued by the more complex patterns of events whether in the "plays" of chess, football, or politics, or in the dynamics of biology, history, or music.

Thus, it can be seen that perceived patterns range from simple to complex, from certain to uncertain, and the designer can choose the pattern appropriate to the needs. Importantly related is the finding from learning research that stimuli that are properly patterned or "chunked" are much more readily learned than the same stimuli presented in an undifferentiated fashion. In fact, where pattern or structure is not evident in the stimulus we generally impose some regularity on it in order to remember it at all.

1.45. *A variety of spatial and temporal arrangements, patterns, or structures influence the perception of relationships.*

The following five types of arrangements have been employed, in varying degrees, to suggest relationships in various subject areas. None, except proximity, have been sufficiently researched to be given the status of a principle.

Proximity. A previous principle has dealt with this factor. It is included here as a reminder of its importance in spatially and temporally arranged messages.

Inclusion. An indicator or stimulus condition of inclusion is the circle, rectangle, or free form around the assorted things. This arrangement gives them in effect the qualities of a good figure. Such a device cuts both ways; it definitely includes some things and equally definitely excludes others. A classic example is the variously overlapping pairs of circles called the Venn diagrams which have been so successfully used to teach the vocabulary and concepts of Set Theory, whether to elementary school children or to college students. Pictures in magazines or books are frequently set apart by bounding lines. Paragraphs are set apart by white space.

Directionality. In general, verbal messages are perceived as proceeding in a left-to-right, top-down direction, at least in most Western cultures. As a consequence, any horizontal linear arrangement of elements will tend to be perceived in a left-to-right sequence. Though obviously a strong tendency for perception of the printed word, it also holds for pictorial elements, as in the case of the comics. There is evidence that people ascribe cause and effect relations as well as before and after relations to visual elements connected left-to-right by lines, and the effect is strengthened by the use of arrows (Fleming, 1968). Time lines in history texts, for example, typically run left-to-right from past toward present. Circles with uni-directional arrows may be perceived as cyclical events, such as life cycles or business cycles (see Figure 1.14). Directionality may depict more subtle relationships, as in the case of a curve relating phenomena on ordinate and abscissa. In a decision matrix or contingency table the intersections of rows and columns are the perceived locus of coordinate relationships. Such heuristic devices appear to provide the message designer with powerful perceptual conditions for denoting relationships. However, use of such devices must be contingent on assurances that the audience understands the "code."

Superordination. Visual elements placed at the top of a display may be perceived as related in particular ways to elements below. Even the words used to mean physically higher (such as above, top, superior, superordinate) can also be used to mean better, more important, more general, more inclusive, more valuable as compared to the words meaning physically lower (such as below, bottom, inferior, subordinate).

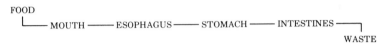

DIGESTIVE SYSTEM

TABLE OF ORGANIZATION

WATER CYCLE

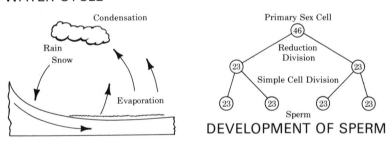

DEVELOPMENT OF SPERM

Figure 1.14. Examples of directionality, superordination, and accentuation factors (Fleming, 1968).

There is evidence that words placed above others may be perceived as "more or better" rather than "less or worse" as compared to those placed below (De Soto, *et al.,* 1968). Clearly consistent with such perceived relationships are such message patterns as verbal outlines, where I, II, III, denote superordinate elements and A, 1, a, denote successively subordinate elements, which are not only indented but placed below the element to which they bear a subordinate relationship. Hierarchical tables of organization (such as those used to present the organization of a company or government, e.g., Figure 1.14,) have been shown to suggest relationships such as greater-lesser and part-whole (Fleming, 1968). Similarly, when people use imagination (mental imagery) to solve problems involving different quantities or values, they typically image the greater above the lesser.

Accentuation. A number of devices for accentuating certain parts of a message have been noted: arrows, underlining, changes in size and type of letter, and color. These function mainly by providing perceptual contrast.

The important point here is that the organization of a message can profitably be accentuated. For example, inserted titles and subheadings which accentuate the organizational outline of a film have been shown to increase learning, particularly where the film was not inherently well organized (Reid and McLennan, 1967).

Summary of Perceptual Distinguishing, Grouping, and Organizing

This section began with the proposition that our perceptions are organized and that consequently the designer can facilitate and control the perceptual process by the way s/he organizes messages.

The three key perceptual principles considered were similarity, difference, and proximity. Quite simply, people group similar things and separate different things. And the process is influenced by the spatial or temporal proximity of these things. Concepts are based on similarities, but learning to use them may depend heavily on the differences that distinguish one concept from another.

A number of more specific principles for the organizing, structuring, or patterning of messages were given and discussed under the heading of spatial and temporal structures. These varied widely in the amount of research behind them but yielded guidelines for the designer, such as:

a. Making the organizational outline of a message apparent (sub-titles in a film or transitional statements in a speech) should improve perception and learning of its essential features.

b. Simultaneous presentation of several objects, such as drawings of various fungi, should facilitate perception of similarities and differences.

c. Lines around, under, between are important perceptual cues for grouping, accentuating, relating.

It seems plausible that stimulus structures that have wide utility across subject matters, such as hierarchical outlines, pie charts, and time lines, should be taught early in the curriculum.

Perception of Size, Depth, Space, Time, and Motion

The preceding section dealt at a general level with the perception of regularities, such as similarity, difference, and relationship, i.e., with some of the basic conditions for identifying concepts. This section extends that discussion to some of the specific relationships and concepts which have been investigated by perception researchers.

Size and Depth

The perception of size and depth are essentially the perception of relationship.

1.46. *Perceived size is reciprocally related to perceived distance, and vice versa, i.e., the greater the size the less the distance, and the greater the distance the less the size.*

Note that perceived size may not always vary with *actual* distance, only with *perceived* distance, and vice versa. Thus, the designer has the opportunity to arrange stimulus conditions such that the apparent (perceived) sizes and distances in messages are as desired. For example, where the designer wishes to compare the size of two animals, s/he must control the distance cues so that the animals appear equidistant from the observer. And where s/he wishes to show distances, s/he must control the apparent size, usually by showing the same object or person at both the near and far points.

1.47. The sizes of unfamiliar objects are perceived as relative to that of familiar objects.

Where cues for distance are lacking, the size of an unfamiliar object can be judged relative to familiar objects. In the case of an unfamiliar rock specimen, for example, the designer would include in the picture a familiar standard such as a ruler or a hand.

Size comparisons can be done verbally as well: your heart is as big as your doubled fists, a mile is as long as 1,760 yardsticks, Texas is larger than Michigan, Wisconsin, Iowa, Illinois, and Indiana all together.

1.48. The size of an object in a field is relative to the other objects there, smallness being perceived where the field contains large objects and largeness being perceived where the field contains small objects.

This is another example of the relativity of perception, and suggests that the designer can somewhat accentuate smallness or largeness of an object by choosing comparison objects of contrasting size.

1.49. The perception of depth in static two-

> *dimensional displays is influenced by the fol-*
> *lowing: relative size (especially of familiar*
> *objects), linear perspective, texture gradient,*
> *upward angular location of grounded objects,*
> *interposition, and filled space (see Figure 1.15).*

Ordinary depth perception is influenced as well by several physiological factors.* However, for most message materials such depth cues are irrelevant, for the materials have no intrinsic depth. The TV or motion picture image, textbook page, and so forth, are all two-dimensional, though often experienced as three-dimensional.

In what follows, the above factors which influence depth perception in two-dimensional displays will be discussed and examples given. Picture an outdoor scene looking down a highway with fields on one side, occasional houses on the other, and mountains in the distance. In general, the relative sizes of cars on the highway and of houses along it should vary inversely with the distance, i.e., the *frontal* (left to right) dimensions of a truck that is half a mile away would be twice the frontal dimensions of one that is a mile away (Rock, 1975).

Linear perspective refers to the *longitudinal* (near to far) dimension of objects and is illustrated by the lines which mark the edge of the road stretching off into the distance. This longitudinal dimension of objects varies inversely with the distance, but at an accelerated rate (Haber and Hershenson, 1973). Thus, longitudinal dimensions are foreshortened or compressed relative to frontal

---

*Probably the most studied are the effects of accommodation, convergence, and binocular disparity. As the eye muscles change the shape of the lens to bring an image into focus (accommodation) they give some cues as to the distance to the object being imaged. As the eyes "toe inward," so to speak, to fixate a near object (convergence) they also produce some cues as to the distance to the object. Binocular disparity, the difference between the retinal images of the two eyes, is more marked as the fixated object moves closer, and hence provides another cue for distance (Forgus, 1966).

Figure 1.15. Examples of several factors influencing depth perception in two-dimensional displays. Can you identify them?

dimensions. If the distance from the near to the far end of a bridge 200 yards away were represented in a drawing by a one-inch line, the same bridge 400 yards away would be represented not by a ½ inch line but by one even shorter, e.g., ¼ inch.

The concept of "texture gradient" combines those just discussed for the edges of objects (relative size and linear perspective) and extends them to the texture of surfaces (Forgus, 1966). For example, if the highway were concrete, the sections would decrease in length at an accelerated rate (following the dictates of linear perspective), while the horizontal or frontal joint between sections would decrease at a constant rate (following the principle of relative size). Similarly, gravel along the edge, clods in a plowed field, and shrubs along the fencerow would form a texture gradient of decreasing size with distance.

The idea of "upward angular location of grounded objects" is simply that near objects are usually grounded (touch the ground) at the bottom of a picture, while the successively more distant are grounded nearer the top or nearer the horizon. In the process, some objects may overlap others, which is called "interposition" (Rock, 1975). Thus, a tree which overlaps and blocks out the view of part of a house is perceived as nearer than the house.

"Filled space" between near and far objects increases the appearance of depth or distance between them as compared to empty space (Murch, 1973). The latter three factors (upper angular location, interposition, and filled space) function essentially independently of image size, while the first three factors, texture gradient, etc., are dependent on image size.

The perceived three-dimensionality of an object involves a degree of distance or depth perception, and some of the above factors apply.

> *1.50.   The perception of solidity and depth in an object is markedly influenced by the illumination, i.e., the shadows cast, and by the sharpness of image features.*

Flat lighting (lighting from the direction of the observer) or diffuse lighting serve to reduce the perceived three-dimensionality of an object (hence the name "flat"), while lighting that is from the side or more directional tends to accentuate three-dimensionality.

Depending on the location of the shadows, either depth or height may be perceived. Shadows *under* an object, assuming normal lighting from above, indicate an object with height. Shadows *over* an area suggest depth, e.g., a hole (Rock, 1975).

Both the gradual brightness gradients and the abrupt ones (shadows which are adjacent to lighter areas) are cues to form or depth or relief. For example, though human eyes may appear darker than the nose even under flat lighting, the two can be "separated" even more by side lighting which puts the eyes in shadow and thus makes them appear deeper in their sockets. Such lighting might also accentuate the shape and size of the nose. Also, the sharpness of the image (due to quality or focus of lens) serves to accentuate perceived depth. A sharply focused figure appears distant from an out of focus or softly focused background.

The above factors facilitate the perception of depth in flat instructional materials. The effect is presumably reduced because of the absence of the physiological cues mentioned earlier, but the illusion of depth can be very convincing. Surface features, such as reflections on the TV tube and texture of the photographic paper, serve to diminish the depth illusion.

Space, Time, and Motion

The previous three sections have considered the spatial and temporal aspects of signs, of modalities, of environmental regularities, and of message structures and patterns. Hence, the perception of space and time will not be belabored here. There will be only brief reviews and a few more principles.

The importance of the perception of spatial relations has been frequently noted in this chapter. The spatial proximity of people, for example, influences whether they are seen as strangers or lovers. The spatial directions in which people are moving (motions toward, away from, or with each other) are also important in perceiving relationship. And, as previously noted, the deployment of objects in space from foreground to horizon markedly influences our perception of their nearness (Forgus, 1966). Objects placed to the left may under some circumstances be perceived as occurring before or as being the cause of those placed to the right (Fleming, 1968). Also, under some circumstances, words placed above are perceived as more or better in relation to those placed below (De Soto, *et al.,* 1968).

1.51.   Spatial perception is strongly oriented relative to the vertical and horizontal.

Perception of the vertical and horizontal accounts for much of our sense of stability and orientation. The static and dynamic sense (located in the labyrinth in the inner ear), the muscle sense, and the perception of upright objects keep us upright oriented and provide a frame of reference for judging the spatial location and form of perceived objects.

In a sense, the frame of a picture or a TV screen provides a substitute anchor point for spatial perception. A tree parallel with the side of the frame is perceived as upright, and one at an angle to the frame is about to fall. A person that fills the frame is close; one that does not is distant.

1.52.   Ordinarily, the perception of time durations and time intervals is relatively inaccurate without a standard or frame of reference.

Temporal structuring or ordering of events is very important to perception. Events are perceived relatively, i.e., as before, after, or during other events. In fact, time is usually counted in reference to something: time for a cup of coffee, time for the bus, faster than you can count to three, slower than molasses. Accurate time estimation requires some external frame of reference such as counting seconds or observing some change such as the position of the shadow on a sundial. For this reason, time is typically portrayed in messages by means of change: the change in position of clock hands, changes from youthful to wrinkled faces, change from summer to winter.

1.53. *Time that is filled with activity appears to pass more rapidly than time that is not.*

The lesson for the designer is clear. S/he should fill the message time slot available. Of course, there is more to it than this, for what the time is filled with makes a major difference. Pleasant, changing, interesting events appear to shorten time durations and intervals, while repetitive and boring events lengthen them.

Time duration in film and TV is a much manipulated dimension. Where an on-going event has been documented, as in a Presidential address, thirty minutes may be reduced to five minutes of highly selected segments. In depicting a lengthy process, the passage of time may be implied by dissolves and fades or by leaving the process for a while and then returning at a later stage. An extension of this is the dramatic device of cutting back and forth between two concurrent events (typically chaser and chased) and thus either stretching or shortening real time. The perceived tempo of an event can be modified by changing the length of each scene.

Also, time relations can be depicted spatially as in the case of a time line or perhaps the ordinate of a curve. For events that recur, the time line is formed into a circle, and the successive events, such as the stages in the reproductive cycle of a plant, are arranged around it.

1.54. *The perception of motion is highly related to both temporal and spatial factors.*

As noted earlier, our perceptual apparatus is very sensitive to movement, even in peripheral vision. Motion attracts attention. So powerful a perceptual phenomenon is it that even minimal cues can suggest it. Motion can be suggested in static figures by blurring or streaking them, and by depicting them in active positions (arms and legs at dynamic angles). An asterisk moving appropriately in a film can be perceived as walking, jumping, or running. (Experiments in which one square moves variously in relation to another have, in darkened rooms, been perceived causally, i.e., "A" is seen to pursue, bump, join, push, repel "B"; Murch, 1973.) And the film medium itself gives an illusion of motion achieved through a succession of static views of objects in different spatial positions, the succession being so rapid that the separate views cannot be distinguished—a clear case of the proper arrangement of spatial and temporal factors.

More basically, time and space are reciprocal with reference to motion: speed = distance/time. An increase in speed is effected by either an increase in distance covered or a decrease in time taken, and the designer frequently has control of both factors.

1.55. The relation of figure to ground is particularly determinative of motion perception.

The sun appears faster-moving at the horizon than it does overhead partly because in the one case it is relative to a static horizon while in the other there is no reference point.

In film animation, a car may be perceived as moving either when it changes position relative to a static background or when it remains still relative to a background which changes position behind it.

As noted earlier with reference to size, the frame of a picture or screen provides a reference point. The less time required for a person to move from one side of the screen to the other, the faster s/he is apparently going.

The perception of motion is highly related to aspects of depth perception discussed in the preceding section. For example, because the retinal image of a car varies in size with its distance, the rate at which the retinal image changes in size is a clue to the speed of an approaching car. Also, a texture gradient perceived when we stand still becomes very dynamic when we move, giving many clues for size, distance, and motion. For example, when we walk down a corridor it appears to open ahead of us and close behind us, this being simply the consequence of a changing gradient of size, perspective, and texture. The gradient of expansion of the landing strip gives the approaching pilot critical cues for altitude, speed, and distance (Hochberg, 1966).

It has been assumed that instruction dealing with some action or motion was best depicted by full demonstration of the motion (live or with motion media, e.g., film and TV). There are apparently some exceptions to this.

Movements, as in a motor skill or procedure, may be adequately perceived from still photos plus verbal descriptions where:

(1) the movements are single, i.e., separate rather than concurrent or interacting;

(2) the movements are codeable, i.e., consistent with labels or directions which employ common or familiar terms; and

(3) there are no orientation difficulties, e.g., possibly ambiguous or disorienting changes of viewpoint between successive movements (Spangenberg, 1973).

However, it will likely take more design time (planning, testing, revising) to adequately represent the movements in a motor skill by still media than by motion media.

Perception and Cognition

At the beginning of this chapter it was asserted that perception is important because it sets limits on all subsequent cognitive processes. Here, in summary, the same idea is restated in positive form.

*1.56.   The better an object or event is perceived,
         according to the foregoing principles of percep-
         tion, the more feasible and reliable will be
         further cognitive processes, e.g., memory, con-
         cept formation, problem solving, creativity, and
         attitude change.*

Reciprocally, the quality of various cognitive processes will markedly influence subsequent related perceptions. What we have learned about our environment and what we consequently come to want to expect from it determine to an important degree what we give attention to, what we selectively perceive, and how we choose to interpret it. Thus, learning and thinking can be seen as facilitating the perceptual process of information extraction from the environment (Forgus, 1966). It is on such grounds that a case is sometimes made for improving, training, and educating the perceptual skills. Teachers of reading, of art, and of science have been particularly supportive of such training. The message designer may even become involved in designing materials to train and sharpen the very perceptual tendencies discussed in earlier sections.

References

Attneave, F. Some informational aspects of visual perception. In P.A. Fried (Ed.), *Readings in Perception: Principles and Practice.* Lexington, Mass.: D.C. Heath and Co., 1974.

Berelson, B. and Steiner, A. *Human Behavior: An Inventory of Scientific Findings.* New York: Harcourt, Brace, and World, Inc., 1964.

Berlyne, D.E. Attention as a problem in behavior theory. In D.I. Mostofsky (Ed.), *Attention: Contemporary Theory and Analysis.* New York: Appleton-Century-Crofts, 1970.

Bishop, P.O. and Henry, G.H. Spatial vision. In P.H. Mussen and

M.R. Rosenzweig (Ed.), *Annual Review of Psychology* (Vol. 22). Palo Alto: Annual Reviews, Inc., 1971.

Boynton, R.M. The psychophysics of vision. In R.N. Haber (Ed.), *Contemporary Theory and Research in Visual Perception.* New York: Holt, Rinehart, and Winston, Inc., 1968.

De Soto, C.B., London, M., and Handel, S. Reasoning and spatial representations. *Journal of Verbal Learning and Verbal Behavior,* 1968, *7,* 351-357.

De Valois, R.L. and De Valois, K.K. Neural coding of color. In E.C. Carterette and M.P. Friedman (Eds.), *Handbook of Perception* (Vol. 5). New York: Academic Press, 1975.

Dodwell, P.C. Contemporary theoretical problems in seeing. In E.C. Carterette and M.P. Friedman (Eds.), *Handbook of Perception* (Vol. 5). New York: Academic Press, 1975(a).

Dodwell, P.C. Pattern and object perception. In E.C. Carterette and M.P. Friedman (Eds.), *Handbook of Perception* (Vol. 5). New York: Academic Press, 1975(b).

Eysenck, H.J. A critical and experimental study of colour preferences. *American Journal of Psychology,* 1941, *54,* 385-394.

Fabun, D. (Ed.). Communications. *Kaiser Aluminum News,* 1965, *23*(3), 1-39.

Fleming, M.L. *Message Design: The Temporal Dimension of Message Structure.* USOE Final Report, NDEA Title VII Project 1401, March 1968.

Forgus, R.H. *Perception.* New York: McGraw-Hill Book Company, 1966.

Foulke, E. *Proceedings of the Louisville Conference on Time Compressed Speech.* October 19-21, 1966, Center for Rate Controlled Recording, University of Louisville, Louisville, Kentucky.

Fried, P.A. The brain—does it have a mind of its own? In P.A. Fried (Ed.), *Readings in Perception: Principles and Practice.* Lexington, Mass.: D.C. Heath and Co., 1974.

Gibson, E.J. Perceptual learning in educational situations. In R.M. Gagné and W.J. Gephart (Eds.), *Learning Research and School Subjects.* Itasca, Illinois: F.E. Peacock Publishers, Inc., 1968.

Gotz, K.O. and Gotz, K. Color preferences of art students: surface colors: II. *Perceptual and Motor Skills,* 1975, *41,* 271-278.

Graham, C.H. *Vision and Visual Perception.* New York: John Wiley and Sons, Inc., 1965.

Gregory, R.L. *Eye and Brain, the Psychology of Seeing.* New York: McGraw-Hill, 1973.

Haber, R.N., and Haber, R.B. Eidetic imagery: 1. Frequency. In P.A. Fried, (Ed.), *Readings in Perception: Principles and Practice.* Lexington, Mass.: D.C. Heath and Co., 1974.

Haber, R.N. and Hershenson, M. *The Psychology of Visual Perception.* New York: Holt, Rinehart, and Winston, 1973.

Helson, H. *Adaption-level Theory.* New York: Harper and Row, 1964.

Helson, H. Current trends and issues in adaptation-level theory. In P.A. Fried (Ed.), *Readings in Perception: Principle and Practice.* Lexington, Mass.: D.C. Heath and Co., 1974.

Hochberg, J.E. *Perception.* Englewood Cliffs, New Jersey: Prentice-Hall, Inc., 1966.

Hoops, R.A. *Speech Science: Acoustics in Speech.* Springfield, Ill.: Charles C. Thomas, Pub., 1969.

Isenhour, J.P. The effects of context and order in film editing. *AV Communication Review,* 1975, *23*(1), 69-80.

Kahneman, D. *Attention and Effort.* Englewood Cliffs, New Jersey: Prentice-Hall, Inc., 1973.

Klausmeier, H.J., Ghatala, E.S., and Frayer, D.A. *Conceptual Learning and Development: A Cognitive View.* New York: Academic Press, 1974.

Kling, J.W. and Riggs, L.A. *Woodworth and Schlosberg's Experimental Psychology.* New York: Holt, Rinehart, and Winston, 1971.

Knowlton, J.Q. On the definition of "picture." *AV Communication Review,* 1966, *14,* 157-183.

Leibowitz, H.W. and Harvey, L.O. Perception. In P.H. Mussen and M.R. Rosenzweig (Eds.), *Annual Review of Psychology* (Vol. 24). Palo Alto: Annual Reviews, Inc., 1973.

Levie, W.H. and Dickie, K.E. The analysis and application of media. In R.M.W. Travers (Ed.), *Second Handbook of Research on Teaching*. Chicago: Rand McNally and Co., 1973.

Mackworth, N.H. and Morandi, A.J. The gaze selects informative details within pictures. *Perception and Psychophysics,* 1967, *2,* 547-552.

Madsen, M.C., Rollins, H.A., and Senf, G.M. Variables affecting immediate memory for bisensory stimuli: Eye-ear analogue studies of dichotic listening. *Journal of Experimental Psychology,* 1970, *83*(3) Monograph Supplement.

McGinnies, E. Emotionality and perceptual defense. In P.A. Fried (Ed.), *Readings in Perception: Principle and Practice*. Lexington, Mass.: D.C. Heath and Co., 1974.

Miller, G.A. The magical number seven, plus or minus two: Some limits on our capacity for processing information. In R.N. Haber (Ed.), *Contemporary Theory and Research in Visual Perception*. New York: Holt, Rinehart, and Winston, Inc., 1968.

Moray, N. Where is capacity limited? A survey and a model. In A.F. Sanders (Ed.), *Attention and Performance*. Amsterdam: North-Holland Publishing Co., 1967.

Mouly, G.J. *Psychology for Effective Teaching.* New York: Holt, Rinehart, and Winston, 1973.

Murch, G.M. *Visual and Auditory Perception.* Indianapolis: The Bobbs-Merrill Co., 1973.

Neisser, U. *Cognitive Psychology.* New York: Appleton-Century-Crofts, 1967.

Paivio, A. *Imagery and Verbal Processes.* New York: Holt, Rinehart, and Winston, 1971.

Pick, H.L. and Ryan, S.M. Perception. In P.H. Mussen and M.R. Rosenzweig (Eds.), *Annual Review of Psychology* (Vol. 22). Palo Alto: Annual Reviews, Inc., 1971.

Plack, J.J. and Shick, J. The effects of color on human behavior. *Journal of the Association for the Study of Perception,* 1974, *9*(1), 4-16.

Posner, M.I. *Cognition: An Introduction.* Glenview, Ill.: Scott, Foresman and Co., 1973.

Rabb, D.H. Audition. In P.H. Mussen and M.R. Rosenzweig (Eds.), *Annual Review of Psychology* (Vol. 22). Palo Alto: Annual Reviews, Inc., 1971.

Reid, J.C. and MacLennan, D.W. *Research in Instructional Television and Film,* USOE Title VII B NDEA, Publication #OE34041. Washington: U.S. Government Printing Office, 1967.

Robson, J.G. Receptive fields: Neural representation of the spatial and intensive attributes of the visual image. In E.C. Carterette and M.P. Friedman (Eds.), *Handbook of Perception* (Vol. 5). New York: Academic Press, 1975.

Rock, I. *An Introduction to Perception.* New York: Macmillan Publishing Co., 1975.

Severin, W. Another look at cue summation. *AV Communication Review,* 1967, *15,* 233-245.

Shepard, R.N. Recognition memory for words, sentences, and pictures. *Journal of Verbal Learning and Verbal Behavior,* 1967, *6,* 156-163.

Spangenberg, R.W. The motion variable in procedural learning. *AV Communication Review,* 1973, *21*(4), 419-436.

Standing, L., Conezio, J., and Haber, R.N. Perception and memory for pictures: Single-trial learning of 2560 visual stimuli. *Psychonomic Science,* 1970, *19,* 73-74.

Swets, J.A. and Kristofferson, A.B. Attention. In P.H. Mussen and M.R. Rosenzweig (Eds.), *Annual Review of Psychology* (Vol. 21). Palo Alto: Annual Reviews, Inc., 1970.

Taylor, S.E. Sensation and perception: The complexity of word perception. *Journal of Developmental Reading,* 1963, 187-206.

Travers, R.M.W., and others. *Studies Related to the Design of Audiovisual Teaching Materials.* Final Report, USOE Contract 3-20-003, May, 1966.

Travers, R.M.W. *Educational Psychology: A Scientific Foundation for Educational Practice.* New York: The Macmillan Co., 1973.

Treisman, A.M. Selective attention in man. In P.A. Fried (Ed.), *Readings in Perception: Principle and Practice.* Lexington, Mass.: D.C. Heath and Co., 1974.

Van Bergeijk, W.A., Pierce, J.R., and David, E.E. *Waves and the Ear.* Garden City, New York: Anchor Books, 1960.

Vernon, M.D. *A Further Study of Visual Perception.* England: Cambridge University Press, 1952.

Vernon, M.D. *The Psychology of Perception.* Baltimore, Maryland: Penguin Books, 1962.

Sources for Principles

The following are largely secondary sources, i.e., reviews, summaries, and generalizations of groups of studies rather than detailed reports of individual studies. Thus, they serve well our purposes of identifying principles based on reliable bodies of research. Readers interested in identifying specific studies and the investigators who conducted them can generally do so through bibliographies in these sources (#1 refers to Principle 1.1, etc.).

1. Helson, 1974; Rock, 1975
1a. Helson, 1974; Helson, 1964
1b. Forgus, 1966; Helson, 1974
2. Berelson and Steiner, 1964; Treisman, 1974
2a. Berelson and Steiner, 1964; McGinnies, 1974.
2b. Forgus, 1966; Treisman, 1974
3. Dodwell, 1975(b); Forgus, 1966
3a. Forgus, 1966; Murch, 1973
3b. Dodwell, 1975(b); Forgus, 1966
3c. Berelson and Steiner; 1964; Dodwell, 1975(b)
3d. Berelson and Steiner, 1964; Murch, 1973
4. Forgus, 1966; Murch, 1973
4a. Forgus, 1966
4b. Berelson and Steiner, 1964

5.   Berelson and Steiner, 1964; Fried, 1974
6.   Neisser, 1967
7.   *
8.   Forgus, 1966; Kahneman, 1973
8a. Berlyne, 1970; Kahneman, 1973
9.   Forgus, 1966; Kahneman, 1973
10. Kahneman, 1973
10a. Helson, 1974; Vernon, 1952
10b. Mouly, 1973; Travers, 1973
11. Berelson and Steiner, 1964; Murch, 1973
12. Kling and Riggs, 1971
13. Plack and Schick, 1974; Vernon, 1962
14. Murch, 1973
15. Plack and Schick, 1974
16. De Valois and De Valois, 1975; Vernon, 1962
17. Graham, 1965; Gregory, 1973
18. Leibowitz and Harvey, 1973
19. Attneave, 1974
20. Murch, 1973; Van Bergeijk, Prince, and David, 1960
21. Berelson and Steiner, 1964; Rock, 1975
22. Murch, 1973
23. Hochberg, 1966; Rock, 1975
24. Hochberg, 1966; Murch, 1973
25. Hochberg, 1966
26. *
26a. *
26b. *
27. Knowlton, 1966
28. *
28a. *
28b. *
29. Moray, 1967; Posner, 1973

*Author's inferences based on research literature.

30. Pick and Ryan, 1971
31. Miller 1968; Murch, 1973
32. Miller, 1968; Murch, 1973
33. Berelson and Steiner, 1964; Posner, 1973
34. Haber and Hershenson, 1973; Vernon, 1962
35. Severin, 1967
36. Madsen, Rollins, and Senf, 1970
37. Pick and Ryan, 1971
38. *
39. Berelson and Steiner, 1964; Rock, 1975
40. Haber and Hershenson, 1973; Rock, 1975
41. Berelson and Steiner, 1964
42. Murch, 1973; Rock 1975
43. Berelson and Steiner, 1964; Rock, 1975
44. Forgus, 1966; Rock, 1975
45. *
46. Forgus, 1966; Rock, 1975
47. Vernon, 1962
48. Pick and Ryan, 1971
49. Forgus, 1966; Murch, 1973
50. Forgus, 1966; Rock, 1975
51. Rock, 1975; Vernon, 1962
52. Forgus, 1966; Murch, 1973
53. Forgus, 1966
54. Forgus, 1966; Murch, 1973
55. Rock, 1975; Vernon, 1962
56. *

*Author's inferences based on research literature.

Chapter 2
MEMORY PRINCIPLES

Given a motivated learner, and given perception of some statement (verbal or pictorial, by teacher, film, book), what are the conditions under which the statement will be learned and remembered? This is the essential question this chapter considers.

There are several current approaches to the analysis of learning and these are generally weighted toward one theoretical position or another. However, no one theory appears adequate to explain all kinds of learning; rather, each theory tends to have its own area of most fruitful application. S-R (stimulus-response) theories, for example, have been quite useful in explaining psychomotor learning and associative memory, while cognitive theories have been more attentive to problem solving. S-R theory has been more analytical, starting with elemental S-R events (associations) as the basic learning paradigm and attempting to explain more complex behavior, e.g., problem solving, as combinations or consequences of such elemental events. Cognitive theory has been more holistic, more concerned with overall understanding than specific memorization. One cognitive theory, called structural learning (Scandura, 1973), sees problem solving as the basic learning paradigm, and simple association (memorization) as a degenerate case of higher level rule learning.

Where discussions of learning are structured around such theories as the above, the distinctions between theories tend to be more apparent than the similarities—probably a desirable consequence where the objective is further inquiry. However, the intent here is the optimal design of instruction.

Hence, without denying the reality or validity of theoretical distinctions, particularly in relation to further inquiry, our strategy will be to emphasize those areas in which the operational conditions of learning are consistent across major theories, though the theoretical explanations may differ. This eclectic approach does not result in contradictory principles for the design of the conditions of learning. However, different theoretical or valuational positions of a designer may result in his emphasizing some principles over others.

A structure for examining a wide range of learning principles is the following (based on May, 1965):

1. Preparation—e.g., attention, perception.
2. Acquisition—e.g., association, discrimination, concept learning, principle learning.
3. Consolidation—e.g., reinforcement, review, practice.

The first group have been considered in the preceding chapter. There remain to be considered the conditions of learning grouped above under Acquisition and Consolidation. All will be dealt with in this chapter except concept learning and problem solving, which will be considered in the next chapter.

Basic Principles of Memory

Five principles appear relevant across many types and levels of learning. These will be considered first and will also be re-encountered in various ways in succeeding sections of this chapter. The first two principles are basic to acquisition, the next two to consolidation, and the final one to the way in which learning is tested and applied.

2.1.   Learning that is meaningful to the learner is acquired more readily and is retained longer

**than that which appears meaningless or arbitrary
to the learner. Aotbe***

Studies of learning nonsense stimuli support this principle. Not only does nonsense learning proceed slowly, but it is marked by striving toward some degree of meaning. This may take the form of seeking something familiar in the stimuli or seeking some pattern or regularity in them. For example, subjects trying to learn nonsense syllables frequently report that they analyze them for some similarity in sound or form to familiar words, or for some feature that is remindful of a familiar object. This gives the designer a clue: to add meaning to a message, incorporate elements from the learner's prior experience. A man's name—Roy G. Biv—can add enough meaning to the learning of the colors in the spectrum (Red, orange, yellow, Green, Blue, indigo, violet) to facilitate acquisition and recall. Thus, learning is meaningful to the extent it deals with familiar objects, events, etc.

Learning is also meaningful to the extent that the situation is organized and the learner is aware of that organization. This characteristic follows directly from the perceptual principle of organization found in the preceding chapter. Examples are the rhymes commonly used as mnemonic devices, e.g.:

General Spelling Rule—
I before E,
Except after C.

Common Exceptions to Spelling Rule—
Either, neither,
Weird, seize, leisure.

Only the rhythmic patterns and rhyming sounds make these meaningful, but this is enough to facilitate learning.

---

*Aotbe means all other things being equal. It means that the preceding statement holds under controlled research conditions but may well vary in applied situations, i.e., other factors may reduce or nullify its effect. Though "aotbe" holds for every numbered guideline in this book, it will appear only at the first of each chapter as a reminder to the reader.

The concept of "meaningful" is difficult to define in a way that a designer could apply it. We have chosen in the above to relate "meaningful" to two more useful concepts, i.e., familiarity and organization, both of which the designer can control to some degree.

> *2.2.   Learning to associate or relate two or more objects or events (stimuli and/or responses) is facilitated where they occur or are encountered in contiquity, i.e., close together in time and/or space.*

This is perhaps too inclusive a principle as stated, for it incorporates several that usually are considered separately. The range of its application will be suggested here, while other principles exemplifying it will be presented later.

The principle follows from the perceptual principle of proximity. Not only are proximate or contiguous experiences perceived as related, but also they are remembered that way.

Three basic branches of S-R psychology rely on contiguity:

    a. classical conditioning, wherein one stimulus is repeatedly paired (made contiguous) with another and comes to elicit the same responses as the other (learning).

    b. paired-associate learning, wherein one event is followed (contiguously) by another, such that the one becomes a stimulus which is the occasion for the other (response).

    c. reinforcement, wherein a response is followed (contiguously) by a consequence (a stimulus), the character of which (pleasant or unpleasant) influences the recurrence (learning) of the response.

Thus, putting things together in a message is a powerful manipulation for the designer. However, the consequent learning is highly dependent on many controllable factors in the situation which will be considered in some detail later.

Learning may at the outset be very tenuous. It fades rapidly without a process of consolidation. Two basic principles follow which affect the *consolidation of learning.*

2.3. *Learning is influenced by the frequency with which the stimuli are encountered and the same or similar responses made.*

This is an old and well-worn truism, "practice makes perfect." It is Thorndike's Law of Frequency. However true in general, it requires much qualifying in terms of the kind of repetition and the rate and spacing of repetition. Also, the kind of learning intended and level of proficiency desired are important determinants of the efficacy of repetition.

Repetition or rehearsal serves well for short-term maintenance of information, but other, more active processes (recoding, elaboration, transformation) are important for retention over longer periods (Postman, 1975).

Repetition is essential for psychomotor skill learning, e.g., typing, playing a piano, swinging a golf club, writing the letter "d."

Repetition is also effective for essentially meaningless (at least initially) kinds of learning, such as memorizing the multiplication table, the alphabet, the thirteen cranial nerves, the meanings of to, two, and too, the spelling of Mississippi, the f/numbers for camera apertures, the name of a new acquaintance, the date of Alaska's becoming a state. In contrast, no repetition will be needed to learn that fingers must be kept out of electrical sockets.

Essentially, the amount of repetition required in learning is reciprocally related to the meaningfulness of the material for the learner. Learning to spell Mississippi, for example, would require less drill where the pattern or rhythm is perceived: M - ISS - ISS - IPP - I. Similarly, learning f/numbers requires less drill where alternative numbers are perceived as being twice (or half) as great, i.e., 2.8, *4,* 5.6, *8,* 11, *16.*

Of course, given enough use (repetition) of Mississippi or the f/numbers, one would tend to learn them anyway. Thus it is that meaningless kinds of content tend to be retained because they are frequently used and each use is a repetition strengthening learning. Meaningless learning that is not repeated tends to be forgotten.

In contrast, concepts and rules tend to be easier to learn and more readily retained providing they are dealt with in a meaningful rather than arbitrary way. For example, the rule for finding the area of a rectangle is $A = 1 \times w$. It can be memorized by practice in expressing it and using it, but may remain relatively meaningless and arbitrary. However, if encountered as a rectangle divided into equal squares, five along one side and three along the other (see Figure 2.1), the otherwise meaningless rule becomes sensible. One can count the squares and thus prove to one's own satisfaction that the rule works. Further, it can be reconceptualized as three rows of five, added in the figure by rows (5, 10, 15), and finally simply multiplied (3 x 5). "Practice" in applying the rule to other rectangles may be seen by the learner to be the interesting task of finding out whether the new rule works with rectangles of different sizes.

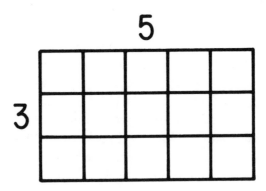

Figure 2.1. Meaningful approach to finding the area of a rectangle.

What we have been discussing is the comparative strengths of principle #2.1 (effect of meaning) and principle #2.3 (effect of frequency or practice). Such is the power of principle #2.1 that the designer would be well advised to maximize its use first and then apply principle #2.3 as much as necessary.

> **2.4.** *Learning is highly dependent on its consequences. Where consequences for the learner are pleasant, interesting, tension reducing, useful, instrumental, rewarding, or informative, learning is more efficient and more lasting.*

This is Thorndike's Law of Effect. It is the most essential condition for learning, in the view of reinforcement theorists.

We speak of the "school of hard knocks" as everyday living in which some kinds of behavior seem effective or enjoyable and are thus repeated (learned) and other kinds seem ineffective or painful and are thus avoided. In formal education the consequences are not left to the "good or bad breaks" of everyday living; rather, the consequences are more often arranged. Learning is controlled by the selective use of reinforcement, i.e., the teacher (or self-instructional program) arranges for pleasant consequences to follow desired responses and neutral consequences or unpleasant ones to follow undesired responses.

While this "rat lab" approach seems mechanistic or sub-human to many teachers, it has been used with undeniable success by researchers and practitioners of "contingency management," i.e., managing people's behavior in any situation (school, business, reformatory) by way of managing the contingencies of reinforcement, i.e., the consequences. Teacher criticism frequently centers on the unworthiness of the selected reinforcers or consequences, e.g., M & M candies instead of genuine interest in the subject matter. However, the consequences can be as diverse and varied as human interests and needs. First-graders can get an extra ten minutes on the playground for desirable reading behavior; and when reading comes to be seen as fun, an extra ten minutes of free reading time can be contingent on desirable mathematics behavior.

Negative consequences have long been used by teachers to control students. "If you don't stop . . . , I'll . . ." "If you don't study for the test, I'll give you a failing grade."

Which kinds of consequences, positive or negative, are most effective? Must every desired response be rewarded? How can a designer employ reinforcement strategies? These and other questions will be considered in later sections dealing with this principle.

> *2.5.*   *Learning as a measurable entity varies not only as a function of conditions during acquisition and during consolidation, as suggested above, but also as a function of the conditions of testing or application.*

That is, whatever a person can be said to "know" in an absolute sense, s/he can demonstrate his or her memory for only part, and that part depends on the type of question or situation involved. In general, aided remembering is more efficient than unaided. The following examples are in increasing order of difficulty (decreasing order of aiding).

1. Recognition—What is the capital of California; (Check one)
   a. Los Angeles   b. Sacramento
   c. San Francisco   d. Hollywood
2. Prompting—The equation for computing the area of a triangle is:
   Area = Base x H . . . . t ÷ 2.
3. Recall—Recite Lincoln's Gettysburg Address.

Thus, the evidence needed by both designer and client regarding the effectiveness of a particular unit of instruction is dependent not only on the characteristics of the unit but also on the characteristics of evaluation. This underscores what has been written both about clarity of intent (objectives) as an essential beginning step in design, and about decisions as to how that intent (learning) is to be measured. During consolidation, the student should be given practice with the type of testing condition that will be used to evaluate performance. Learning to recognize may be fundamentally different from learning to recall. Also, greater frequency of practice (Principle #2.3) may be required where measurement is by recall than where it is by recognition.

We have examined briefly two basic acquisition principles, two basic consolidation principles, and finally a basic evaluation principle. There follow numerous other principles and discussions of their application. These are grouped under four headings: Acquisition of Associative Learning, Consolidation of Associative Learning, Discrimination Learning, and Observational and Motor Learning.

Acquisition of Associative Learning

Memorization problems differ in several dimensions. One fundamental difference is that between memorizing two or more things as a group (association) and memorizing them as distinct and separate (discrimination). In general, the more similar two or more elements are perceived to be, the more readily they are associated and the less readily they are discriminated. Conversely, the more different the two or more elements, the more readily they are discriminated and the less readily they are associated.

Within each of these two categories of memorization, the learning problem may vary according to the number of things memorized, e.g., paired or multiple associations and paired or multiple discriminations. Here, the effect of the number of elements is the same for both categories of memorization, i.e., the greater the number of elements, the more difficult both the problem of association and that of discrimination. An important distinction among multiple associations is that of degree and kind of organization, i.e., whether the elements to be memorized are disordered, spatially ordered, temporally ordered (serial learning), hierarchically ordered, or other. In general, as the number of elements to be memorized increases, the more important it is for the designer to employ such factors as order, organization, and other instructional conditions which facilitate memory, conditions with which this unit deals.

What can the designer/teacher do to facilitate the acquisition of associations? Some of the possible environmental manipulations will be considered in what follows under the following categories: modality and sign types; cues and prompts; unit size and organization; learner activity and strategy.

Modality Effects and Sign-type Effects

In the Perception chapter, several modality differences were noted, e.g., visual perception was characterized as spatial and simultaneous, while auditory perception was characterized as temporal and sequential. The haptic (touching) and kinesthetic modalities have other characteristics which may be used to advantage for representing certain kinds of subject matter in instruction. Modality characteristics have consequences for learning.

> 2.6.   *In general, the modality used in the final testing or application situation should be the modality employed during instruction.*

Thus, the designer's analysis of a problem must include the final performance conditions. If the learner is to write a description of a chemical test for sodium, he should practice that response; if he is to make such a test in a laboratory, he should practice that. Instructional messages will vary accordingly.

Similarly, language instruction for the purpose of reading literature will emphasize vision, while that for the purpose of conversing in the language will include a great deal of oral and auditory practice.

It was noted earlier that perceptual capacity was larger where two modalities were simultaneously employed than where only one was employed. Presumably, there is a corresponding effect on learning.

> 2.7. *More learning can occur where information is received concurrently in two modalities, e.g., vision and audition or vision and touch, than where received in only one modality.*

This principle only states a possibility, which numerous circumstances can negate. Conflicting information in two modalities can interfere with learning. Redundant information in two modalities may have no effect except, for example, where a pictured object and a spoken name for it may be doubly recorded in memory, and thus better remembered. However, excessive redundancy in two modalities (hearing and seeing the same words) may induce boredom or inattention to one modality.

Nonetheless, the potential for better learning under two-modality conditions is apparent, the potential including both quantitative and qualitative dimensions.

In the Perception chapter, differences between digital signs (words) and iconic signs (pictures) were noted, e.g., the relative output advantages of digital signs (easily spoken or written) as compared to the iconic (generally poorly-developed skills in drawing). Clearcut differences have been established as well in the effects of pictorial and verbal signs on learning.

> 2.8. *The more concrete the things to be associated, the more readily they are learned and remembered.*

For example, in order to teach a student to associate a state with its principal crop, a designer might use a simple outline map and a picture of the product instead of or in addition to the words

"Indiana" and "corn." This assumes that in both word and picture versions the learner already knows the meaning of, or referent for, each sign (picture or word).

> *2.8a.   More specifically, objects and pictures of objects are better remembered than their names. These results have been found for a variety of learning conditions, including recognition, paired-associate, and free recall (see Figure 2.2).*

Explanations are varied, but a common one is that objects and pictures are recoded into names during perception, the result being essentially the same as if the name had been the stimulus. But the object or picture exhibits additional features which make it more memorable (see Figure 2.2). For example, a simplified drawing of a man may still indicate his expression, stance, clothes, or height, while the word "man" indicated little except type style, which is probably so common as to be unnoticed (Jenkins *et al.,* 1967).

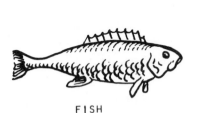

FISH

APPLE

Figure 2.2. Examples of pictures and words used in a memory comparison study. (Deno, S.L. Effects of words and pictures as stimuli in learning language equivalents. *Journal of Educational Psychology,* 1968, *59*(3), 202-206.)

Although we retain some iconic information by recoding it into verbal form, this would not account for the remarkable efficiency of our visual recognition memory for objects and events. We readily recognize the faces of friends, though we could not easily draw accurate likenesses of them.* Further, it is difficult to see how a sufficiently definitive memory list of verbal descriptors could be accessed and tested with sufficient rapidity to account for the immediacy of the experience of recognizing a friend's face. The same holds for our recognition memory for myriad objects and places we have encountered.

Some people possess what has been called photographic memory or eidetic imagery. They can recall vividly and in detail a picture or event previously perceived. As they are doing so their eyes move as though surveying a scene. (Rapid eye movement also frequently accompany dreams during sleep.) Eidetic imagery appears in some children (approximately 8%) but in very few adults (Haber and Haber, 1974).

2.8b. Concrete words are better remembered than abstract words.

There is even some evidence that noun concreteness is more important in learning than is meaningfulness (number of verbal associations) or frequency of usage (Tulving and Madigan, 1970).

The designer should note the consistency between the last two principles. They seem to agree that throughout the concrete to abstract continuum (from objects to abstract words) the more concrete is better remembered.

---

*Studies requiring subjects to reproduce from memory a pictured object (iconic sign) have typically yielded inaccurate or much simplified reproductions. It is not clear, however, whether the simplification occurred as a part of the perceptual and memory processes or as a consequence of subjects' inability to draw with greater precision. Requiring subjects to draw more carefully has resulted in greater accuracy of reproduction (Neisser, 1967).

Again, concreteness appears to aid memory partly because of the extra attributes it provides, whether perceived in pictures or associated with concrete words. Following this lead, the designer might want to greatly embellish messages with exotic pictures or colorful phraseology so as to provide more extras and further facilitate memory. However, in this way processing and memory capacity would soon be exceeded.

Further, it would certainly be a mistake for the designer to conclude that the more abstract messages are generally undesirable or to be avoided. Rather, abstraction is the goal toward which learning typically moves within a subject matter. The more concrete phases of instruction are to be seen as initial means to that eventual end.

> *2.9.   In general, instruction for the new learner in a subject area should begin with the more con-crete messages and move to the more abstract as the learner proceeds to higher levels of the subject. This principle holds for learners of all ages.*

This principle further qualifies the prior two principles. It places greater or lesser emphasis on message concreteness, depending on the age of the learner and the extent of his knowledge.

A distinction must be made between the conreteness of a message and the concreteness of the concept being presented. They need not be the same. Often the teaching of concrete concepts can benefit by abstraction which reveals the relevant attributes. Also, it is often the teaching of abstract concepts that can profit most from concrete messages: examples, illustrations, analogies, models, diagrams.

> *2.10.   Concreteness is more facilitating at the stimulus side of the association than the response side.*

This fits nicely with our everyday learning experiences as well as the more contrived classroom learning situation, i.e., we regularly respond in more abstract terms than we perceive. We describe (abstract R) our experiences (concrete S). We learn to name (abstract R) geographic features (concrete S). We write reports (abstract R) about laboratory experiments (concrete S). We assign weights, numbers, colors, etc. (abstract R) to the objects of our experience (concrete S).

Thus, the very common classroom task of learning to associate names with objects and relationships is facilitated where the designer depicts that object relatively concretely.

2.10a. An effective combination of iconic and digital signs appears to be a pictorial stimulus and a verbal response, e.g., label or description.

Studies of paired-associate learning show pictures to be most effective in the stimulus position and words most effective in the response position. This principle is consistent with much of our encounter with the world. We meet people and learn their names; we observe moisture forming on windows and hear the term condensation.

As this principle implies, one way to solve the digital versus iconic dilemma is to use both. Within the limits of channel capacity, this strategy appears to have much merit.

The principle is also consistent with the concept of coding discussed previously. To the extent that a word labels or categorizes a pictured object or event, it can facilitate the coding process.

2.10b. An effective combination of digital signs usually is a more concrete word as stimulus and a less concrete word as response.

Note that both this principle and the preceding one are

consistent with the principle that learning is facilitated where the stimulus is more concrete (whether digital or iconic) and the response is less concrete (or more abstract).

Cues and Prompts

One of the most obvious manipulations of the learning environment is that of modifying the instructional stimuli to be presented. What are some of these S manipulations, and what are their consequences for the learner?

An important distinction that is made in learning research literature is that between the *nominal stimulus* and the *effective stimulus.* The nominal S is what is presented to the learner; the effective S is that part of the nominal S which a particular learner selects out, attends to, and employs in making his/her response. A common designer/teacher error has been to overlook this distinction and to assume that the obvious (to designer) relevant attributes of the nominal S will become the effective S for the learner.

Several principles encountered in the Perception chapter have already suggested the general problem, i.e., we are selective perceivers, and our attention is drawn to novel and to complex stimuli. To be considered are several principles for the specific purpose of controlling attention in instructional situations.

> *2.11.   Learning what is relevant or criterial in a situation is influenced by the degree to which instruction controls the effective stimulus.*

> *2.11a. In general, instructional messages can control the effective stimulus either by adding or subtracting cues or by making cues more or less salient (prominent, noticeable).*

For example, words (cues) can be added to or edited from a description, and a pictured object can be made more or less salient by removing or adding a competing background.

2.11b. The cues manipulated* can be either criterial (substantively definitive) or non-criterial for the task or concept being taught.

An initial question is: What are the criterial attributes of a skill or task? An adequate skill analysis will yield much of the answer, but further analysis may be needed. For example, Gibson (1969) made a feature analysis of the ways in which printed letters of the alphabet differ, e.g., straight segments (horizontal, vertical, oblique), curved segments (closed, open), etc. This analysis yielded a chart which made possible the identification of the features of each letter which were distinctive or criterial, i.e., which were sufficient to identify each letter and distinguish it from others. Instruction based on such analyses could be narrowed to the essential distinguishing cues.

Obviously, a designer can choose what S manipulations to employ. S/he can use all the above manipulations. For example, biology instruction dealing with photosynthesis can add criterial cues (add a drawing to a verbal definition), subtract criterial cues (omit details of the organic chemistry involved), add non-criterial cues (lines under key words), subtract non-criterial cues (use schematized drawings), or make some cues more salient (emphasize the significance to man of the process). The question is: How many different kinds of such cue manipulations should the designer employ? Perhaps the most tenable answer is: Use all those and only those found to be necessary. But without extensive prototyping and formative evaluation this answer is difficult to apply.

*Stimulus manipulations which increase the probability of correct responding (accurate learning) have been called prompts, though the term will not be used here because of the varied and sometimes negative meanings it has acquired. We will use the word "cue" to refer to all stimulus manipulations, e.g., size, shape, color, detail, background, contrast, etc. "Criterial cues" are those that define the concept or are essential to the skill, i.e., they are what the learner must learn. Non-criterial cues are all others and include such as arrows and underlinings which call attention to but are not the criterial cues.

It does seem that a "bare bones" message design, especially where limited to criterial cues, will be more effective than an embellished one (despite a designer's desire to add certain niceties or production values), especially where the added color or realistic detail constitutes irrelevant complexity (McKeachie, 1974).

The problem is sometimes clouded by theoretical issues. In general, S-R theories stress the dire consequences of learner error (s/he learns incorrect Rs) and hence the virtue of maximum cueing to assure correct responding. In contrast, cognitive theories accentuate understanding (more than just correct responding), which includes knowledge of incorrect responses and why they are incorrect; thus, maximum cueing is not a virtue and criterial cues are preferred over non-criterial. The issue is unresolved. Anderson and Faust (1973) cite two studies which indicate negative consequences, both conceptual and motivational, from student errors. However, in neither study was the learner informed of the reason why his/her incorrect Rs were in error.

There appear to be no theoretical grounds for objecting to corrective feedback when necessary. So the main issue may be one of *when* to manipulate cues (either before instruction or after incorrect Rs have been made) and *how much* to manipulate cues rather than whether to manipulate cues at all.

One could argue that maximum cueing (minimum error) should be employed with mediators which do not readily provide corrective feedback, e.g., ITV and film; whereas minimum cueing could (not necessarily should) be employed with mediators which readily provide corrective feedback, e.g., teacher, branching program PI, and CAI. The more flexible strategy of providing cues only as needed is most available to those mediators which typically provide the most detailed record of student errors, e.g., PI and CAI, and which thus give the designer the option of either revising the program to prevent error or providing branching (corrective and informative feedback) to prevent the repetition of an error.

> *2.12. Learning is facilitated where criterial cues are salient (dominant, apparent, conspicuous). Add non-criterial cues only if and as necessary (see Figure 2.3).*

Stated differently, the designer should try first to "magnify" or accentuate the criterial features and "reduce" or eliminate the non-criterial features. Elimination or reduction of non-criterial features is especially important where they are "noisy," i.e., more salient or dominant than the criterial features. Magnification and reduction are most readily done where the features are continuously variable, i.e., size, brightness, weight, loudness. Thus, in teaching the parts of a flower, the features peculiar to a petunia can be eliminated and those characteristic of flowers generally can be retained and accentuated with bold outlines. This accentuation of criterial cues is preferred over simply adding arrows (non-criterial) to a color photo of a petunia.

The reasoning behind this is that an added non-criterial cue is a temporary crutch which, though effective in early stages of learning a concept or skill, must eventually be removed or faded so that responding will be under the control of the criterial cues, i.e., so that the student will understand.

For example, in teaching sight reading of the word "boy," the learner is expected to say "boy" when shown the printed word. The teacher can provide non-criterial cues, e.g., pointing at the word, saying "boy," and asking the learner to also point and say. Or, as noted earlier, a picture of a boy could also cue the desired response. In any case, none of these non-criterial cues can be continued, for the printed word alone must become a sufficient cue. See Figures 2.3a and 2.3b for examples of the above principle.

> *2.13. Learning can be facilitated where initial instruction is maximally cued to assure correct responding and where in subsequent instruction the non-criterial cues and the added-salience*

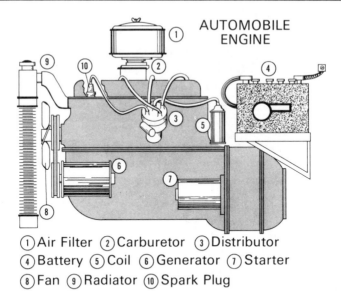

① Air Filter ② Carburetor ③ Distributor
④ Battery ⑤ Coil ⑥ Generator ⑦ Starter
⑧ Fan ⑨ Radiator ⑩ Spark Plug

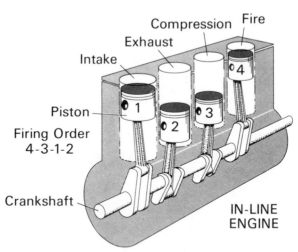

Figure 2.3. Two representations of an automobile engine in which different sets of criterial cues have been made salient. (From Barnard, J.D., Stendler, C., Spock, B., and Beeler, N.F., *Science: A Way to Solve Problems,* Copyright © 1962 The Macmillan Co. Reprinted by permission of The Macmillan Co.)

> **cues are faded, i.e., gradually reduced and finally eliminated.**

The indication is that the abrupt removal of such cues tends to result in errors, whereas the gradual removal does not. The principle is particularly pertinent for fixed-pace media, where errors are more likely, and for non-responsive media, where errors are least readily corrected.

Proponents of the fading technique begin with maximally cued instruction and gradually eliminate the non-criterial and the added-salience cues. There is an alternative strategy called brightening (Ellson, Barber, Engle, and Kampwerth, 1965), which is essentially the opposite of fading. It has been found superior to conventional instruction, but has not been given controlled comparison with fading.

> **2.14. Learning can be facilitated where initial instruction is minimally cued and where cues are added gradually (brightened) if and as necessary till the learner can respond correctly.**

Brightening is *not* the same as small step programming. Whereas the latter consists of small additions of *content* (leading to additional responses), the former consists of additions of *cues* for a single response. The learner is given a question or problem in a relatively difficult form, i.e., without supporting cues. If his response is adequate, he is reinforced and presented with another question or problem. If not, instruction on the problem is "brightened" by means of a series of cues, which gradually increase the probability of adequate responding. For example, where the student is learning to sound out new words, a series of cues for a tutor to present might be:

1. Point to word and ask learner to sound it out.
2. Point to first letter(s) of word and ask learner to make the sound.

3. Tell learner the sound of the first letter(s) and have him repeat it.

Cue #2 is employed only if #1 fails, cue #3 only if #2 fails.

Or, the series of cues may be much longer. For example, where a beginning reader is being taught to understand printed instructions, e.g., "Point to Jack" (i.e., to a picture of a boy), the progression of cues might be as follows:

1. "Read the sentence."
2. Wait (to increase duration of stimulus).
3. "Read it again."
4. "Read it again, faster."
5. "What does it say?"
6. "What does it tell you to do?"
7. "Do what it tells you to do."

Where the learner might not understand "point," still further cues may be needed.

8. "Point to the window."
9. "Point to me."
10. "Point to the book."
11. "Point to the sentence."
12. "Now, what does the sentence tell you to do?"
13. "Do what it tells you to do." (Ellson, 1976, p. 160)

At whatever cue level the learner responds correctly, he/she is reinforced and the next task presented. Cued tasks can be repeated later till no further cueing is required. The process has many of the characteristics of discovery learning and, similarly, generally requires a responsive mediator such as a teacher, tutor, or CAI. Its merits appear to include an avoidance of over-cueing and the accompanying problems of subsequent fading. Also, it is adaptable to individual learner differences, for the amount of cueing (0 to maximum) depends on the learner's responses. Further, it would seem to provide greater incentive for many learners than would over-cued instruction.

The brightening procedure, beginning as it does with minimal cueing, will typically be accompanied by more errors than the fading procedure. These errors can be followed by added cueing, and/or by explanation of errors.

These are several ways of following up on errors which have been advocated in various instructional procedures and conceptualized with reference to various theories:

1. overlook errors or at least don't acknowledge them,
2. inform learner that he/she responded incorrectly,
3. same as 2 plus give the correct response,
4. same as 3 plus explain the correct response,
5. same as 4 plus explain why the incorrect response was wrong (Anderson, 1973).

Actually, there are additional combinations and variations of the above possibilities. Further, there is a comparable array of ways to follow up on correct responses, which will be considered later.

It seems probable that learning should increase as the amount of information regarding errors increases, i.e., as the procedures move from #1 to #5 above. However, the evidence based on PI (well controlled conditions of instruction and feedback) is not conclusive for #s 4 and 5.

NOTE: Consideration of knowledge of results (whether correct or incorrect) and of the presumably related concept of reinforcement is frequently done in one unit. Here, the handling of errors will be dealt with as an acquisition problem and the handling of correct responses and of positive reinforcement will be dealt with as a consolidation problem. Though the distinctions are not so clearcut as this treatment implies, the instructional procedures and consequences appear sufficiently different to justify the separation of corrective feedback from the confirmation of correct responses. Essentially, the distinction is between the informational effects and the motivational or affective effects.

2.15. *Informing the learner of errors increases learning over not informing him, and then providing him*

***with the correct responses is additionally facili-
tative.***

(The fact that knowledge of correct responses, where *no* error
has been made, has frequently been shown in PI studies to be
*in*effective in increasing learning will be discussed subsequently
with reference to reinforcement.)

There is nothing very surprising in principle #2.15. Feedback as
a principle in engineering (human and otherwise) is of long
standing, and it has been a basic tenet of programmed instruction.
However, research on knowledge of results has produced numerous
findings of no significant difference. Recent studies suggest the
need of conceptual and procedural refinements, i.e., distinctions
must be made between knowledge of correct and knowledge of
incorrect responses, and knowledge of results should be provided
only after the learner responds. In some programs, e.g., programmed textbooks, it is possible for the learner to look ahead,
find the correct answer, and simply copy it. This is not really
knowledge of results *after* responding, for the learner made no
independent response. The result is that the learner responds
accurately within the program but does poorly on the test
afterwards. Perhaps this is because the learner doesn't have to
attend critically to either question (S) or answer (R), or perhaps it's
because the learner is given no practice in associating S and R
(Anderson, Kulhavy, and Andre, 1971).

2.16.   *Informing the learner of errors and of correction*
for those errors should occur as soon as practical
after the incorrect R.

This principle can be seen as another example of contiguity,
Principle #2.2, in this case the temporal contiguity of error and
correction.

The principle is supported more by reinforcement theory and
by animal studies than by PI studies (Anderson and Faust, 1973).

Arguments for the principle are particularly persuasive where the learner might rehearse or practice an error not immediately corrected or where the subject matter is hierarchical such that correct responses to (understanding of) subordinate concepts or tasks is prerequisite to learning superordinate material.

However, where the material to be learned is meaningful (both S and R familiar) some delay in feedback is not critical (McKeachie, 1974) and may even be beneficial (More, 1969).

2.17. Repeating a previously missed item and responding to it correctly aids learning, particularly complex learning.

This can be seen as a special case of the frequency principle (#2.3), though practice beyond one correct trial is not implied above. It is more clearly a case of contiguity, i.e., to arrange for the correct R to be made contiguously with the criterial S. Simply informing the learner of the correct R, following his/her error, does not typically provide contiguity with the criterial S. However, the whole item can be repeated such that the learner attends to it just before giving the correct R.

Lindgren (1972) considers feedback to be a more meaningful event for the learner than some of the preceding discussion has implied. He sees it as a situation in which the "learner makes corrections in strategy as a result of errors he perceives" (p. 203). This refers to something more than making the correct R to the criterial S, though such is presumably involved. The implication is that the learner changes his/her strategy or approach to the question, which change is based on awareness of the errors, rather than simple recall of the·answer.

The practical differences between providing S-R contiguity and providing understanding of "why" may be considerable. Perhaps the designer's most functional approach to such differences in conception and implementation of feedback or knowledge of results is with reference to the kind of learning involved in a particular situation. If essentially rote or meaningless learning is required, then principles 2.11 to 2.17 apply. However, principle #2.1 reminds us of the power of meaningfulness (familiarity and pattern) in learning. Often, it may be the case that a given bit of content can be taught at several different levels, rote memory to concept or principle. Consequently, it seems desirable to invoke additional principles where possible, principles that raise rote learning to meaningful learning. This is not to recommend the ignoring of principles 2.11-2.17 but rather to add to them wherever possible.

The likelihood that a cue *becomes* meaningful (as we have defined it) to the learner is affected by its two characteristics. Is the cue familiar? Does the cue relate to others or does it suggest a pattern?

2.18. *Added cues which are familiar and/or which direct attention to relationships can facilitate learning.*

The kinds of relationships which a designer may employ are many, e.g., conceptual, spatial, temporal, causal, functional, hierarchical, quantitative, qualitative.

There are numerous ways of making stimuli more familiar. An example would be the analogy (verbal or pictorial) which illuminates a new or difficult idea by comparison with attributes of a familiar one, e.g., the tug-of-war game familiar to youth, which provides a useful analogical way of depicting meaningfully some of the stressful, seesaw, human conflicts (of ideas, ambitions, politics, trade, war) common in history. Also, simply reminding the learner how new facts relate to old both adds an element of familiarity to the new and changes isolated (meaningless) new facts into meaningful additions and extensions of previous cognitive structures and relationships. Further discussion of organizational and relational factors follows in a later section.

Unit Size, Spacing, and Pacing

Whereas the preceding section included principles for analyzing and selecting the kinds of elements (cues) to be included in a unit, this section includes several principles for gauging the amount of such cues (information) to provide and the rate at which to provide it.

The optimum size of an instructional unit is difficult to determine short of field testing it. The teacher/designer's tendency is typically toward trying to cover too much in a given time. For persons enthusiastic about their subject, there is always something very interesting or apparently essential which should be added to a unit.

Size was considered in the Perception chapter with reference to the concept of perceptual span, i.e., the number of familiar items that could be perceived at a glance. The "magic number" of 7 +/- 2 was reported to be quite stable across a diversity of situations. However, use of that number in design was seen to be impaired by two factors: (1) the size of an item varied widely depending on the perceiver's familiarity with it; (2) there was no rate prediction for glances, i.e., the time necessary between glances was not established.

The unit size problem for material to be learned has been investigated extensively with PI under the label "size-of-step," but with no consistency of results. There is apparently no way of reliably estimating unit size by counting sentences or minutes. There are too many important variables, e.g., difficulty or familiarity of the subject, interest or age of the learner. However, there are apparently outside limits to human ability to process information, and 7 +/- 2 is an example of such a limit.

> **2.19.** *The more mature and/or the more motivated the learner, the greater can be the size of an instructional unit.*

Although intended to refer to the size or length of a continuous instructional session, the above probably also applies to the number of such sessions (dealing with a certain topic) with which the learner can cope.

While the above principle can be seen as referring to continuous instruction on a given topic, regardless of method or activity, unit size can more analytically be dealt with by dividing instruction into presentation and testing (or demonstration and practice). The question then becomes: How much information or how long a presentation is desirable before the learner responds by rehearsing the material, by answering questions, or by discussing or applying what has been encountered? Margolius and Sheffield (1961) conceive of the problem as that of finding the "demonstration-assimilation span." Establishing the span depends on field testing, the optimum span being the amount of material for which 75 percent of learners tested immediately can score 100 percent correct. Units of this size, interspersed by student responding, were found by Margolius and Sheffield to be superior to larger size units for a mechanical assembly task.

Knowledge factors, e.g., the structure of the skill or concept, probably interact with psychological ones, e.g., the demonstration-assimilation span. Skill or concept analyses yield units (sub-skills, or sub-concepts) or instructional phases (introduction, problem, definitions, examples) which provide useful segments of instruction. Probably the best procedure is to use such subject matter units as the primary determiners of unit size, modulated as necessary by psychological factors, e.g., the demonstration-assimilation span.

There is an extensive history (before PI) of inquiry into the problem of unit size under the labels: part or whole learning, spaced or massed practice. Conceptually, the part vs. whole issue is centered on the stimulus, i.e., the amount of subject matter presented; whereas, the spaced or massed practice issue is centered on the response, i.e., the amount or extent of practice.

The part vs. whole issue has in the main been seen as a theoretical concern, the S-R theorists preferring the teach-a-small-part-at-a-time approach and the cognitive theorists preferring the teach-the-whole-first (or at least introduce-the-whole-first) approach. Both pose difficulties. The teach-a-part-at-a-time approach poses problems in getting the parts effectively linked so that an eventual whole is synthesized. The teach-the-whole-first approach is difficult to initiate, for it's easier to begin with a small (simple) part than the whole (complex), even where that initial whole is simplified. An eclectic view for the designer is to employ both strategies, i.e., first provide a simplified overview (see principle #2.26b to follow) and then provide the parts one-at-a-time. The parts (judging by Margolius and Sheffield's demonstration-assimilation span) would be larger than initially employed by programmers but smaller than is typical of texts or lectures.

2.20. For non-meaningful subject matter the part method appears preferable, for meaningful subject matter the whole method appears preferable.

There is some evidence for and some logic in this principle. First, non-meaningful subject matter, as defined here, is not intrinsically patterned and hence has no apparent whole with which to begin. The opposite, of course, is characteristic of meaningful subject matter (familiar and patterned), and there is some evidence that meaningful subject matter is more readily learned with the whole method. There is also evidence that the more intelligent the learner, the more likely s/he will benefit from the whole method (Mouly, 1973).

Second, non-meaningful learning (lists of words, spelling, foreign language vocabulary) is frequently more difficult and requires more practice than meaningful learning. Hence, employing small increments of new material (parts) followed by practice appears sensible. In contrast, where important meanings are in the relationships between parts of a subject matter, delayed consideration of those relations, as in a pure part method, would likely inhibit learning.

2.21.   *Spaced or distributed practice in general results in greater learning than massed practice.*

This means that interspersing rest periods between practice periods is preferable to continuous practice. The principle apparently applies over diverse kinds of learning, nonsense to meaningful.

There is some difficulty in applying the principle because the manipulation (length of practice) is relative, being influenced by the difficulty of the task, age and motivation of the learner, etc. For example, a motivated learner at the end of the semester can study for longer periods (massed practice) than s/he could earlier.

There is some conceptual difficulty with "practice," for in early stages of learning it contributes to acquisition and in later stages to consolidation. Here, with reference to acquisition, we are primarily interested in practice sufficient for initial learning to some beginning criterion or level of proficiency.

The negative effects of massed practice are at least two. First, the learner becomes fatigued and less efficient. Not only is the learner inefficient, but also, as Bugelski (1964) observes, where the learner is frequently tired when s/he studies s/he may come to associate the two, i.e., become convinced that books induce sleep or that learning is very tiring.

Second, the likelihood of interference with preceding and succeeding learning is increased. The effects of interference are complex, and will be considered in the following sections.

Organization, Pattern, and Relationship

The preceding chapter emphasized organization as a basic characteristic of the perception process. For the designer, influencing perceptual organization by means of stimulus organization was treated as a means of increasing the predictability and the capacity of perceptual information processing.

For learning, the consequence of organization can be more acquisition and better retention. In what follows, a diversity of relationships will be considered, from that between S and R to that between inserted questions and the material to which they refer.

2.22. The more meaningful the relation between the things associated, the greater the learning.

This is, of course, an example of the basic principle (#2.1) of meaningfulness. The classical example from research is that word pairs are easier to associate than nonsense syllable pairs.

As noted earlier, meaning includes at least two dimensions: familiarity and order or pattern. Thus, words that the learner has used and knows the referents for are more readily associated than new words or those with unclear meanings. The designer can choose familiar words or arrange for unfamiliar words to become more meaningful through association with familiar synonyms, objects, or contexts. From a cost/benefit point of view, it might be more economical to increase the meaningfulness of a pair of words than to increase the number of trials required for associating the otherwise meaningless pair. Contrariwise, there is some evidence that where words are to be simply recognized, rather than recalled, a degree of novelty or uncommonness or unfamiliarity appears to facilitate recognition memory (Sheppard, 1967).

Structures or patterns of the simplest kinds can facilitate associative learning. Where two meaningless words have similar first letters or sounds, or where their first letters are adjacent in the alphabet, etc., association may be improved. The designer can contrive relations by making the things to be associated part of a common figure. For example, placing corn in a field the shape of the state of Indiana (see Figure 2.4) yields a contrived figure which provides a perceptual basis for associating the two. More powerful are relational factors which are conceptual, e.g., contrasts such as before-after, cause-effect, subordinate-superordinate, etc.

Figure 2.4. Related or combined images of "corn" and "Indiana" which may facilitate associating the two.

From a quite different theoretical perspective, the essential condition for acquiring an association is not the meaningfulness of the relationship between things but the contiguity of the relationship, i.e., the closeness of the things in time or space. From our eclectic perspective, it is useful to consider both meaningfulness and contiguity as determinative influences on learning and hence as useful kinds of manipulations.

The general contiguity principle previously stated (#2.2) will here be made explicit in a situation in which an existing S-R association is employed by the designer to effect another S-R association, one in which the S is new.

> **2.23.** ***A change in S-R relations can occur in which an old R becomes associated with a new S. Specifi-***

> *cally, where a strong habit or association or*
> *reflex exists, i.e., a particular S dependably*
> *elicits a particular R, the response can be shifted*
> *to another S by arranging for the new S to be*
> *repeatedly paired with the old S. Under these*
> *conditions, the new stimulus becomes associated*
> *with (conditioned to) the old response by being*
> *contiguous with it (Principle #2.2). Eventually,*
> *the new stimulus elicits the old response (see*
> *Figure 2.5).*

This change in S-R relations is called classical conditioning. It can also be referred to as S substitution. While prominent in texts on learning, classical conditioning has usually served more to explain certain kinds of already-learned behavior than to suggest procedures the teacher or designer can use in facilitating or

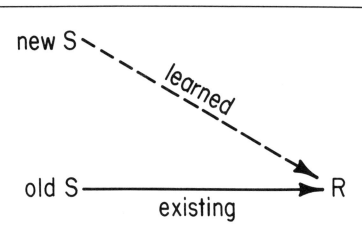

Figure 2.5. Diagram of the conditioning process. Note that both the S-S and the S-R relations are contiguous. The contiguity in time of the two Ss (old and new) is the essential direct manipulation arranged by the designer. The resulting contiguity of new S and old R is what presumably leads to the new association.

controlling learning. For example, much early learning is explained by classical conditioning, e.g., how the infant's responses to mother come to be elicited also by the spoken word "mother." Responses of fear are also explained in this way, e.g., a child encounters a dog amid loud sounds of barking and/or being jumped upon or knocked over. The unpleasantness previously associated with loud sounds or falling becomes linked to a new stimulus, dog.

Bugelski (1964) describes in a similar way a student's learning to like or dislike a subject. A student may from the outset like or dislike his teacher's personality or style (presumably because of prior associations of those traits with other persons). This provides ideal circumstances for conditioning, i.e., all semester the teacher is paired with a particular subject matter. The student's sub-vocal response to the teacher, e.g., "I dislike," comes to be made to the contiguous subject matter as well, i.e., the student learns to dislike the subject. Bugelski in this context asserts that the proper role of the teacher is that of conditioner of favorable emotional reactions to subject matter. Similarly, one can say that an important role of other mediators, e.g., film, book, tape, is conditioning favorable responses (attitudes) to the subject matter and, more broadly, to the school and to education.

Other kinds of learning processes are involved where prior S-R relations interact with present S-R relations. In one process, prior learning facilitates present learning; there is a transfer of learning. In another process, prior and subsequent learning interact negatively in what is called interference. Prior learning interferes with present learning, and present learning may interfere with recall of prior learning (Travers, 1973). Thus, both the concept of interference and that of transfer deal with the effects of earlier learning on later learning, or, vice versa, but the predictions are opposite, inhibition vs. facilitation. The next two principles attempt to clarify the relationships between the S and R of earlier learning and that of later learning.

2.24. *When a stimulus is similar to previously learned stimuli, learning will be facilitated if the new response to be learned is similar to those previously made.*

For example, one learns in elementary school to use the word "batteries" (flashlight) to refer to certain cylindrical objects which power lights. Transfer of the R (the word "battery") is quite easy to similar looking (cylindrical) objects which power lights, e.g., larger batteries and smaller penlight batteries.

However, the opposite effect is likely where the new response is dissimilar, as the following principle indicates.

2.25. *When a stimulus is similar to previously learned stimuli, learning will be inhibited if the new response to be learned is dissimilar to those previously made.*

An example of this would be learning to respond in a friendly, positive manner to stimuli (other races, other political parties) which have previously been responded to in an unfriendly or negative manner. Similarly, habitual Rs to familiar situations in teaching or in child rearing are difficult to modify. In a word, responses are resistent to change.

These effects (Principles #2.24 and #2.25) are summarized and extended in Table 2.1.

Response	Stimuli	
	Similar	Dissimilar
Similar	1. High positive effect	2. Slight positive effect
Dissimilar	3. Negative effect	4. No effect

Table 2.1. Interfering-facilitating relations between old S and R and new S and R (after Berelson and Steiner, 1964, p. 161).

Cell # 1 in the table refers to Principle #2.24, i.e., where both the S and R of the earlier learning are similar to both the S and R of later learning, transfer is maximum and interference minimum. Cell #3 refers to Principle #2.25, i.e., where in later learning a dissimilar (new) R must be learned for a similar (old) S, the interference is maximum. Where the stimulus to be learned is dissimilar from previous stimuli, there is little effect (cell #2 and #4) regardless of the R.

Another observation can be made from comparing cells #2 and #3 in Table 2.1. It appears easier to learn different Ss (same R) than it is to learn different Rs (same S).

In addition to the relationships discussed in the foregoing, other relational or organizational factors are pertinent to design. The Perception chapter suggested that our perceptions are organized and that the rate of information processing is influenced by perceived organization of the stimulus. Skill and concept analysis procedures suggest some of the ways in which subject matter is organized. The issue here is the influence of various organizations of substantive elements on the acquisition of associative learning.

2.26. *Where material to be learned is organized and that organization is apparent to the learner, acquisition will be facilitated.*

One can suggest further that some ways of organizing instruction are likely to be more facilitative than others. For example, while alphabetizing is a widely applicable way of organizing material, there are frequently other organizations which are more substantively relevant. The names and locations of the states can be learned in alphabetical order, but a more relevant ordering would be by regional groupings.

Units of instruction are commonly organized on apparently logical bases, e.g., from simple to complex (from single-celled organisms to mutlicellular organisms), from concrete to abstract (from examples of inflation to theories explaining it), or from the familiar to the unfamiliar. There seems little reason to question these rationales.

There is some counter evidence, namely that instruction can be sequenced too predictably and hence lack interest, at least for the more able learner (McKeachie, 1974).

Memory for elements within a unit varies according to the serial position of the elements (serial position effect).

> *2.26a.* ***Cues encountered earliest and latest within an instructional unit tend to be better remembered than cues in the middle.***

These effects are called primacy (superior learning of initial or first material) and recency (superior learning of last or more recent material). It may be that these are basically the consequence of greater isolation or reduced interference, i.e., no potentially inter-fering events before the first of a series or after the last of a series.

While these effects are strong for recall of word lists, there is some evidence that they are of less importance for meaningful prose and of little importance for recognition memory of picture series.

The effect of introductory material on subsequent learning has recently been investigated under the label "advance orga-nizer."

> *2.26b.* ***Where the beginning of a unit provides an introduction to the material which is relatively abstract and general, subsequent learning of related details within the unit can be facilitated.***

The introductory material is called an advance organizer. The principle seems valid for learning material that is meaningful, or perhaps it is that the material *becomes* meaningful for the learner because an advance organizer provides familiarity and pattern.

The principle is consistent with the whole-first preferences of cognitive theorists. The difficulty with either applying it or investigating it more analytically is in the designing or operationalizing of the advance organizer.* Obviously, it precedes further instruction and is intended to give some organization to what follows. But just what would "give organization" and, in particular, how abstract should it be? Answers to these questions are slow in coming.

The characteristics of advance organizers which facilitate learning have included: (1) previewing or outlining of topics to be covered, and (2) contrasting new material with what the learner already knows. An example would be a topic sentence at the beginning of a paragraph. There are numerous other kinds of introductions which *might* facilitate subsequent learning, e.g., directions about how to perform a task, advance selectors which alert the learner to isolated facts or features (in contrast to relations and patterns), motivational statements (arousal stimuli, per Bull, 1973), e.g., If you learn the following material, you can . . . .

The concept of advance organizer is strongly remindful of another advance stimulus called "set" (discussed in the Perception chapter), which would explain the effects of organizers in terms of perceptual readiness for or selective sensitivity to what follows.

However, organizers can be located in other than advance positions, as the following states.

2.26c. Intra or post unit organizers can facilitate learning.

---

*A recent review of numerous studies revealed that fewer than half found differences favorable to advance organizers. Part of the problem is conceptual and operational (What is an advance organizer?) and part is theoretical (How would an organizer function?) (Barnes and Clawson, 1975). Many explanations of negative findings are possible, including the fact that an advance organizer may function only when organization is otherwise lacking in the subject matter, the instruction, or the learner (cognitive structure).

Examples would be internal or subordinate topic headings and end-of-unit summaries.

The organizers studied have generally resembled topic sentences or summary sentences and have presumably functioned (in part at least) in an organizing role. However, the insertion of *questions* in prose instruction has also been studied, and its effects are presumably not organizational.

> *2.27. Questions inserted frequently in instructional prose facilitate prose learning, particularly where the questions follow the passage. The effect is large where the criterion test consists of the same questions, though there is sometimes a positive effect on new questions as well.*

In contrast, the effect of pre-questions seems to be smaller and limited to the question-relevant aspects.

Inserted questions are called adjunct questions and are spaced throughout the text, i.e., after each paragraph or each page rather than listed at the end of the chapter. Generally, too, the effect appears greater on short-answer questions than on multiple-choice (Anderson and Biddle, 1975).

Such results for inserted questions are remindful of those in programmed instruction, where frequent questions are integral to the instructional design from the outset rather than subsequently inserted. However, the above principle is important because it is based on studies done separately from other aspects of programming, e.g., active responding and feedback, and hence has relevance outside of typical PI contexts.

The reason for such effects is still being debated, e.g., added review, arousal, added activity, and processing.

> *2.28. The kind of inserted question influences the amount and kind of learning.*

The kind of question asked (rote recall of details, application of principles) seems to selectively facilitate the kind of learning characterized by the question (Anderson and Faust, 1973).

Of perhaps greater theoretical interest is the finding that higher level questions may induce greater recall, presumably because of the additional levels of processing required. Greater recall (as compared to rote questions) has been found for meaningful questions of various types, e.g., inferential, application, comprehension, abstract, and interrelational (relating details to topic sentence). Note the following example passage and questions (Rickards, 1976, p. 14):

> The southern area of Mala can best be described as a desert. Rainfall is less than 2 inches per year in southern Mala. The soils of the area are either rocky or sandy. In the summertime, temperatures have been recorded as high as 135 degrees in southern Mala.
>
> - *Rote learning of facts postquestion:* How many inches of rainfall are there per year in southern Mala?
> - *Rote learning of ideas postquestion:* What geographical term best describes southern Mala?
> - *Meaningful learning postquestion:* Why can it be said that southern Mala is a desert?

In most cases post questions were used, though there is some evidence that such conceptual questions function as well or better in a pre-passage position (Rickards, 1976).

The use of inserted questions seems advisable as well with mediators other than text, and hence should be widely useful for the designer. For example, Anderson (1970) recommends inserting questions in lectures. He suggests that the facilitating effect can be distributed throughout the class by first asking the question, then pausing so all will think of an answer, and finally calling on one student. It seems likely, too, that questions instead of captions for textbook illustrations would induce higher levels of processing and of learning.

There is also some evidence that poor readers who read in a word-by-word fashion may recall more and may comprehend more where meaningful (as compared to rote) post questions are employed (Rickards, 1976).

Other ways of ordering words also have consequences for learning.

> *2.29.* *The organization of words within sentences influences learning. Specifically, the more nearly a string of words approximates English word order, the more readily it is learned. Further, the active form of sentence structure is easier to learn and use in solving problems than is the passive form.*

Thus, though novel word orders may be useful in attracting attention, they may not be learned as readily as normal word orders.

Learner Activity, Strategy

Some theorists essentially equate learning (acquisition) with doing. We presumably learn by doing, and whatever we do in a particular context, i.e., with reference to a particular S, we associate with that context. However, there is plenty of contrary evidence, i.e., learning without activity, at least observable activity. For example, we learn from lectures or films even when we don't take notes. And numerous studies of PI have shown no difference between overt and covert responding.

Part of the conflict is definitional. The tendency, as in the above paragraph, has been to equate active responding with overt or observable responding. Contrariwise, Anderson and Faust (1973) distinguish three levels of activity: (1) attending (reading, looking, listening); (2) covert responding (repeating words sub-vocally or generating mental images); and (3) overt responding (oral, written, or drawn Rs). Obviously, if one considers even level

#1 (attending) to be an active R, there is little doubt that active responding is necessary to learning. Under this definition, a useful question is: What kind(s) of active responding are most facilitative of learning?

> *2.30.   In general, where the learner reacts to or interacts with the criterial S, learning is facilitated, and that facilitation increases with the degree of learner activity or involvement.*

There is evidence that as the degree of activity increases (from attending to overt responding) the amount of learning increases; however, the difference between covert and overt may be slight. There are residual advantages for the overt R. From the teacher-designer's viewpoint, the overt R can be evaluated and changes made in instruction as necessary; from the learner's viewpoint, external feedback, corrective or reinforcing, can be received.

However, overt responding can readily be overdone and can degenerate into meaningless drill. Some of the ways to use practice fruitfully to consolidate learning are considered in the next major section, Consolidation of Associative Learning.

Overt activity can vary importantly in the degree and kind of learner involvement or, as Lindgren (1972) conceives it, the degree to which the learner processes and transforms the stimulus. If s/he repeats a paragraph word-for-word, s/he is overtly active but makes no transformations and learns little. If s/he restates it in other words or generates a mental image of the situation, s/he is involved in transformation and will likely retain more. Such processing and transforming activities* are highly subject to

*In a more theoretical formulation of this idea (Craik and Lockhart, 1972), learning is hypothesized to be proportional to the level of processing of the information. For example, studies have shown that where subjects only note the sound or spelling of a word (low level processing) their recall of the word is less than that of subjects instructed to assess the meaning or value of the word (high level processing). Similarly, where subjects only judge the sex of a

control by the instructional designer, e.g., by the set given, the task assigned, the questions asked.

A special term for certain cognitive transformations is "mental elaboration" (Rohwer, 1972), and its effect seems to be a recoding of the input information such that it can be stored in additional ways and/or in more individually consistent and meaningful ways. Thus, facilitative covert activity can take the form of recoding, elaboration, or transformation of the information received. Several principles based on such activities follow shortly.

Implicit in the idea of learner activity is that of learner choice of what to attend to, what way to process it, and what kind of covert or overt R to make, if any. These choices we can call learner strategy. The teacher-designer can influence learner strategy to some degree by way of organizers, choice of subject-matter, kinds of cues presented, rate of presentation, etc. On the other hand, learners develop preferences for certain strategies, presumably on the basis of the variety of strategies they have encountered and the relative effectiveness of the strategies tried.

2.31. *The strategy employed by the learner markedly influences the time required to form an association and the probability of recalling it.*

Simple repetition or drill, by itself, is one of the least effective strategies. Other methods which employ both familiarity and structure are more effective and can be included by the designer in instructions to the learner.

2.31a. *Where a learner's strategy involves the genera-*

---

pictured person, their recognition memory for the picture is less than that of subjects instructed to judge the character of the pictured person (Bower and Karlin, 1974). The level of processing (Craik) or degree of learner involvement in transforming the stimulus (Lindgren) appears to strongly influence learning.

*tion of a relational mental image, associative
learning can be markedly facilitated.*

For example, the designer could instruct learners to form their own mental image of Indiana and corn, i.e., one image incorporating both, as vivid or exotic an image as possible. This will require a few seconds, but will markedly improve recall of the association. Note that the essential characteristic of the image, i.e., unified whole, is the same whether the learner generates his/her own or studies one presented by a designer.

Some writers emphasize the need for the imagery to be interactive, i.e., imaging an ear of corn on top of a map of Indiana is not as useful a relational structure as an interactive image such as a large corn plant growing out of the map. Further, a vivid image which adds novelty by embellishing or elaborating the objects to be associated is effective, e.g., the head of an Indian (Indiana) who has corn cobs in place of feathers in his headdress.

An example of the degree of memory facilitation possible with an imagery strategy is a study reported by Bower (1972). A sample of university students were given arbitrary pairs of concrete nouns to associate under instructions either to form a mental image of the two named objects interacting or to learn the pairs of words so that the left word of each pair could cue recall of the right. Pairs were presented for five seconds. After presentation of each 20 pairs, recall was tested by presenting the left word of each pair. Subjects were informed of the correct responses after testing. Five such 20-pair lists were presented, after which all 100 pairs were tested again. Recall for the imagery instructions condition was about 50 percent greater than for the standard recall instructions condition (see Figure 2.6). Subsequent studies in which control subjects were prevented from using imagery techniques have yielded recall scores for the imagery condition which were 100 percent greater than those for the control. Such differences between experimental and control groups appreciably exceed those for most other kinds of manipulations of instructional conditions reported in the recent learning literature.

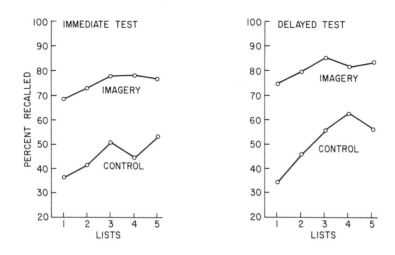

Figure 2.6. Amount of recall over five lists of words by imagery vs. control subjects, tested both immediately and delayed. (Bower, G.H. Mental imagery and associative memory. In L.W. Gregg (Ed.), *Cognition in Learning and Memory.* New York: John Wiley and Sons., Inc., 1972.)

Where an association should include more than two items, a more complex and exotic image can be generated by learner or designer which incorporates the several items in interactive and elaborated relationships.

There is good evidence of a developmental effect regarding learner strategies. Rohwer's (1972) work, for example, suggests that an imagery strategy for memorizing is not spontaneously used by learners before about 18 years of age. However, younger learners can successfully use the strategy provided the objects and relations are demonstrated or pictured (ages 3-9) or the process of generating interactive images is described in instructions to the learner (ages 12-18). Thus, where the cognitive process (interactive imagery) cannot be performed by younger learners, it can be demonstrated (supplanted) by objects or pictures.

There is evidence (Salomon, 1972) that certain other cognitive processes can be supplanted as necessary by media. For example, films and TV can supplant (serve as substitutes for) the mental process of visualizing (imaging) certain spatial events or relations, such as making a cross-section through the earth. For a learner who has never observed or learned about such processes, the supplantation is necessary; for more experienced learners, presentation of just the label might be a sufficient cue for the generation from memory of the appropriate visualization, either as a mental image or as a drawing.

> *2.31b. Where a learner strategy involves the generation of a relational sentence or paragraph, associative learning can be facilitated, i.e., words embedded in a sentence or paragraph are more readily associated than those processed in isolation.*

For example, it is easier to learn to associate the noun pair, "fork" and "cake," when they are embedded in the context or pattern of a sentence, "The fork cuts the cake" (Rohwer, Lynch, Suzuki, and Levin, 1967). In these and other cases, it is somewhat of a puzzle as to why it is easier to memorize both the elements and the structure, such as a five-word sentence, than it is to simply memorize the elements, the two words. A string of digits presented orally is more readily learned if a rhythmic pattern is introduced. Again, it would seem that the pattern would introduce an additional load on memory instead of effectually decreasing the memory load (Neisser, 1967). Apparently, the explanation lies in the large facilitating effect of structure in perception and learning.

The evidence is that learners instructed to create narrative stories incorporating lists of unrelated nouns can readily do so. In one study (Bower and Clark, 1969) subjects took about one to two minutes to create stories which included ten nouns. They repeated this procedure for a dozen different lists. Recall by the story group was 93 percent, while recall by control subjects using their own methods for an equivalent time was only 13 percent.

Bower (1973, p. 63) provides an example of a story incorporating the twelve cranial nerves as follows:

> At the oil factory (olfactory nerve) the optician (optic) looked for the occupant (oculomotor) of the truck (trochlear). He was searching because three gems (trigeminal) had been abducted (abducents) by a man who was hiding his face (facial) and ears (acoustic). A glossy photograph (glossopharyngeal) had been taken of him, but it was too vague (vagus) to us. He appeared to be spineless (spinal accessory) and hypocritical (hypoglossal).

A designer might employ a similar narrative or a rhyme in a message designed to teach a list of items. Or s/he might instruct students to generate their own. The thematic unity of such stories plus the syntactic structure of the sentences provides the necessary relational structure, and the addition of numerous common story elements provides the desired familiarity factor. Thus, pattern or structure plus familiarity yield a kind of meaningfulness which, though synthetic, is nonetheless quite effective for memory purposes.

However, it is still an open question as to whether the designer should provide a relationship in the message or encourage the learner to generate one. It seems probable that where a meaningful structure exists or can be provided for the verbal or pictorial elements, it should be employed by the designer along with specific instructions to notice and use it. Otherwise, where there is no meaningful structure, i.e., where the relationships are arbitrary and rote memory is needed, the designer should encourage the learner to generate some verbal, numerical, or pictorial structure.

At the beginning of this section it was indicated that there are noticeable differences in the strategy employed by learners in a given situation, and that these differences may reflect in part differences in knowledge of alternate strategies and in part differences in preference for or success with certain strategies. The designer can take these differences into account in any of several ways: (1) adapt instruction to the preferred strategy of the learner; (2) inform the learner of an effective strategy for coping with each unit and even train the learner to employ it; or (3) incorporate varied instructional approaches in each unit, such that the learner can find some representation of the content which is acceptably consistent with his/her strategies.

In addition, one can make a strong case for systematic instruction in alternative information processing strategies as an early and perhaps ongoing part of the school curriculum. The intent would be to assure each learner of a varied and adaptable repertoire of learning methods such that s/he would have educated preferences, i.e., would choose for each kind of learning a relatively efficient strategy.

This idea of teaching structures that have wide utility would apply to such commonly used graphic patterns as pie graphs, time and number lines, and hierarchical outlines and tables. Learning the pattern of the alphabet obviously yields a comparable payoff by greatly simplifying access to a dictionary, to a textbook through its index, and to a library through its card catalog.

Kumar (1971) cites evidence that scanning skills can be improved with training, and recommends more widespread instruction in encoding procedures for students.

Salomon (1972) found that visualization skills could be developed through repeated exposure to special films. For example, learners shown films of the laying out or unfolding of solid objects (cubes, etc.) onto a flat plane were later able to perform better than control Ss on visualization tasks. Similarly, learners encountering a film which showed many zooms in on details of a painting subsequently performed significantly better than control Ss in the skill of attending to details in a display.

Perhaps the concept of "visual literacy" can become better studied, understood, and applied with reference to such information processing skills as the above.

Consolidation of Associative Learning

Once learning at some initial level has been acquired, retention over longer periods of time is influenced by several factors which can be said to consolidate learning. Principles #2.3 and 2.4 (frequency and reinforcement) are basic to much of the discussion of consolidation principles which follow.

Knowledge of Correct Responses, Reinforcement

> *2.32. What occurs (S_2) immediately following an act (R) strongly influences the probability the act will be repeated in the existing context (S_1). That is, the likelihood that S_1 and R become associated (learned) is dependent on S_2, the consequences.*

This principle combines two basic principles previously discussed, i.e., contiguity and effect or consequence. It is called instrumental conditioning, as compared to classical conditioning, Principle #2.23.

The power of this principle as compared to classical conditioning is the comparative ease with which a teacher can control it, e.g., a mere smile or nod or "That's correct" or "Good work," can provide the consequence, the reinforcement, which strengthens learning. However, other mediators (film, TV, books, etc.) do not so readily provide such reinforcement.

It is essential here to distinguish between contingent and non-contingent reinforcement. The intent in the former is to reinforce the learner only if and when s/he displays the desired behavior. If a teacher smiles and nods only when a correct answer or desirable approximation is given, s/he is employing contingent reinforcement. It is this kind of control that other mediators, except programmed instruction, typically lack.

Non-contingent reinforcement presumably occurs when a whole lesson or presentation is interesting, exciting, or otherwise has positive consequences for the learner regardless of his/her responses. Thus, non-contingent reinforcement is a more general concept that is essentially indistinguishable from other techniques for "motivating" the learner. It is, however, something that mediators other than the teacher and PI can readily provide. Such mediators can be designed so as to interest and excite the learner and make the general consequences of learning positive. Techniques discussed in other chapters for attracting attention and persuading would be pertinent for non-contingent reinforcement.

A key point is that, by definition, a reinforcing stimulus makes more likely the recurrence of the response it follows.* Thus, the selective use of reinforcement is appropriate where the learner gives a correct R (an event the designer wants to recur) to the criterial S, and the general use of reinforcement is desirable to make the learning process seem worth participating in again.

Though a central principle of PI, much research with PI fails to show any positive effect for reinforcement where that consists of knowledge of results following a correct response. One study (Anderson, Kulhavy, and Andre, 1971) suggests the reason may be that most programs permit peeking at answers before responding. Where this is prevented and the learner must respond *before* receiving reinforcement, learning is reliably facilitated. This suggests that knowledge of correct responses is not apt to aid learning from programmed texts and other mediators which do not control for peeking.

A central design issue is: What kinds of stimuli are reinforcing? It is clear that many stimuli in a learning situation may not be reinforcing, even some of those which are intended to be. For example, knowledge of results is supposed to be reinforcing, but where a learner correctly answers a series of easy questions, it is

---

*This concept of reinforcement ignores the fact that the consequences of some acts are negative, i.e., they make recurrence of a response *less* likely. Punishing a noisy student is an example. There is evidence that while punishment may have an immediate deterrent effect, it may result in little long-range behavior change. The withholding of positive reinforcement can be more effective. Hence, positive reinforcement (given or withheld) is the more effective manipulation and is the focus of the above discussion.

apt to be counter-productive to tell him/her the correct answers and/or praise him/her. If no effort has been expended, no plaudits are expected.

Basically, a reinforcer is anything that works, i.e., that results in the recurrence of the desired R. One strategy for choosing a reinforcing S_2 is to allow the learner to choose from a list of possibilities. For example, a first-grader might choose one of the following: an extra dessert, extra time for an art project, or an extra story read by the teacher. Most reinforcing stimuli for older students are not under the control of teachers, e.g., peer approval, an increased allowance, a place on a ball team. Grades appear to be the most potent reinforcer for older students, though added comments in class or on papers can be effective. Also valuable are opportunities for greater independence in choosing study topics and more options in instructional method.

Further, the motivational aspects (praise, tangible rewards) are more important for non-achieving children, while the informational aspects (knowledge of results) are more important for middle class achievers (McKeachie, 1974).

Reinforcers can be seen as satisfying basic needs or motives. Numerous listings of such motives have been made, but only a few will be mentioned here as suggestive of kinds of reinforcers. Beyond such physiological needs as food, there are many learned needs which are more appropriate to school learning, e.g., need for affiliation or social contact; need for status or esteem; need for achievement. There is evidence, too, that humans seek variability in stimulation and have intrinsic interest in puzzles and problems (Berelson and Steiner, 1964).

Basic problems in the management of contingent reinforcement are those of *timing* and *frequency*. How soon after the desired R has been made should reinforcement be given? What proportion of desirable Rs should be reinforced? The following principle deals with timing.

2.32a. Generally, reinforcement should occur soon

> *after the desired R is made. This facilitates*
> *identification of the desired behavior and associ-*
> *ation of it with the criterial stimulus. Where*
> *reinforcement must be delayed, care must be*
> *taken to make sure the learner knows what it's*
> *for.*

Although there is considerable evidence indicating that immediate reinforcement is more effective than delayed, it is also clear that humans learn to do work for which reinforcement (grades, prizes, achievements) is delayed. Perhaps the essential factor is that the person knows which of his/her behaviors lead to which reinforcement or consequence.

A teacher's "OK," "Well done," "Good thinking" after students' oral responses are examples of immediate reinforcement, while comments on a paper returned the next day or later are examples of delayed reinforcement. Programmed Instruction and Computer-Assisted Instruction provide built-in capacity for immediate reinforcement, whereas typical books and films do not. However, class discussions of books and films provide many opportunities for teachers to reinforce learning from such mediators.

There is some evidence against immediate reinforcement (knowledge of correct Rs). More (1969) found that where knowledge of results was delayed from two to 24 hours, both recall and retention were higher than where knowledge of results was immediate. This evidence is based on school learning of several pages of science and social studies material of medium difficulty. Probably immediate reinforcement would have been more effective if the material had been more difficult. The delay time may have provided opportunity for the learner to think about or interact with the material and thus recall it better (Principle #2.30).

In addition to these reinforcement timing considerations, there is the problem of frequency.

> **2.32b. In general, it appears desirable to reinforce all correct responses during initial learning. Subsequently, a fairly frequent though random pattern appears preferable for consolidation and maintenance of behavior.**

At early stages of learning, or throughout difficult learning, the student benefits from feedback as to the correctness of his/her behavior, and also frequently needs encouragement. The more confident the student becomes of his/her correct performance, the less effective the external feedback, for s/he will likely be providing it internally.

Practice, Application, and Review

Principle #2.3 emphasized simple repetition of learned behavior, the more frequent the better. Principle #2.22 indicated the desirability of spaced practice. Principle #2.30 indicated the importance of learner activity. The emphasis here will be on distinctions between different kinds of practice as they affect the consolidation of learning.

A first distinction is that of the kind or level of learning.

> **2.33. In general, psychomotor skills and rote verbal learning require more practice for consolidation than do concept or principle learning.**

For example, learning to play a musical instrument requires years of practice to acquire competence, and continued practice thereafter to maintain and perfect it. In contrast, learning the concept "geologic strata" may require only reading a definition and seeing descriptions or pictures of several examples, there being essentially no practice. Certainly, subsequent experience identifying strata in the field, observing their displacement, etc., would greatly enrich the concept, but would not change its basic definition.

2.34. *In general, the newer the material the more*
practice is required overall and the more time is
required per repetition.

This fits nicely with Principle #2.32b, which recommends frequent reinforcement of initial learning, for frequent practice provides the occasions for frequent reinforcement. In fact, some writers see the reinforcement possibilities as the primary reason for practice.

2.35. *In general, practice in varied contexts can both*
increase retention of learning and extend its
range of utility.

The influence of varied practice on retention is explained in S-R terms as the linking of an R to a variety of different aspects of an S such that the R is more likely to be recalled. That is, more aspects of the available S become effective for the learner, thus increasing the number of ways in which recall can be cued.

A similar effect, called transfer or generalization, occurs when different, but similar, stimuli are encountered and the learner repeats the previous R. As a consequence, the learning is transferred or generalized to other situations and its range of utility is broadened. An example of this is in the use of reviews at the end of units which not only repeat essential ideas but also extend them with reference to new contexts, problems, or relations.

An extension of this "review plus new" idea has been called the progressive part method in which earlier learned parts are periodically and systematically re-introduced in subsequent instruction. The effect is to compensate for some of the weaknesses of part-learning by providing spaced practice (Principle #2.22) and, especially, by relating old learning to new contexts and new learning (Principle #2.35), i.e., by making some partial wholes out of the parts. For example, words from earlier vocabulary lists are re-introduced periodically in subsequent lists, sentences, and stories.

Transfer is sometimes considered a natural consequence of a well-learned unit. A more rational view is that while it can occur without apparent pre-planning, it is best seen by the designer as the consequence of deliberate instructional design.

> *2.36.* *Transfer is facilitated where the learning situation resembles the testing or application situation, or where the learning is practiced in various "realistic" contexts (simulation).*

As suggested earlier, with reference to acquisition, transfer is facilitated where the new S and R are similar to the previous (Principle #2.25).

A systematic extension of transfer and generalization processes is the learning of a concept, in which an R (the concept name) is learned for a carefully defined *group* of stimuli (concept examples) which may appear different but have certain attributes in common. More on this in the Concept Learning chapter.

Not all the consequences of transfer or generalization are positive. Frequently overgeneralization occurs such that the R is inappropriate in the new context. When this happens a discrimination must be learned.

Discrimination Learning

When faced with a collection of stimulus objects, a learner can group them (form a concept) and refer to each item in the group by the same name (acquired equivalence), or s/he can distinguish between the objects and refer to each by a different name (form a discrimination). To discriminate two things is to distinguish between them. Perceptual discrimination, the perception of difference, was discussed in the Perception chapter as one of two basic dimensions of perception, the other being the perception of similarity. We tend to separate our world of objects, events, and ideas into distinguishable entities or groupings, within which are identified similarity, consistency, and regularity, and between which are observed difference, inconsistency, and irregularity.

While the preceding principles of learning have dealt with the associating or relating of things, the following principles will deal with the learning to distinguish or discriminate things. It was noted earlier that stimulus item similarity facilitates association, whereas item dissimilarity facilitates discrimination; and that for both, the more items to be learned (multiple associations and multiple discriminations) the more difficult the task.

Many of the preceding association principles apply as well to discrimination learning, i.e., discrimination learning is facilitated by practice, benefits from corrective feedback and reinforcement, etc. What seems particularly pertinent to discrimination learning are manipulations of criterial cues.

> *2.37.   Discriminations are most readily learned where the differences between stimuli are maximal.*

> *2.37a. Differences can be maximized by exaggerating the criterial features, by increasing the number of feature differences, and by eliminating or reducing the dominance of the non-criterial features (see Figure 2.7).*

> *2.37b. Training should begin with examples which are most different and proceed to those with finer differences to the extent required.*

For example, in teaching the difference between a high quality and low quality photographic print or jackknife dive or microscopic slide, the designer would begin with the gross differences (examples which are "obviously" different) and train toward the subtler differences (requiring finer discriminations).

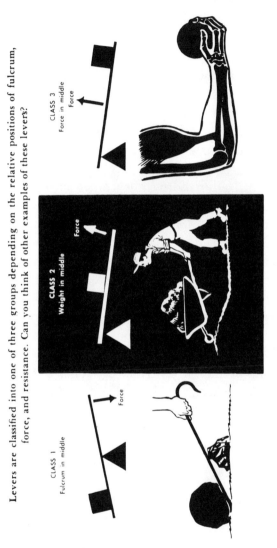

Figure 2.7. Differences in classes of levers are represented three ways: (1) verbally, (2) abstract figures, (3) concrete examples. These several differences should facilitate the discrimination of types of levers. (From Jacobson, King, Killie, and Konicek, *Broadening Worlds of Science,* Copyright © 1964 American Book Co.)

2.38. *Prior training with the criterial attributes facilitates discrimination learning.*

Perhaps the most questionable of association principles as applied to discrimination learning is that of stimulus contiguity. Some authors assert that discrimination learning is facilitated where the items are placed side-by-side in space or close-together in time, the intent being to make differences apparent. Others contend that the characteristics of the items should be learned in situations quite separate in space and time and not made contiguous until after thoroughly learned in isolation, the intent being to avoid interference.

A compromise position is to teach the characteristics of one item, e.g., the letter "m," separately until moderate competence is reached and then introduce the item to be discriminated, e.g., "n," and provide for practice in identifying "m" in the presence of "n." The latter requires a contiguous situation but could be graduated in difficulty. For example, begin with a simultaneous presentation and a matching task, e.g., Which one(s) (in the comparison group) match "m"? Then end with a successive presentation and a choice task, e.g., Choose the "m"(s) from the series of letters. (Based on Anderson and Faust, 1973.) Possibly, the simultaneous vs. separate issue is related to the meaningfulness of the distinction to be learned, i.e., where the differences are sensible and meaningful the comparison could be simultaneous, but where the differences are arbitrary, e.g., m and n, the initial presentation would be separate.

Depending on theoretical preferences or practical considerations, a designer might attend primarily to the stimulus features to be discriminated, e.g., to adding or accentuating criterial cues and/or removing or deemphasizing non-criterial cues; or s/he might control the consequences, e.g., reinforce correct Rs and/or withhold reinforcement of errors and/or provide corrective feedback. Where possible, do both.

Observational and Motor Learning

Studies of imitation and of modeling have enlarged our understanding of a kind of learning sometimes referred to as observational learning.

2.39. *Observing the actions of another person (model) can lead to the acquisition of new learning or the facilitation or inhibition of prior learning.*

Reported observational learning has been of many kinds (cognitive content, pro- and anti-social behavior, racial and sex-role attitudes) and across a wide age range (kindergarten to adult) (Leifer, 1976).

Of particular interest to instructional designers is the evidence that the model may be either live or recorded (film, videotape).

Of interest relative to learning theory is that plausible explanations of observational learning have included elements of both S-R and cognitive perspectives. In the view of one of the primary investigators (Bandura), the observed behavior is processed and stored both in imaginal and verbal codes. Later, the verbal response may be elicited, which activates the imagery, which in turn guides the learner's imitation of the previously observed behavior (Baldwin, 1973). Overt imitation can take place during observation of the behavior, immediately after, or some time later.

2.40. *Imitation by children has been shown to be influenced by the nurturance (friendliness) of the model and by the observed consequences of the model's behavior. Observed punishment may inhibit imitation of the punished behavior.*

It appears that for children in particular, observational learning is very important in the acquisition of social skills. Further, observational learning is credited (in varying degrees by different authors) with an important role in early language learning (Baldwin, 1973).

Accounts of observational learning are remindful of those of motor learning, particularly where the motor learning involves behavior already in the learner's repertoire. Under these circumstances, observing a motor skill performance may be a sufficient basis for its acquisition.* For example, the skill of operating an overhead projector (for one who has operated other projectors) involves several familiar behaviors: inserting plug in receptacle, placing device with lens facing screen, flipping a switch, operating focusing knob. Little is new except sequencing and adapting these already-practiced actions, so the skill can largely be acquired by observational learning.

However, where new motor skills must be learned, particularly complex ones such as serving a tennis ball or parallel parking, learning by observation alone is insufficient; more knowledge of the nature and sequence of the acts is required and much more practice is necessary.

> **2.41.** *Motor learning commonly involves both knowledge of the form and sequence of actions and proficiency in implementing them. Knowledge of the form and sequence may be acquired by verbal instruction and/or by observing a model, while proficiency in the actions may require practice, sometimes very extensive practice.*

---

*Or as noted in the Perception chapter, even still pictures of stages of the action may suffice for motor learning so long as accompanied by verbal descriptions and so long as the words refer reliably to actions which the learner has previously observed and performed. Also, verbal description by learners of observed action has been shown to improve imitation of a model (Baldwin, 1973). Presumably, verbal instructions alone may suffice where the words cue recall of images of prior actions.

Older conceptions of motor learning placed greater emphasis on the chaining together of separate moves such that (with much practice) each move would arouse the following one, i.e., aspects of each response (arousal of muscle senses, etc.) would become the stimulus for the next response in an associative chain. Training focused on establishing the linkages through practice.

More recent conceptions (Posner and Keele, 1973) place emphasis on higher-level processes called motor programs, i.e., a representation in memory of an entire movement pattern. The implication is that whereas at first the learner's knowledge of the movement is applied consciously, haltingly, and with benefit of much feedback (visual and kinesthetic), later control of the movement is smooth and requires little conscious attention. Presumably, the control becomes partly automatic, i.e., a motor program is formed. The training implied would focus on establishing an image or internal representation of the movement pattern, perhaps through repeated observation of an expert. The intent of subsequent practice would be to bring execution closer and closer to the internalized model.

The conflict between the above alternative conceptions is unresolved, so principles to be applied are wanting. However, task or skill analysis procedures (described in Duncan, 1972; and Anderson and Faust, 1973) are functional in establishing the sequence of moves, the most difficult moves, and the possible sources of difficulty.

Also operative in observational learning contexts are numerous of the memory principles encountered earlier, e.g., frequency, contiguity, reinforcement, spaced practice, knowledge of results, and part-whole learning.

Conceptually, observational learning is difficult to distinguish from other forms of learning in which a stimulus is observed by a learner. The distinction in current usage seems to reside more in the stimulus (a model's behavior) than in the act of observing. Also, there may or may not be any intent to instruct on the part of the model, so that observational learning may occur more frequently outside formal classrooms than inside. In a social situation, we each are potential participants, both as models and as observers of models.

Also, the learning of cognitive skills such as visualization—the zooming in on details and the laying out of solid objects (noted earlier in this chapter under learner strategy)—can be seen as the consequence of repeatedly "observing" those operations and internalizing them.

In a still broader sense, much concept learning can be said to be based on the learner's "observation" of regularities or invariances in his/her world.

References

Anderson, R.C. Control of student mediating processes during verbal learning and instruction. *Review of Educational Research,* 1970, *40,* 349-369.

Anderson, R.C. and Biddle, W.B. On asking people questions about what they are reading. In G.H. Bower (Ed.), *The Psychology of Learning and Motivation* (Vol. 9). New York: Academic Press, 1975.

Anderson, R.C. and Faust, G.W. *Educational Psychology, The Science of Instruction and Learning.* New York: Dodd, Mead & Co., 1973.

Anderson, R.C., Kulhavy, R.W., and Andre, T. Feedback procedures in programmed instruction. *Journal of Educational Psychology,* 1971, *62,* 148-156.

Ausubel, D.P. *Educational Psychology: A Cognitive View.* New York: Holt, Rinehart, and Winston, 1968.

Baldwin, A.L. Social learning. In F.N. Kerlinger (Ed.), *Review of Research in Education* (Vol. 1). Itasca, Ill.: F.E. Peacock Publishers, 1973.

Barnes, B.R. and Clawson, E.U. Do advance organizers facilitate learning? Recommendations for further research based on an analysis of 32 studies. *Review of Educational Research,* 1975, *45*(4), 637-659.

Berelson, B. and Steiner, G.A. *Human Behavior: An Inventory of Scientific Findings.* New York: Harcourt, Brace, and World, 1964.

Berliner, D.C. and Gage, N.L. The psychology of teaching methods. In N.L. Gage (Ed.), *The Psychology of Teaching Methods.* NSSE Yearbook (Vol. 75, pt. 1). Chicago: University of Chicago Press, 1976.

Biehler, R.F. *Psychology Applied to Teaching.* Boston: Houghton Mifflin Co., 1971.

Bower, G.H. How to . . . uh . . . remember. *Psychology Today,* 1973, *7*(5), 62-70.

Bower, G.H. Mental imagery and associative memory. In L.W. Gregg (Ed.), *Cognition in Learning and Memory.* New York: John Wiley, 1972.

Bower, G.H. and Clark, M.C. Narrative stories as mediators for serial learning. *Psychonomic Science,* 1969, *14*(4), 181-182.

Bower, G.H. and Karlin, M.B. Depth of processing pictures of faces and recognition memory. *Journal of Experimental Psychology,* 1974, *103*(4), 751-757.

Bugelski, B.R. *The Psychology of Learning Applied to Teaching.* Indianapolis: Bobbs-Merrill Co., 1964.

Bull, S.G. The role of questions in maintaining attention to textual material. *Review of Educational Research,* 1973, *43,* 83-87.

Craig, R.C. *The Psychology of Learning in the Classroom.* New York: Macmillan Co., 1966.

Craik, F.I.M. and Lockhart, R.S. Levels of processing; a framework for memory research. *Journal of Verbal Learning and Verbal Behavior,* 1972, *11,* 671-684.

DeCecco, J.P. *Psychology of Learning and Instruction: Educational Psychology.* Englewood Cliffs, N.J.: Prentice-Hall, 1968.

Duncan, K. Strategies for analysis of the task. In J. Hartley (Ed.), *Strategies for Programmed Instruction: An Instructional Technology.* London: Butterworths, 1972.

Ellson, D.G. Tutoring. In N.L. Gage (Ed.), *The Psychology of Teaching Methods,* NSSE Yearbook (Vol. 75, pt. 1). Chicago: University of Chicago Press, 1976.

Ellson, D.G., Barber, L., Engle, T.L., and Kampwerth, L. Programmed tutoring: A teaching aid and a research tool. *Reading Research Quarterly,* 1965, *1*(1), 77-127.

Gagné, R.M. *Essentials of Learning for Instruction.* Hinsdale, Ill.: The Dryden Press, 1974.

Gagné, R.M. and Rohwer, W.D. Instructional psychology. In P.H. Mussen and M.R. Rosenzweig (Eds.) *Annual Review of Psychology* (vol. 20). Palo Alto: Annual Reviews, Inc., 1969.

Gibson, E.J. *Principles of Perceptual Learning and Development.* New York: Meredith Corp., 1969.

Glaser, R. and Resnick, L.B. Instructional psychology. In P.H. Mussen and M.R. Rosenzweig (Eds.), *Annual Review of Psychology* (vol. 23). Palo Alto: Annual Reviews, Inc., 1972.

Jenkins, J.R., Neale, D.C., and Deno, S.L. Differential memory for picture and word stimuli. *Journal of Educational Psychology,* 1967, *58*(5), 303-307.

Kumar, V.K. The structure of human memory and some educational implications. *Review of Educational Research,* 1971, *41,* 379-417.

Leifer, A.D. Teaching with television and film. In N.L. Gage (Ed.), *The Psychology of Teaching Methods,* NSSE Yearbook (Vol. 75, pt. 1). Chicago: University of Chicago Press, 1976.

Lindgren, H.C. *Educational Psychology in the Classroom.* New York: John Wiley, 1972.

Mager, R.F. and Beach, K.M. *Developing Vocational Instruction.* Belmont, Calif.: Fearon Publishers, 1967.

Margolius, G.J. and Sheffield, F.D. Optimum methods of combining practice with filmed demonstrations in teaching complex response sequences: Serial learning of a mechanical assembly task. In A.A. Lumsdaine (Ed.), *Student Response in Programmed Instruction.* Washington, D.C.: National Academy of Science–National Research Council, 1961.

May, M.A. *Word-Picture Relationships in Audiovisual Presentations.* USOE Report NDEA-VIIB-530, No. 2 (ERIC #ED 003 164), 1965.

McKeachie, W.J. Instructional psychology. In P.H. Mussen and M.R. Rosenzweig (Eds.), *Annual Review of Psychology* (Vol. 25). Palo Alto: Annual Reviews, Inc., 1974.

More, A.J. Delay of feedback and the acquisition and retention of verbal materials in the classroom. *Journal of Educational Psychology,* 1969, *60,* 339-342.

Mouly, G.J., *Psychology for Effective Teaching.* New York: Holt, Rinehart, and Winston, 1973.

Neisser, U. *Cognitive Psychology.* New York: Appleton-Century-Crofts, 1967.

Packard, R.G. *Psychology of Learning and Instruction.* Columbus, Ohio: Charles E. Merrill, 1975.

Paivio, A. *Imagery and Verbal Processes.* New York: Holt, Rinehart, and Winston, 1971.

Posner, M. and Keele, S.W. Skill learning. In R.M.W. Travers (Ed.), *Second Handbook of Research on Teaching.* Chicago: Rand McNally, 1973.

Postman, L. Verbal learning and memory. In M.R. Rosenzweig and L.W. Porter (Eds.), *Annual Review of Psychology* (Vol. 26). Palo Alto: Annual Reviews, Inc., 1975.

Rickards, J.P. Stimulating high-level comprehension by interspersing questions in text passages. *Educational Technology,* 1976, *16*(11), 13-17.

Rohwer, W.D. Decisive research: A means for answering fundamental questions about instruction. *Educational Researcher,* 1972, *1*(7), 5-11.

Rohwer, W.D., Lynch, S., Suzuki, N., and Levin, J.R. Verbal and pictorial facilitation of paired-associate learning. *Journal of Experimental Child Psychology,* 1967, *5,* 294-302.

Salomon, G. Can we affect cognitive skills through visual media? An hypothesis and initial findings. *AV Communication Review,* 1972, *20*(4), 401-422.

Scandura, J.M. Structural learning and the design of educational materials. *Educational Technology,* 1973, *13*(8), 7-13.

Severin, W. Another look at cue summation. *A V Communication Review,* 1967, *15,* 233-245.

Shepard, R.N. Recognition memory for words, sentences, and pictures. *Journal of Verbal Learning and Verbal Behavior,* 1967, *6,* 156-163.

Travers, R.M.W., *Educational Psychology.* New York: The Macmillan Co., 1973.

Tulving, E. and Madigan, S.A. Memory and verbal learning. In P.H. Mussen and M.R. Rosenzweig (Eds.), *Annual Review of Psychology* (Vol. 21). Palo Alto: Annual Reviews, Inc., 1970.

Sources for Principles

The following are largely secondary sources, i.e., reviews, summaries, and generalizations of groups of studies, rather than detailed reports of individual studies. Thus, they serve well our purpose of identifying principles based on reliable bodies of research. Readers interested in identifying specific studies and the investigators who conducted them can generally do so through bibliographies in these sources (#1 refers to Principle 2.1, etc.).

1. McKeachie, 1974; Mouly, 1973
2. DeCecco, 1968; Packard, 1975
3. DeCecco, 1968
4. Craig, 1966; Packard, 1975
5. *
6. Severin, 1967
7. *
8. Gagné and Rohwer, 1969; Paivio, 1971
8a. Gagné and Rohwer, 1969
8b. Gagné and Rohwer, 1969; Tulving and Madigan, 1970; Paivio, 1971

*Author's inferences based on research literature.

9. Packard, 1975; Travers, 1973
10. Gagné and Rohwer, 1969
10a. Gagné and Rohwer, 1969
10b. Paivio, 1971
11. *
11a. *
11b. *
12. Anderson and Faust, 1973
13. Anderson and Faust, 1973
14. Ellson, Barber, Engle, and Kampwerth, 1965
15. Anderson and Faust, 1973
16. Anderson and Faust, 1973
17. Anderson and Faust, 1973
18. *
19. *
20. Mouly, 1973
21. Bugelski, 1964; Postman, 1975
22. Berelson and Steiner, 1964
23. Packard, 1975
24. Anderson and Faust, 1973
25. Anderson and Faust, 1973
26. Biehler, 1971
26a. Berelson and Steiner, 1964
26b. Ausubel, 1968
26c. Anderson and Faust, 1973
27. Anderson and Biddle, 1975
28. Rickards, 1976
29. Neisser, 1967
30. Lindgren, 1972; McKeachie, 1974
31. *
31a. Paivio, 1971
31b. Bower, 1973
32. Craig, 1966; Packard, 1975; Glaser and Resnick, 1972

*Author's inferences based on research literature.

32a. Craig, 1966; Mouly, 1973

32b. Anderson and Faust, 1973

33. DeCecco, 1968

34. Kumar, 1971

35. Anderson and Faust, 1973; Craig, 1966

36. Anderson and Faust, 1973; Craig, 1966

37. Gibson, 1969

37a. Gibson, 1969

37b. Mager and Beach, 1967

38. Gibson, 1969

39. Berliner and Gage, 1976

40. Baldwin, 1973

41. Gagné 1974; Mager and Beach, 1967

Chapter 3
CONCEPT LEARNING PRINCIPLES

Concepts are an essential part of learning to cope with our world. Without the ability to group objects, events, or ideas by common characteristics, we would be forced to learn about and deal with each separate object, event, or idea as altogether unique. The memory load would be impossible. Concepts enable us to simplify, categorize, and thus better cope with the diversity surrounding us. Of course, such grouping together of different things, such attention to selected similarities while overlooking apparent differences, sometimes gets us into trouble. We mis-identify and we stereotype. We mistake poisonous mushrooms for edible, and we ascribe erroneous characteristics to groups of people differentiated by color, sex, nationality, etc. That is, we can learn erroneous, sterotypic, non-functional concepts.

"Concept" has been variously defined. Some definitions have employed the response characteristics, i.e., the common response (typically, the name for the concept) given to a group of discriminably different objects.* For example, where a learner says "square" with reference to appropriate geometric figures, but not with reference to inappropriate figures, s/he can be said to have the concept, particularly if some of the individual figures are

---

*It should be clear that while the verbal label is a very important response, there are many others, e.g., pointing to examples, drawing examples, or otherwise behaving consistently toward them. For example, where a driver consistently stops at all red traffic lights, s/he can be said to have the concept "stop" whether or not s/he can say, write, or understand the verbal label.

new to him/her. The utility of this definition is in the testing of
concept acquisition. There are two critical aspects of the test.
First, the same response must be made to a *variety* of different
examples, e.g., small and large squares; red, green, and black
squares, etc. Second, the test should involve objects *not seen
before* e.g., a large orange square. This definition points up a
fundamental distinction between memorization and conceptualiza-
tion. Memory processes may include the recognition of a
particular object, or the association of a *particular* word label with
that one object, while concept formation involves a common label
for a diverse *group* of objects. A concept can be applied whether
or not the learner has ever before encountered certain examples of
it or had occasion to associate them with the name. While useful
for testing, such response-oriented definitions are not the most
functional for design purposes.

Other definitions of "concept" have emphasized stimulus
characteristics, i.e., the common characteristics of all examples of
the concept. For example, "square" can be defined as "a closed
geometric figure which has four equal sides and four equal angles."
The concept is operationalized as the ability to state the definition
or to recognize and identify correctly any geometric figure which
exhibits the above stimulus attributes. This definition of concept
is functional for the designer because it indicates what the learner
must attend to, i.e., the criterial attributes which distinguish
examples from non-examples of the concept (figure, closed, four
equal sides, equal angles). Thus, these are the very stimulus
attributes that the designer must emphasize. We will consider a
concept to be that set of attributes (characteristics) shared by all
examples in the group and only by those examples (Engelmann,
1969).

Because of the centrality of the criterial attributes in the above
definition and in the design principles to follow, it is essential that
the designer analyze concepts prior to designing messages to teach
them. The process of concept analysis* can begin with a formal or

---

*See other sources, such as Engelmann (1969); Markle and Tiemann (1974);
Merrill and Tennyson (1977); and Tennyson, Woolley, and Merrill (1972).

dictionary definition, but must proceed at least three steps further.

1. Extract the criterial attributes from the definition, e.g., figure closed, four equal sides, four equal angles.
2. Check (preferably with naive learners) whether the attributes are both necessary and sufficient to reliably distinguish examples from non-examples, e.g., squares from triangles, parallelograms, etc.
3. Consider whether other attributes (or a smaller set of the above attributes) would suffice.

The above steps reflect a considerable skepticism on the part of instructional designers relative to the traditional definitions given in text and dictionary, both with reference to whether they function (provide a reliable basis for identifying examples) and with reference to whether they are economical (provide the simplest or most cost/effective basis for identifying examples). For example, Markle and Tiemann (1974) conducted a concept analysis of "morpheme" which yielded eight attributes (step one above). Further analysis and testing (step two) revealed that six of the attributes were irrelevant and that only two were criterial. Further analysis (step three) revealed that the addition of one criterial attribute significantly increased the accuracy of the learner's concept, i.e., their skill in distinguishing examples of morpheme from non-examples.

Implied in step three is the fact that a learner's first contact with a concept need not (probably should not) be intended for complete understanding.* Concepts are typically built throughout a curriculum, i.e., refined over time as the learner's capacity and need develop. Accordingly, beginning concepts can be taught relative to the local context in which the learner will perform. For example, of the several formal attributes of the concept "insect" (exo-skeleton, three main body parts, six legs, etc.) it may suffice

---

*Klausmeier, Ghatala, and Frayer (1974) describe four levels in the attainment of a concept, from the concrete level to the formal level.

for primary students to use only the six-legs attribute. This will serve to distinguish insects from most other small animals which such students are likely to encounter, including spiders (eight legs). Such a concept is efficient to teach and functions well. Other attributes can be added when and if they become important to identifying a greater range of animal forms.

The concept analysis phase, briefly noted above, is largely comprised of logical procedures. There follows the synthesis phase, largely comprised of empirically derived principles for instructional design. The designer has analyzed learners and knowledge (concepts) and is now ready to consider how s/he will answer the design question: What instructional conditions will lead to the desired effect?

Concept learning has been investigated quite extensively. Hence, it is possible to devote a chapter to instructional design principles based on that research. However, it is probably correct to observe that most of the experimental work to date has employed what is basically a concept discovery situation. The subject is shown examples and non-examples of the concept and is to discover the defining attributes. Such research is highly relevant to inductive or discovery kinds of instruction. However, many findings cannot be applied without qualification to other kinds of situations, e.g., deductive ones which begin with a definition or description of the concept followed by examples.

Predictably, there are concepts by which we simplify and systematize our dealing with the concept of concept. Several of these follow.

- *Conjunctive concepts*—defined by "and," by this attribute *and* that one *and* another one, i.e., the attributes which all examples have in common. For example, "apple" can be defined by such attributes as: edible fruit *and* from rosaceous tree *and* roundish *and* usually redish.
- *Disjunctive concepts*—defined by "or," i.e., examples having either one attribute (or set) *or* another attribute (or set). For example, "strike" in baseball can be defined as: batter

swings *or* umpire calls *or* batter hits outside baselines.

- *Relational Concepts*—defined by a *relation between* attributes rather than by their presence or absence. For example, "mountain" can be defined as an elevation of the earth's surface that is *greater than* a hill and *less uniform* than a plateau.

Additionally, concepts are grouped by the concreteness of the attributes which define them: concrete concepts, abstract concepts. While concrete concepts will often be referred to in what follows, the principles also apply to abstract concepts, the attributes being named or described instead of pictured or pointed to.

In what follows, principles of concept learning are discussed with reference to: type of concept; selecting, sequencing and presenting examples of rules; and consolidating conceptual learning. There is also a brief section on problem solving and creativity.

Types of Concepts

3.1.   *Conjunctive concepts are the most easily attained, relational concepts next, and disjunctive concepts least easily attained. Aotbe***

Fortunately, most concepts in school subjects are conjunctive and, hence, relatively amenable to instruction and learning.

3.2.   *Concepts of concrete objects appear to be more readily formed than some more abstract concepts, e.g., concepts of spatial forms and of numbers.*

*Aotbe means all other things being equal. It means that the preceding statement holds under controlled research conditions but may well vary in applied situations, i.e., other factors may reduce or nullify its effect. Though "aotbe" holds for every numbered guideline in this book, it will appear only at the first of each chapter as a reminder to the reader.

Whether or not this difference is attributable to fundamental differences in concrete vs. abstract concepts is unclear. It may simply reflect the relative difficulty in identifying the criterial attributes and making them apparent to the learner.

However, the fact that concrete words are more readily memorized than abstract words (see Memory Chapter) may explain in part the greater ease of concrete concept attainment. Further, examples of concrete concepts can be readily processed as mental images and thus be better retained.

> ***3.3.*** ***Abstract concepts can be learned from a variety of verbal structures, e.g., definitions (including criterial attributes), sentence contexts, described examples, and synonyms.***

While concepts of some level can be formed from sentence contexts and synonyms, we view the use of definitions (featuring criterial attributes) and described examples to be more reliable means of developing accurate concepts.

> ***3.4.*** ***Ease of concept attainment generally increases as the overall number of both criterial and non-criterial properties decreases.***

That is, the less information the learner must deal with, the better, but how much control does the designer have over numbers of attributes in examples?

Clearly, by judicious selection of examples or by simplified representation of those examples (verbal or pictorial manipulation) the designer can reduce the number of *non*-criterial attributes.

Less apparent is the possibility of reducing the number of criterial attributes for school subject matter. This may be especially important in teaching complex concepts. A rational basis for reducing the number of attributes without introducing learner error was presented in the initial paragraphs of this chapter. Basically, the range of potential attributes can be reduced to those *necessary* to the distinguishing of examples from non-examples in the context in which the learner will use the concept. This approach may result in considerable instructional advantage, for the definitions of common curricular concepts are frequently encrusted with verbalized intricacies which are super-fluous in most contexts or which are non-functional in distinguishing examples from non-examples.

Further, such concept analysis procedures require a close examination of numerous examples and non-examples in order to discover which attributes are sufficient for distinguishing them. The fringe benefit of this analysis process is that it yields lists of common examples and non-examples. These examples and non-examples are shown in what follows to be of immediate use in deciding which to employ in instruction and how to present them. Strategies and principles for *selecting* examples will be considered first, followed by principles for *presenting* examples.

Selection of Examples and Non-examples

It should be noted that pertinent throughout this section are several perceptual factors (see the first chapter) such as selective attention, grouping by similarity, and separating by difference.

3.5. *Choose both examples and non-examples* for instruction.*

Essentially, the examples demonstrate what the concept is, and

---

*Some writers refer to positive examples and negative examples. We have chosen the simpler designation: examples and non-examples. Also, the words "instance" and "exemplar" are frequently used instead of the more common "example," which we will use.

the non-examples show what it is not. Both are apt to be important to the learners' understanding of the concept. The practice of presenting only one example can readily induce a concept that is either too broad (overgeneralization) or too narrow (undergeneralization) (see Figure 3.1). For example, if only "human" is given as an example of the concept "mammal," then undergeneralization may result, for the learner may extend the concept to include upright animals such as monkeys. If another example is given, such as "whale," then overgeneralization is likely to occur to fish. So "fish" should be presented as a *non-example* to prevent overgeneralization to other aquatic animals. Thus, by judicious selection of examples and non-examples, the concept can be exposed and delineated.

3.6.   *Choose a wide variety* of examples for instruction.*

This has the effect of showing the breadth of the concept and thus prevents undergeneralization. For example, the concept "mammal" could be considerably broadened by adding dog, elephant, mouse, and kangaroo to the initial set of man and whale. Such broadening and diversifying of concept examples has the effect of not only demonstrating the extent of the concept but also of clarifying the concept definition, i.e., showing that such features as size, uprightness, etc., are irrelevant because they vary across examples.

*How concepts are formed from various examples or how they are stored in memory is a current lively research issue. There is evidence that for some concepts at least we develop a preferred or prototypic example, i.e., a rose standing for the concept "flower" and a dog standing for the concept "animal." There is also evidence that subjects exposed to a varied series of examples, e.g., geometric figures, come to form an abstracted memory image or scheme which represents the common properties of the figural concept. Further, there is evidence that for formal concepts we can recall or generate a verbal list of defining attributes, which leads some theorists to conclude that concepts are stored as verbal-like lists of attributes or as verbal-like propositions.

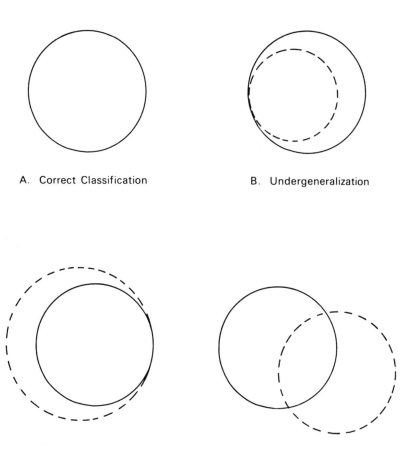

A. Correct Classification   B. Undergeneralization

C. Overgeneralization   D. Confusion

Figure 3.1. Graphic depictions of how a learner's concept (dotted lines) may differ from the correct concept (solid lines). The area in each circle represents the extent of the concept, i.e., the number and kind of examples included. (After Sheppard, 1971.) An example of B (Undergeneralization) would be the use of "dog" to refer to only one kind, e.g., spaniel, or only dogs with long hair or brown color. An example of C (Overgeneralization) would be to use "dog" to refer to cats or to wolves as well.

3.6a. *Try to choose a group of examples across which the criterial attributes show least variation and the non-criterial attributes show most variation.*

The logic here is straightforward, because criterial or definitive attributes are understood to be what is common or similar across all examples. Thus, *any* characteristics which do *not* change across examples will be understood by the learner to be criterial. Hence, examples should be chosen so that no change in criterial attributes is observable. For example, in Figure 3.2 *all* examples (in the circle) are closed figures and have three sides. On the other hand, any characteristics which *change* across examples will be understood to be non-criterial. Hence, all examples (Figure 3.2) vary systematically in non-criterial attributes, such as size, orientation, and relative length of sides.

3.6b. *Try to choose examples in which the criterial attributes are as obvious as possible and the non-criterial attributes are as non-obvious as possible. Or depict or simplify the examples in a way to accomplish the same effect.*

This is a special case of the "make criterial attributes apparent" principles discussed in the previous chapter with reference to memory. However, as with memory processes, any stimulus manipulation which maximizes criterial attributes or minimizes non-criterial ones must eventually be faded so that the learner can identify real examples in real contexts.

3.7. *Choose close-in (little variety) non-examples, i.e., that have numerous attributes similar to the examples, and that differ from them only with respect to one (or two or three) criterial attributes.*

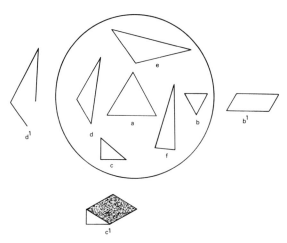

Figure 3.2. Possible examples and non-examples for teaching the concept of "triangle," examples inside the circle and non-examples outside. Choosing a variety of examples a-f instead of only one, typically "a," prevents undergeneralization. Choosing close-in non-examples b^1-d^1 accentuates the criterial attributes and prevents overgeneralization by showing the concept boundaries. What criterial attributes do c^1 and d^1 show?

Note that the characteristics of non-examples here are just the opposite of those for examples (Principle #3.6), i.e., similarity for non-examples and diversity for examples. The effect is to call attention to the criterial attributes. This clarifies the boundaries between the concept and others similar to it and thus prevents confusion and overgeneralization. Notice in Figure 3.2 that the non-examples b' to d' are similar to examples b to d, differing in fact on only one criterial attribute apiece. For instance, d differs from d' only by being a closed figure (criterial attribute). Close-in non-example d' thus serves to accentuate that criterial attribute of closedness.

Contrariwise, using an altogether different non-example does little for understanding. For example, a drawing of a face would be such an obvious (divergent) non-example of a triangle that it would serve no purpose. Similarly, using car or daffodil as a non-example of mammal contributes little, whereas using fish as a non-example delimits the concept relative to whales, as noted earlier.

This principle assumes that there are potentially confusing non-examples in the context, i.e., there are other concepts which have many attributes in common with examples (perhaps all attributes but one). Adequate concept analysis procedures would have revealed whether or not such competing concepts are present and would have identified the close-in non-examples and their attributes.

As a practical matter, experienced teachers will typically be well aware of close-in non-examples, for these will have been troublesome to learners, and hence to teachers, in previous classes.

> *3.8*   *Choose enough examples to demonstrate the practical range of the concept and enough non-examples to cover the most common close-in ones, i.e., the most frequently confused ones.*

The practical range of the concept refers to breadth and variety of examples which would logically be encountered in the context under consideration. For example, providing "Emu" as an example of the concept "bird" is likely to be dysfunctional.

This suggests general criteria for deciding on the number of examples and non-examples that the designer should employ for concept acquisition. Additional examples and non-examples may be necessary where attributes are difficult to remember or where distinctions are subtle. Still more would surely be required for consolidation and confirmation of the learner's concept.

In sum, a handy way for the designer to think about choosing examples and non-examples is as follows:

A. Choose examples sufficient to:

    (1)   suggest the range or diversity of the concept,

    (2)   eliminate the extraneous or non-criterial attributes.

B. Choose non-examples sufficient to:
  (1) delimit the concept,
  (2) accentuate the criterial attributes.
Examples chosen to meet these criteria can be called a "minimum rational set" (Markle, 1975).

Prerequisites and Instructions

There may be some important prerequisites to learning a concept.

3.9. *Prior learning of relevant words, e.g., names of attributes, of examples, or of concepts, can facilitate concept learning. The same would hold for prior encounter with relevant objects, events, or relations.*

For example, observing and learning differences between certain attributes (large-small, red-green, 3-4, etc.) is obviously necessary before the learner can cope with concepts whose criterial attributes are of that kind.

Similarly, knowing prerequisite or constituent skills or concepts may be essential. As Gagné's (Gagné and Briggs, 1974) learning hierarchies suggest, certain skills or other forms of knowledge may be prerequisite to later learning. For example, learning the concept "balanced chemical equation" may require math skills as well as knowledge of the valences of constituent chemical elements. Similarly, where a definition includes other concepts, those constituent concepts must be understood before the definition can be. For example, the definition of city, "large or important town," is of little value unless the learner understands three other concepts: large, important, town.

Such considerations can be pertinent to the pre-testing of learners' prior knowledge and to the design of an introductory unit to teach the prerequisite knowledge.

> *3.10. Providing the learner with appropriate instructions can facilitate concept learning, including information about the stimulus (attributes, etc.), the desired response (concept identification, etc.), and a strategy to apply.*

Thus, the designer can not only take account of the learner's prior learning, s/he can add to it in preparation for concept instruction.

Presentation of Examples and Definitions (Rules)

Basically, what the designer has available for presentation are two types of information: (1) definitions and/or lists of attributes; (2) examples and/or non-examples. Ways of effective presentation for each type of information will be considered here. The relative emphasis to be given each and the sequencing of each will be considered in a subsequent section.

There follow several principles dealing with ways of *presenting examples.*

> *3.11. There is evidence that examples in verbal form facilitate concept learning over those in picture form, presumably because the former exhibit fewer irrelevant attributes. Similarly, simplified examples such as line drawings, cartoons, charts, and diagrams have been found more effective than realistic pictures.*

This principle appears to largely reiterate and exemplify principle #3.6b. The issue is not only concrete vs. abstract or words vs. pictures, it is criterial attributes vs. non-criterial. If *either* picture or word examples contain *non-criterial* attributes which are too numeorus or too obvious, the designer must somehow reduce their number and/or dominance. He may do this by modifying his pictures or words or by changing from one to the other.

3.12. Use of the concept name in contiguity with each presented example facilitates concept learning.

Apparently, the concept name (e.g., the word "corpuscle") serves as a mediator for the concept learning process. At minimum it indicates to the learner that all the pictures of different blood cells presented have something in common which s/he is to detect.

While concepts can certainly be formed from examples alone, without the use of the concept name, it is generally highly desirable that a concept name be acquired so that the learner can thereafter readily and efficiently refer to the concept by means of a single word.*

Not all concepts we use have names, but essentially all of those important to school curricula have names, and the utility of the concept is dependent on the acquisition of both the name and all that it refers to.

3.13. Presenting examples in close succession or simultaneously in small groups, and keeping previous examples in view while others are added facilitate concept acquisition (see Figure 3.3).

These procedures facilitate comparisons so that similarities

*We should be careful to distinguish the concept label from what it refers to, i.e., the common properties of all examples. Both are important to instruction, but while a concept can be useful without a label, a label without knowledge of what it refers to is empty. Hence, the insistence by instructional designers on testing concept acquisition, not through recitation of a definition or recall of a label, but through some observable performance that indicates functional knowledge of the criterial attributes, e.g., distinguishing examples from non-examples.

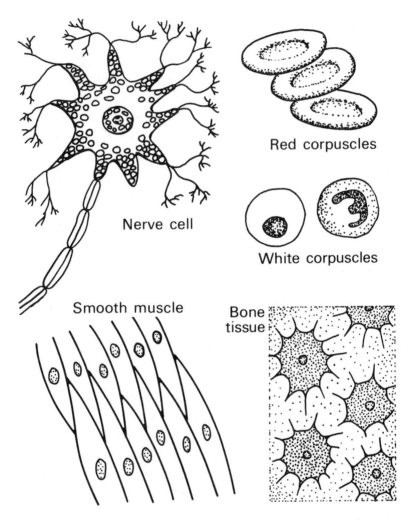

Red corpuscles

Nerve cell

White corpuscles

Smooth muscle

Bone tissue

Figure 3.3. Simultaneous presentation facilitates observation of criterial similarities and non-criterial differences for examples of the concept "body cell." Also the wide range of cell types is useful in suggesting the range of the concept. (See also Figure 3.4.) (From Davis, I.C., Burnett, J., Gross, E.W., and Prichard, L.B., *Science 2: Experiment and Discovery*, Copyright © 1965 Holt, Rinehart, and Winston, Inc. Reprinted by permission of Holt, Rinehart, and Winston.)

become apparent and criterial attributes can be identified. Leaving examples in view further facilitates learning by reducing memory load. See Figure 3.3. In contrast, where examples are presented one-at-a-time and not left in view the learner must keep in mind all previous examples for comparison with each new one.

In addition to presenting examples there is also the problem of *presenting definitions.*

3.14. Presenting a definition as a list of criterial attributes can facilitate concept acquisition over presenting it in typical sentence form.

The effect of a list is to delineate each criterial attribute which might otherwise be overlooked in the more undifferentiated sentence form. For example, the dictionary definition of "indene" is "a colorless liquid hydrocarbon, C_9H_8, obtained from coal tar by fractional distillation." A preferred format for instructional presentation would begin with the superordinate class and then list the distinguishing attributes.

Hydrocarbon
1. colorless
2. liquid
3. formula C_9H_8
4. distilled from coal tar

The effect is to place the concept in a definitive class of chemicals (hydrocarbon) and to differentiate it from others in the class by four explicit attributes.*

Sequencing of Examples and Definitions (Rules)

A long-debated issue in instruction is that of induction vs. deduction; or in our terms, presenting examples first and deriving

*Concept analysis may reveal that not all these attributes are criterial.

from them the rule (called egrule) vs. presenting the rule first and illustrating with examples (called ruleg).

Mechner (1967) resolves the issue with reference to the initial difficulty of the concept for the particular learners. If it is relatively easy for the learners and they can understand it in its most abstract and general form (verbal definition), then use the rule-first or ruleg approach. This assumes the learners understand the words (other concepts) included in the definition. However, if the concept is difficult and the learners are not likely to understand initially the verbal definition, then use the example-first or egrule approach. The criterial attributes of the concept are identified in the examples; and, only later, if at all, stated abstractly as a definition.

Other authors (Engelmann, 1969; Hickey and Newton, 1964) recommend a combined approach called egruleg, i.e., give examples first, derive from them the rule (definition or set of attributes), and then apply it to further examples. This egruleg sequence appears to have much to recommend it, though hard data on the issue are wanting. Adding Mechner's (1967) view to this would yield a plausible strategy as follows:

1. Where the concept is difficult (too abstract) for the learner, use egruleg.
2. Where the concept would be understood in abstract form, use ruleg.

In applying this, the designer would, after choice of 1 or 2, organize instruction accordingly and apply the preceding principles relative to examples and definitions as needed. However, there remains an important issue in concept instruction: Does one provide the criterial attributes, i.e., list them or point them out in examples (exposition), or does one encourage the learner to find them (discovery)? The egrule approach can be employed in either way. The next two principles deal with this question.

3.15.   Presenting the criterial attributes (by rule, definition, or list) or otherwise directing attention

to them in examples increases concept attain-
ment over expecting the learner to discover
them.

This is not to disparage the discovery method except where the criterion is learning efficiency. Discovery may well have the edge when it comes to arousing student interest and to learning the process of discovery or inquiry. Otherwise, pointing out the criterial attributes in examples or describing the criterial attributes as in a definition yields more rapid concept learning. However, learning the definition alone is inadequate without use of examples.

In fact, presenting the definition or a list of the defining attributes is necessary for many concepts because one or more of the criterial attributes is not readily observable in examples. This holds not only for obviously abstract concepts (democracy, power, brotherhood, catalyst, intelligence) but also for some apparently concrete concepts. For example, a vertebrate animal is characterized by a backbone, which is not directly observable in examples. Also, numerous objects are partly defined by their use, i.e., a hat by being worn on the head, a ball by being used in a game, a hammer being used to pound things. Just showing the physical attributes of these objects is not enough to define them; their function must also be shown or described.

A caution in using principle #3.15 is that the words (actually, other concepts) used in the definition must already be familiar to the learner or must be specially taught before the definition can be used in instruction.

3.16.   *In employing a discovery-type method (as com-*
pared to an expository method) a greater num-
ber of examples will generally be required and
the criterial attributes in the examples must be
fewer in number and more dominant and appar-
ent to the learners.

That is, discovery of the criterial attributes must be highly probable if a valid concept is to be learned. This may frequently require considerable guidance of the discovery process by both designer and teacher, as the above principle suggests.

Further, there is evidence that instructing the learner in a problem-solving strategy, e.g., focusing, can facilitate discovery of the criterial attributes (the solution). The focusing strategy involves testing one attribute at a time across examples to ascertain whether they all evidence it (Bourne and Dominowski, 1972.)

> *3.17. The initial examples presented should be as familiar to the learner and as representative of the concept as possible. Initial presentations should include only examples (no non-examples), and these should display the criterial properties as unambiguously as possible, and should include as few non-criterial properties as possible (see Figure 3.4).*

The intent is to simplify initial learning by eliminating what might be irrelevant and distracting. Likewise, the intent is to minimize the possibility for error by directing attention to the criterial attributes.

The amount of error during learning would depend also on the instructional method: more for discovery and less for expository. Some of the pros and cons of permitting learner error were discussed in the previous chapter.

There is some evidence (Clark, 1971) that the above principle (examples presented first) is applicable to conjunctive concepts, whereas for disjunctive concepts the initial presentation of a sequence of non-examples is more facilitative.

> *3.18. Subsequent presentations should be a mixture of examples and non-examples. Both should gradu-*

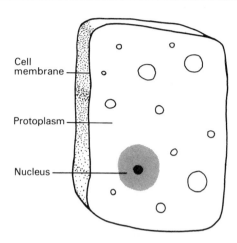

Cell
membrane

Protoplasm

Nucleus

Figure 3.4. Simplified example of "body cell" useful for initial presentation of the concept. (See also Figure 3.3.) (From Davis, I.C., Burnett, J., Gross, E.W., and Prichard , L.B., *Science 2: Experiment and Discovery,* Copyright © 1965 Holt, Rinehart, and Winston, Inc. Reprinted by permission of Holt, Rinehart, and Winston.)

> *ally increase in difficulty, i.e., examples becoming more varied (increasing non-criterial attributes) and non-examples becoming closer in (increasingly similar to examples).*

This and Principle #3.17 reiterate a basic rule of instruction: begin with the familiar and simple and move toward the unfamiliar and complex.

Consolidation and Confirmation of Concept Learning

3.19.   *Obtain responses from learners during subsequent presentations of examples and non-examples and provide corrective feedback after each response.*

This is a reiteration of similar principles (Frequency Principle and Feedback Principle) from the preceding chapter on memory. These principles apply to concept learning as well, though the Frequency Principle is generally of less importance to learning a concept than to learning a skill.

> *3.20.   Allow time for the learner to study examples and non-examples, to respond, to think about the feedback s/he receives.*

> *3.21.   Where learners verbalize the criterial attributes of the concept and/or the concept name, learning is increased as compared to where they do not or where they verbalize non-criterial attributes.*

> *3.22.   Where learners put newly-formed concepts to use, the concepts will be better learned.*

This is remindful of principles in the previous chapter dealing with active learner responses.

> *3.23.   Verify the learner's concept by presenting additional examples and non-examples not used during instruction and having learners identify them.*

> *3.24   As further verification of the learner's concept, have the learner define the concept or state the criterial attributes.*

In sum, a workable *expository* presentation method for concepts would be the following.
1. Present one simple clear example.
   a. Label it.

   b. Point out the criterial attributes in the example.

2. Present the rule in list form.
3. Present other examples of greater complexity and diversity (more irrelevant attributes).

   a. Repeat labeling and pointing out criterial attributes.

   b. Get learners to label the examples and provide feedback.

   c. Get learners to point out the criterial attributes.

   d. Leave all examples in view.

4. Begin to introduce close-in non-examples.

   a. Use different labels for non-examples.

   b. Point out differences in attributes.

   c. Give learners practice in differentiating examples and non-examples and provide feedback.

In contrast, for a *discovery* method, several of the preceding principles are particularly pertinent (3.6, 3.6b, 3.13, 3.17, 3.18) as well as those in the following section on problem solving.

Problem Solving and Creativity

Generally speaking, the message designer faces a quite different kind of task in arranging the conditions for problem solving as compared to those for concept formation. For concept formation, the designer is trying to maximize stimulus support, whereas for problem solution s/he is intending to minimize such support.* Also, a concept will usually be defined by a small and prescribed number of attributes, whereas there may be multiple solutions to problems, each involving different approaches and different attributes.

---

*These latter distinctions do not characterize concept formation as typically thought of by either the psychologist studying concept identification or the teacher employing the inquiry approach to concept discovery. Both tend to approach concept formation as a problem for the learner to solve.

*3.25.   Problem solution can be facilitated by instruc-
tions which develop a relevant set toward the
problem and by situational support which emphasizes or groups the crucial elements or reveals
the crucial relations in the situation.*

Frequently, in problem-solving situations, it is the case that familiar objects and concepts must be used in an unfamiliar way. Unusual perceptions and responses may be required (Berelson and Steiner, 1964). The problem solver must look at the situation in a new way.

For such problems, perceptual set may be the major deterrent. The usual way of looking at things is ineffective. In a way, it can be said that there is more information available in the situation than the problem solver at first perceives (Posner, 1973). The designer can arrange to make crucial elements or relations in the display more evident, or s/he can simply arrange elements in an unusual way so as to upset stereotyped perception and thought. Whether or not any such help is given is another issue, and may depend on the purposes of instruction and the stage in the process.

In addition to providing problem-solving information (crucial elements and relations) the designer can also provide general strategies of problem analysis and problem solution. For example, instruction in the use of a conservative focusing strategy (testing out one feature of the stimulus at a time) can facilitate solution in a concept discovery task (Bourne and Dominowski, 1972). Probably the long range payoff is greater for teaching generalize-able strategies than for providing problem-specific information.

It is no doubt possible to control the difficulty of a problem by the instructions given and by the various kinds of contextual cues provided. Also, it is probably desirable to exercise such control so as to provide the learner with a graduated series of problems, such that the situational support is initially high and then gradually removed as the learner finds effective strategies for problem solution.

Language is importantly related to both concept formation and problem solution. Words represent the world view of those who use them, in that words stand for or label many of the concepts which a particular language community has found necessary. In a sense, then, language tends to stereotype or channel thinking. This process can be a constraint to problem solving where new concepts and new ways of thinking are required (Posner, 1973). Consequently, the words used by the designer to describe the problem or to label its constituents may either facilitate or inhibit solution. Perhaps problems "stated" nonverbally would induce or permit less restricted and more creative solutions.

3.26. *Provision of situational support for problem solving can take the form not only of relevant information but also of opportunity to record, test, and manipulate various alternatives.*

Pencil and paper, chalk and chalkboard, charts and models, feltboards and magnetic boards, audio and video recorders, calculators and computers, and manipulanda of various other sorts may facilitate problem solution. They provide means of recording, comparing, rearranging, and modifying the elements of the problem.

Similarly, induced mental imagery provides a dynamic process for generating and transforming alternative elements, configurations, and solutions (Arnheim, 1969). Such use of imagination has frequently been reported by persons whose profession involves creative problem solutions, e.g., theoretical physics, art and architecture, design engineering, or chess playing.

Creative behavior is even further distinguishable from concept formation; it is like problem solving, only more so. Stimulus support is necessary but quite different. Whereas stimuli for concept formation were chosen so as to direct, control, and converge perception and response, stimuli for creative behavior should be chosen so as to allow or cause perception to diverge or to escape from restrictive sets.

> *3.27. The development of creative behavior is facilitated by materials which increase sensitivity to the attributes or features of the environment (objects, events, relations, people), and which encourage and give practice with alternative ways of dealing with the environment under low risk conditions.*

Various kinds of materials have been used to test or train creativity. Some, like clay or construction paper, move the student to create something from nothing. Others like a tin can or brick, provide familiar simple forms, but ones with minimal constraints where the student is encouraged to conceive of as many uses for them as possible. More structured are games which provide certain constraints but allow many possible moves. These are particularly useful in the study and development of strategies for creative problem solving.

Thus, materials for creative behavior will tend to be such as will permit and encourage adapting, rearranging, substituting, modifying, reversing, combining, and removing.

References

Anderson, R.C. and Faust, G.W. *Educational Psychology: The Science of Instruction and Learning.* New York: Dodd, Mead and Co., 1973.

Arnheim, R. *Visual Thinking.* Berkeley and Los Angeles: University of California Press, 1969.

Berelson, B. and Steiner, G.A. *Human Behavior: An Inventory of Scientific Findings.* New York: Harcourt, Brace, and World, 1964.

Bourne, L.E. and Dominowski, R.L. Thinking. In P.H. Mussen and M.R. Rosenzweig (Eds.), *Annual Review of Psychology* (Vol. 23). Palo Alto: Annual Reviews, Inc., 1972.

Clark, D.C. Teaching concepts in the classroom: A set of teaching prescriptions derived from experimental research. *Journal of Educational Psychology,* Monograph, 1971, *62,* 253-264.

DeCecco, J.P. *The Psychology of Learning and Instruction: Educational Psychology.* Englewood Cliffs: Prentice-Hall, 1968.

Engelmann, S. *Conceptual Learning.* San Rafael, Calif.: Dimensions Publishing Co., 1969.

Forgus, R.H. *Perception.* New York: McGraw-Hill, 1966.

Gagné, R.M. and Briggs, L.J. *Principles of Instructional Design.* New York: Holt, Rinehart, and Winston, 1974.

Hickey, A.E. and Newton, J.M. *The Logical Basis of Teaching: 1. The Effect of Subconcept Sequence on Learning,* Final Report, Office of Naval Research, Contract Nonr 4215 (00), January, 1964.

Katz, A.N. and Paivio, A. Imagery variables in concept identification. *Journal of Verbal Learning and Verbal Behavior,* 1975, *14,* 284-293.

Klausmeier, H.J., Ghatala, E.S., and Frayer, D.A. *Conceptual Learning and Development: A Cognitive View.* New York: Academic Press, 1974.

Markle, S.M. They teach concepts, don't they? *Educational Researcher,* 1975, *4*(6), 3-9.

Markle, S.M. and Tiemann, P.W. Some principles of instructional design at higher cognitive levels. In R. Ulrich, T. Stachnik, and J. Mabry (Eds.), *Control of Human Behavior* (Vol. 3). Glenview, Ill.: Scott Foresman, 1974.

Merrill, M.D. and Tennyson, R.D. *Teaching Concepts: An Instructional Design Guide.* Englewood Cliffs, New Jersey: Educational Technology Publications, 1977.

Mechner, F. Behavioral analyses and instructional sequencing. In P.C. Lange (Ed.), *Programmed Instruction* (Vol. 66), NSSE Yearbook Pt. 2, Chicago: University of Chicago Press, 1967.

Posner, M.I. *Cognition: An Introduction.* Glenview, Ill.: Scott Foresman, 1973.

Sheppard, A.N. *Changing Learner Conceptual Behavior Through* the Selective Use of Positive and Negative Examples, Ed.D. thesis, Indiana University, 1971.

Tennyson, R.D., Woolley, F.R., and Merrill, M.D. Exemplar and nonexemplar variables which produce correct classification behavior and specified classification errors. *Journal of Educational Psychology,* 1972, *63,* 144-152.

Thiagarajan, S. *Instantial and Contrastive Teacher Moves and Students' Conceptual Behavior,* Ph.D. thesis, Indiana University, 1971.

Sources for Principles

The following are largely secondary sources, i.e., reviews, summaries, and generalizations of groups of studies rather than detailed reports of individual studies. Thus, they serve well our purpose of identifying principles based on reliable bodies of research. Readers interested in identifying specific studies and the investigators who conducted them can generally do so through bibliographies in these sources (#1 refers to Principle 3.1, etc.).

1. Clark, 1971
2. Clark, 1971
3. Klausmeier, Ghatala, and Frayer, 1974
4. Clark, 1971
5. DeCecco, 1968
6. Sheppard, 1971; Thiagarajan, 1971
6a. Clark, 1971
6b. Clark, 1971
7. Sheppard, 1971; Thiagarajan, 1971
8. DeCecco, 1968
9. Clark, 1971; Klausmeier, Ghatala, and Frayer, 1974
10. Klausmeier, Ghatala, and Frayer, 1974
11. DeCecco, 1968
12. DeCecco, 1968
13. DeCecco, 1968

14. Markle, 1975
15. Anderson and Faust, 1973; Clark, 1971
16. Anderson and Faust, 1973
17. Anderson and Faust, 1973; Clark, 1971
18. Clark, 1971
19. DeCecco, 1968; Klausmeier, Ghatala, and Frayer, 1974
20. Clark, 1971
21. Clark, 1971
22. Klausmeier, Ghatala, and Frayer, 1974
23. DeCecco, 1968
24. DeCecco, 1968
25. Forgus, 1966
26. Forgus, 1966
27. Forgus, 1966

Chapter 4
ATTITUDE CHANGE PRINCIPLES

When a learner encounters an instructional message, three classes of response may occur: perception, learning, and acceptance. While all three responses may occur more or less simultaneously, perception and learning must precede acceptance, which may or may not follow.

Accepting-responses have generally been studied under the terms "attitude change" or "persuasion." Since this book is concerned with instruction, one might question the appropriateness here of principles for attitude change and persuasion. One might even suggest that professional ethics demand that teachers avoid using their influential positions for persuasive purposes. If this is so, why should educators be interested in principles for changing attitudes?

First, there is considerable question whether information-versus-propaganda and teaching-versus-persuading can be validly discriminated. However, even the most ethical educator would probably agree that there are cases in which it is legitimate to urge learners to accept the truth of certain ideas. In fact, educators express increasing concern with changing attitudes not only toward subject matter, but also attitudes about social issues such as treatment of minority groups. Educators might also be concerned about attitudes because of their impact upon perception and learning. Attitudes may affect perception through vigilance (e.g., people are on the lookout for the things they enjoy) or through distortion (e.g., people sometimes misinterpret objects and events to be consistent with their attitudes). Similarly, people generally learn and retain information which agrees with their attitudes better than they learn counter-attitudinal information. Finally, some educators might be interested in attitude change techniques if for no other reason than that they can avoid unintentionally biasing their teaching.

The division of content in this chapter is based upon a simple model of the communication process: A SOURCE presents a MESSAGE through a CHANNEL to a RECEIVER. Principles of attitude change for each of these components are introduced in the order named. Principles dealing with the message are divided into those concerned with the *message content* (WHAT to say) and the *message structure* (HOW to say it). The placement of principles within sections is somewhat arbitrary. For example, the effects of the receiver's group affiliations in persuasion could reasonably be discussed under the message, the channel, or, as was chosen, the receiver.

First, however, a brief introduction to the concept of attitude is in order.

The Concept of Attitude

Attitude has long been one of the central concepts of social psychology and considerable debate concerning its most useful conceptual and operational definition has appeared. Someone can be found who disagrees with almost any statement about the concept. However, a few of the more generally agreed upon characteristics of the concept are:

Attitude is a *latent variable.* Attitudes, like many other constructs in psychology, are not directly observable but are inferred from behavior. In real life, these behaviors are usually people's verbal statements or their observable actions. In experimental research, these behaviors are usually subjects' responses to various paper-and-pencil self-report attitude measures.

Attitudes *have objects*. People have attitudes toward specific referents (particular individuals, works of art, etc.), toward classes of referents (police officers, expressionism, etc.), and toward events or behaviors (being arrested, painting with oils, etc.).

Attitudes have an *affective component*. Probably the most fundamental aspect of the concept is the emotional approach-avoidance tendency. An individual's affective evaluation of an object can vary in *direction,* either positive or negative; in *degree,* the amount of positiveness-negativeness, from strongly positive to mildly positive through neutral to mildly negative and strongly negative; and in *intensity,* the amount of commitment or involvement with which a particular position (direction and degree) is held. These affective reactions serve as implicit responses to objects that arouse motives for behavior. Accordingly:

Attitudes have a *behavioral component*. Attitudes imply a predisposition to behave in an evaluative way. However, both researchers and practitioners have frequently found that people's attitudes toward some class of objects fail to predict their behavior toward a member of that class in some particular situation. Thus, a person who holds a negative attitude toward police may nevertheless behave very courteously toward an officer who stops his/her car. Behavior is multiply determined. Any particular act is the product of a blend of several personal predispositions (only one of which is attitude) and of the demands the particular situation places upon the performer. Actually, many theorists prefer to exclude action tendencies from the concept of attitude.

Attitudes have a *cognitive component*. Attitudes toward police, for example, may involve beliefs about the honesty and effectiveness of police officers. Such cognitions are, of course, teachable, and attitudes *are learned*. People are not born with a set of attitude structures. However, it has often been observed that information alone may not be sufficient to change attitudes. Also, researchers have been puzzled by the repeated failure to obtain a correlation between people's recall of the information in a persuasive message and their agreement with the conclusions of the message. Perhaps, as Greenwald (see Insko, Lind, and LaTour, 1976) suggests, people's retention from a persuasive message is not of the information *per se,* but of their "cognitive reactions" that were aroused by the message.

Attitudes are relatively *stable and enduring.* An individual's attitude toward the police does not shift from day to day and is relatively resistent to change. However, the individual may have only an *opinion* about Officer Smith, a policeman with whom the individual has had little contact. *Opinions* are more transitory and subject to change. This distinction between attitudes and opinions lies in the importance the object holds for the individual, and in his/her involvement with the issue. *Values* deal with higher-order concepts such as security and freedom, and are generally even more stable and resistant to change than attitudes. Finally, *motives* are drive states that may be aroused by attitudes, but which appear and disappear with given circumstances. Other writers define these terms differently (see McGuire, 1969, for a sample).

The Source

Some people are interested in hearing what Johnny Carson has to say about anything—even brands of coffee and political candidates. Celebrities attract attention, and since attention is a necessary condition for persuasion to occur, sources are often selected on the basis of their attention-getting features. However, the attention-getting aspects of different sources are not the focus of this section. Here, we are concerned with the persuasive aspects of sources. Given a message with a particular content and structure, what are the characteristics of the source which may lead the receiver to accept or reject the conclusions in the message?

A research strategy that has often been used to study this

question involves presenting the same persuasive message to two or more groups of subjects but attributing the message to different sources for each group. For example, in one of the classic studies of this kind, Kelman and Hovland (1953) asked three groups of subjects to listen to a "transcribed radio program" which argued for lenient treatment of juvenile delinquents. One group was told that the source was a judge from juvenile court who had authored several books on the topic. Another group was led to believe that the source was a nere-do-well who had "gotten into many scrapes" and who might have been involved in dope-peddling. The third group was told only that the source had been chosen at random from the studio audience. Afterwards, the investigators assessed the degree to which each group of subjects accepted the conclusions of the message. (As expected, the judge was most persuasive, the nere-do-well least.)

Sources in such experiments have been identified as particular individuals, groups, or organizations, or they have simply been defined as communicators possessing certain characteristics. The kinds of characteristics that have received the most study may be grouped into three classes: (1) the credibility of the source, (2) the attractiveness of the source, and (3) the nature of the source-receiver relationship.

Source Credibility

The likelihood that a receiver will accept the conclusions advocated in a given message is in part a function of the receiver's perception of the source's credibility. Note the phrase "the receiver's perception." Source credibility is not a constant property of a source; rather it is an attribution that is conferred upon the source by the receiver.

*4.1.   High credibility sources exert more persuasive
        influence than low credibility sources. Aotbe.**

*Aotbe means all other things being equal. It means that the preceding

A wide variety of characteristics contribute to perceptions of high source credibility. For example, Singletary (1976) told subjects to imagine the most credible or believable news source they could, and then to describe that source. The person imagined was described as being knowledgable, attractive, trustworthy, articulate, satirical, and stable. Other investigators have identified other characteristics. Two characteristics have been identified and studied repeatedly: expertise and trustwoithiness.

4.1a. *Expertise is usually the most important component of high source credibility.*

Does the source "know what s/he's talking about?" Certainly, it seems reasonable to inquire about the credentials of the communicator. Does the receiver believe that the source has the information, experience, and intelligence to know the correct stand on the issue? Generally, the expertise of a source is content-specific. That is, a person may be viewed as being an expert on topic A, but not on topic B. However, some persons who are perceived as highly intelligent and generally well-informed may be accorded high credibility over a wide range of issues. For example, studies of the diffusion of innovations have shown that opinion leaders (individuals who frequently influence others in their social system or group) tend to have higher social status and greater exposure to media than their followers (see Rogers and Shoemaker, 1971).

4.1b. *Trustworthiness may contribute to high source credibility.*

If the source is perceived as being biased or insincere, attempts at persuasion may be ineffective. When the source's motives are

---

statement holds under controlled research conditions but may well vary in applied situations. Aotbe should be applied to every numbered guideline in this book, but appears only at the first of each chapter.

suspect, trustworthiness suffers. Communicators who are judged to be arguing in their own self-interest or who are thought to have an ulterior motive may be viewed with skepticism. On the other hand, several researchers have found that communicators who appear to be arguing against their own best interests are rated as being particularly believable. But even when the receiver suspects that the source is untrustworthy, some attitude change may occur. The trustworthiness of the source appears to be a less important matter than the source's expertise, particularly when the basis for persuasion is the legitimacy of the factual content in the persuasive message. Even so, it is generally to the source's advantage to be rated high in trustworthiness.

4.2.   The effects of source credibility tend to diminish with the passage of time.

People who show high initial acceptance of a message from a high credibility source may show less acceptance later on. This should not be too surprising. It might be expected that people's initial strong agreement with a high credibility source would soften; they "forget their attitude," just as information is forgotten over time. Somewhat surprisingly, though, researchers have found that people who receive a message from a low credibility source show an increase in acceptance of the message as time passes. This later phenomenon is called the "sleeper effect." A hypothesis advanced to explain both effects is that with the passage of time the message content becomes disassociated from the source and people become increasingly influenced by the content of the message. In the sleeper effect, people who were initially suspicious of the source and tended to reject the conclusion on that basis are increasingly affected by the strength of the agruments themselves (see Figure 4.1).

The sleeper effect is an example of a more pervasive "discounting-cue" hypothesis which states that the influence of any cue that is present when the message is presented and which would tend to

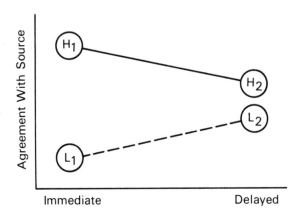

Figure 4.1. H_1 represents agreement with a high-credibility source immediately following a message. H_2 is the level of agreement after a delay of several weeks. L_1 represents agreement with a low-credibility source immediately following a message and L_2 is the agreement after the delay. The dotted line is the "Sleeper effect." (Adapted from Hovland, Janis, and Kelley, 1953, p. 255.)

lead the receiver to accept or reject the conclusion will become less salient with the passage of time, and that the persuasive impact of the message content will become paramount. Thus, many persuasion techniques that may be effective in the short run will lose their effectiveness in the long run.

4.3.   The amount of factual information learned from a message is independent of the credibility of the source.

High credibility sources result in no more learning of message content than low credibility sources. This principle must be qualified by the caveat that when people have free choice of whether or not to expose themselves to a message, they may be less likely to attend to messages from low credibility sources.

However, when attention is assured, degree of source credibility does not affect the amount learned. There is some indication (see McGuire, 1969) that when a message is attributed to a source of unknown or neutral credibility, more learning may occur. Perhaps people feel a greater need to understand the arguments when they lack the cue of high or low source credibility to guide them in judging the acceptability of the conclusion.

4.4. The receiver's evaluation of the message will affect the receiver's evaluation of the source.

The source-message relationship is a two-way street. What a source has to say about issues has a bearing upon how we feel about the source. Message factors such as the quality of the arguments may affect source credibility. Triandis (1971) cites evidence relating the extremity of a source's argument to his perceived trustworthiness and expertise. A source who takes an extreme position in opposition to the receiver may be judged as being more sincere but less competent than a source who takes a moderately opposed position. A source who takes an extreme position that agrees with the receiver may be judged as being both more sincere and more competent than a source who takes a moderate position in agreement.

Attractiveness

Source credibility tends to be topic-specific. The receiver evaluates the source's expertise and trustworthiness relative to the particular issue involved. There are, however, other characteristics which are largely irrelevant to topical concerns that may enhance the source's persuasive effectiveness. These characteristics are usually grouped under the rubric of "attractiveness."

4.5. Attractive sources are more influential.

A variety of factors appear to contribute to attractiveness,

among them similarity, familiarity, liking, and appearance. These
characteristics overlap and are mutually reinforcing. Often it is
difficult to specify exactly why we are attracted to other people.
Even so, some factors may be isolated—at least conceptually.

4.6.   *Source-receiver similarity contributes to the attractiveness of the source.*

People are more likely to accept influence from sources with
which they can identify. Experiments manipulating subjects'
perceptions of their similarity to the source have generally shown
a positive effect across a wide variety of bases for similarity.
Probably the more ways in which the source appears to be similar,
the more attractive the source will be. Nevertheless, some kinds of
similarity may be more critical than other kinds.

4.6a.   *Source attractiveness is particularly enhanced by perceived ideological similarity.*

It is particularly effective if the receiver perceives the source as
holding similar values and beliefs. Considerable research has been
conducted comparing the effectiveness of source-receiver similarity in belief (for example, political beliefs) versus some demographic characteristic (race, age, etc.). Although the evidence is
not one-sided (particularly regarding race), ideological similarity
appears to be more critical. Additionally, it appears that the more
relevant the nature of the shared belief is to the attitude issue in
question, the more effective the source will be in persuading the
receiver. Even so, it is probable that ideological similarities that are
irrelevant to the topic of concern often help. Probably the
important thing is that the receiver views the source as being
someone who "has the same ideas and thinks like I do."

A different kind of contributory factor to the positive effect of
similarity in natural communications situations is that there is
greater fidelity of communication between people with similar
backgrounds.

4.6b. More effective communication occurs when the source and receiver are similar.

Rogers and Shoemaker (1971) note that when the source and receiver "share common meanings, a mutual subcultural language, and are alike in personal and social characteristics, the communication of ideas is likely to have greater effects in terms of knowledge gain, attitude formation and change, and overt behavior change" (p. 14). Communication failure can often be traced to a dissimilarity between the implicit assumptions held by the two parties. The extreme difficulties experienced in cross-cultural communication forcefully demonstrate the problem.

4.7. Familiarity correlates with source attractiveness.

Does familiarity breed contempt or make the heart grow fonder? The latter, say social psychologists. It is not clear whether this occurs because people arrange conditions so that they can become more familiar with those they find attractive, or because familiarity leads to perceptions of attractiveness. Perhaps both. In any event, the relationship is well established. In a related line of research, it has been found that repeated contact with stimuli may result in more positive evaluations of those stimuli. (See the discussion on the attitudinal effects of mere exposure in the section about experience with attitude objects.)

Of course, all rules have their exceptions. In this case, several researchers (see McGuire, 1969) have found that praise from a stranger is sometimes more effective in influencing children's behavior than praise from a friend or parent.

4.8. Liking is related to source attractiveness.

One approach to the study of attitudes emphasizes cognitive consistency, the concept that people strive to keep related cognitions in a balanced, harmonious state. An early expression of the concept was Heider's (1946) balance model. The model deals with the relationships between the three necessary elements in a persuasive communication situation: a source (S), a receiver (R), and an attitude object (O) about which the source makes some assertion. When a source makes a positive statement about an object toward which the receiver also feels positive, the system is in balance (see "a" in Figure 4.2). But what might happen if the source made a negative assertion about the object ("b")? Figure 4.2 shows the two possible modes the receiver may use to regain cognitive consistency.

The balance model is obviously an extreme oversimplification of actuality. Among other things, degrees of liking (positiveness-negativeness) and the importance of the attitude object are not represented. However, the basic concept is sound and is the springboard for other, more detailed formulations.

4.9. *Physical appearance contributes to attractiveness.*

Studies of computer dating matches show that physical appearance affects ratings of attractiveness. Other research shows that good-looking damsels in distress are helped more speedily than their less comely counterparts. Physical appearance affects evaluations of competence and sincerity. For example, Miller (1976) found that a liberal-appearing source (long hair and a beard) was judged as being more sincere when he argued in favor of granting amnesty to draft evaders, whereas a conservative-appearing source (short hair, no beard) was judged as more sincere when arguing against amnesty.

Credibility vs. Attractiveness

The effectiveness of source credibility lies in the receiver's belief that the source has the ability to know the proper stand on an issue and the objectivity to communicate that stand truthfully. By accepting influence from a high credibility source, the receiver

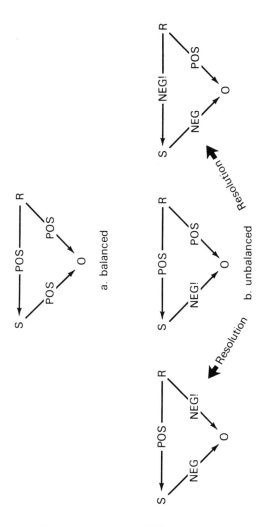

Figure 4.2. Heider's balance model. "S" represents the source, "R" the receiver, and "O" an attitude object. In "a" an S makes a positive statement about an O. Since R feels positively about both S and O, the system is in balance. In the imbalanced condition shown in "b," S makes a negative statement about O. R can resolve this imbalance either by changing his/her attitude to the O (represented on the left) or by changing his/her attitude toward the S (represented on the right).

could be said to be engaging in a rational decision-making process. Attractive sources exert influence simply through their association with a particular point of view. The rationale for the receiver's acceptance is on a more emotional level. These two types of influence may hold implications for the design of the message.

4.10. The quality and structure of the arguments in a persuasive message are more critical for credible sources than for attractive sources.

If the receiver is inclined to accept a source's conclusions because of the source's attractiveness, providing supporting arguments will be of minor importance. However, if the receiver is inclined to accept a source's conclusions because of the source's expertise, supporting arguments may be of considerable importance (see Figure 4.3).

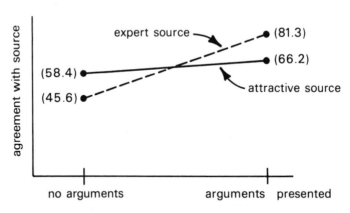

Figure 4.3. Norman (1976) found that a message containing no arguments was ineffective when attributed to an expert source (a source of 45.6 as compared to a score of 43.5 for a control group who received no message). On the other hand, subjects showed considerable agreement with an attractive source presenting the message without arguments (58.4) and agreement did not improve significantly with the inclusion of arguments.

This principle could be stated in a different way: When the message includes complicated argumentation, use an expert source; when the message consists of little more than the conclusion, use an attractive source. Stone and Hoyt (1974b) found that attractiveness alone was not effective in changing attitudes on a complicated, controversial issue. They also found that expertise was effective only when coupled with attractiveness (and presumably trustworthiness). Thus follows the obvious conclusion that the best approach is to employ sources who are both credible and attractive. The identification of such sources is a problem in cases when expertise implies a lack of similarity to the receiver.

The relative effectiveness of credibility and attractiveness is also related to the nature of the source-receiver relationship.

The Source-Receiver Relationship

Behavior must be looked at in terms of the context in which it occurs. Kelman (1961) has identified three persuasion situations based upon the social relationship between the source and receiver: compliance, identification, and internalization. In *compliance* the source has control over rewards and punishments. These controls may be either formal in nature, such as exist in an employer-employee relationship, or informal in nature, as when the source can permit or block the receiver's admittance into a group or social set. Compliance may even exist in cases where the only rewards and punishments the source controls are his own personal approval or disapproval. In persuasion situations involving *identification,* the receiver holds a satisfying relationship with the source, and may accept influence from the source for the purpose of perpetuating this relationship. In persuasion situations involving *internalization,* the source does not have any leverage over the receiver. If attitude change occurs, it is for reasons related to the content of the persuasive message itself and not for source-related reasons that are extrinsic to the topic. These three types of persuasion situations hold implications for the importance of the source's credibility and attractiveness, and for the degree to which their influence can be expected to persist.

> **4.11.   In compliance, the credibility and attractiveness of the source are of minor importance, and the source's influence will persist only so long as the source can audit the receiver's behavior.**

Here the receiver expresses opinions in agreement with the source in an attempt to influence the source's behavior. Through compliant behavior, the receiver hopes to obtain some reward—perhaps only a favorable reaction. In such occasions people often say things they do not really believe. Paradoxically, the receiver's own credibility may be enhanced, by expressing an opinion at variance with the more powerful person. "Thus," note Katz and Bernstein (1975, p. 215), "even the simple-heart, seeking a reliable guide to another's true feelings and being aware of the social obligations under which this person labors, will discount behavior consistent with these obligations and pay special attention to behavior inconsistent with the same."

In general, opinions expressed in compliant situations will terminate when the source is no longer in a position of control. However, if people are repeatedly led to say something that contradicts their inner belief, they may come to believe in the publically expressed position (see the upcoming discussion of cognitive dissonance.)

> **4.12.   In identification, the attractiveness of the source is of prime importance, and the source's influence will persist only so long as the receiver obtains satisfaction from the relationship.**

If you wish to become identified with a particular group, it is necessary to express the viewpoints held by the group. Kelman (1961) compares this situation to compliance:

> Identification is similar to compliance in that the individual does not adopt the induced behavior because its content *per se* is intrinsically satisfying. Identification differs from compliance, however, in that the individual actually believes in the opinions and actions that he adopts. The behavior is accepted both publicly and privately, and its manifestation does not depend on observation by the influencing agent (p. 64).

Should the receiver find that the individual or group has lost its attractiveness, the attitudes associated with the relationship are very susceptible to change.

> **4.13.** **In internalization, the credibility of the source is of prime importance, and the attitude will persist as long as it is congruent with the receiver's belief system.**

It might be argued that in education the ethical position is to attempt to exert influence in the context of internalization rather than compliance or identification. The content itself, and consequently the expertise and trustworthiness of the source, should predominate. Also, if the teacher is interested in finding out what the learner's true beliefs are, care must be taken to avoid situations of compliance, or the learner will simply tell the teacher what s/he thinks the teacher wants to hear.

Compliance, identification, and internalization are not always discrete. Two or more processes can occur simultaneously. If the source has control over a person, but the relationship is also satisfying, both compliance and identification may occur. If, in addition, the attitudes and actions required by the situation are also congruent with other attitudes, internalization may take place.

Message Content—WHAT to Say

The second major component of a persuasion situation is the

message. First we consider the problem of selecting the informational content of the message. Given that the communicator has decided on the conclusion s/he wants the receiver to adopt, how can s/he determine what information to present? Which arguments will be convincing and which arguments will be unconvincing? One means of determining the most effective message content is to pretest alternative messages. However, extensive pretesting is sometimes not feasible. Furthermore, how can the communicator think up potentially effective agruments in the first place?

The first type of message content discussed in this section is information that could be presented about the source of the message. Second, guidelines are presented for determining the content of the arguments in the message. In determining what arguments to present, the receiver's needs and values should be considered. Another question is whether or not some opposition arguments should be included. Third, guidelines for deciding about two aspects of expressing the conclusion are considered: Should the conclusion be left unstated; thus allowing the receiver to draw his/her own conclusion; or should the conclusion be stated explicitly, and if so, how strongly should the conclusion be stated?

Information About the Source

One kind of message content that is frequently overlooked is information about the source. Often, particulary in education, the information provided about the source is sparse. If attitude change is an objective, and if the source is not well known by the receiver but possesses characteristics that may facilitate attitude change, then this information should be made a part of the message.

4.14. *Be sure the receiver is informed of the expertise of a high credibility communicator.*

While it has often been shown that communicators who are perceived as being experts on a topic are more persuasive, exactly what constitutes expertise for a given receiver may not be obvious.

For example, Cantor, Alfonso, and Zillmann (1976) found that a tape-recorded message recommending the use of an intrauterine device was more effective when attributed to a source who had used the IUD herself than a source who had not. However, the same message was not affected by manipulating the level of medical expertise of the source. In another study, Shrigley (1976) asked third-year elementary education students to indicate the characteristics of instructors for elementary science methods courses that relate to teaching credibility. He found that practical teaching experience was rated high while involvement in research and authoring science textbooks was rated low. As noted earlier, credibility, including the factors that are associated with expertise, are percepts of the receiver and not properties of the source.

The source's attractiveness can also be enhanced by message content. One technique is to increase the perceived similarity of the source by establishing belief congruence between the source and receiver.

> **4.15. To enhance communicator attractiveness, establish belief congruence with the receiver by arguing in favor of positions the receiver is known to hold.**

Research has shown that establishing co-orientation between source and receiver on one topic can increase the source's effectiveness on another topic. This tactic is known as "flogging a dead horse." Praise the things the receiver likes (freedom and peace) and criticize the things the receiver dislikes (crime and taxes). Other research has shown that expressing affection for the audience may facilitate attitude change. Finally, Aronson, Willerman, and Floyd (1966) report an interesting technique for enhancing the likeablness of an expert, but austere, source. Revealing the source in the act of making a human pratfall (spilling a cup of coffee) may increase effectiveness by showing the source to be "more human."

Another aspect of information about the source that could be introduced into the message concerns how the source might stand to profit or lose from acceptance of his arguments. Self-serving messages may not be credible.

4.16.   *Persuasion may be facilitated if it is shown that the source is advocating a position that is opposed to the source's own best interest.*

Walster, Aronson, and Abrahams (1966) found that any communicator will be more effective when arguing a position against his/her own interest, and that the effectiveness of a low credibility source will be particularly enhanced. For example, in one experiment, a criminal (Joe "The Shoulder," serving a 20-year sentence for smuggling and peddling narcotics) was not persuasive when arguing for less powerful courts, but was highly effective when arguing for more powerful courts. A high credibility source (a prosecutor) was somewhat more effective when arguing against his own best interest (less powerful courts) than when arguing in favor of his interests.

The Needs of the Receiver

In teaching subject matter content, you begin where the student is; in attempting to persuade, you should also begin where the receiver is in terms of relevant needs.

4.17.   *Arguments are more effective if they are relevant to the receiver's needs.*

Show the receiver how an existing need can be satisfied by adopting your point of view. People are generally quite amenable to having their existing needs met. Of course, the need may not be apparent to the receiver, hence it may be necessary to remind him/her of the need and to point out the importance of satisfying it. However, once the need is apparent to the receiver, persuasion will be greatly facilitated if your objective can be related to the receiver's objectives.

Often the need which an attitude object can serve is quite obvious. For example, if the receiver has a need to wash his/her clothes, soap will facilitate the fulfillment of that need. It might be the communicator's job to convince the receiver that a particular brand of soap will do the best job. But, sometimes the need which an attitude itself can serve is not so clear.

4.18.   Attitudes perform psychological functions, and attitude change is facilitated by relating message content to those psychological functions.

Why do people hold the attitudes they do? Daniel Katz emphasizes the notion that attitude formation and change must be understood in terms of the psychological needs which attitudes serve, and that as these motivational processes differ, so too will the conditions necessary for attitude change. It is these motivational bases, not the attitudes themselves, that are the real causes of behavior. Unless you know the psychological need that is met by the holding of an attitude, you are in a poor position to predict how it might be changed. Katz (1960) describes four functions which attitudes can serve:

The knowledge function. People need standards or frames of reference for understanding their world. Attitudes help supply such standards. Adopting an attitude about a class of objects introduces stability into the world. Thus, stereotyping is sometimes only a matter of convenience used for reducing the information processing that would be necessary if each member of a class were treated as a unique event. Modifying attitudes based upon the knowledge function would seem to involve leading the receiver to attend to different cues about the object and to learn new discriminations.

The utilitarian function. People generally feel positively toward things that bring them rewards and negatively toward punishing stimuli. Manipulating perceptions of reward and punishment is the most common way to attempt attitude change. Holding a particular attitude may also be utilitarian if some social gain may accrue from expressing the attitude. Under conditions of compliance and identification, it may be useful to ingratiate one's self by expressing particular points of view.

The value-expressing function. The holding of a particular attitude may serve the function of providing you with a means of giving positive expression to the type of person you wish to be. Value-expressive attitudes give clarity to the self-image. If you view yourself as being politically liberal, adopting positive stances on issues such as civil rights legislation will help you demonstrate your ideological identity.

The ego-defensive function. While value-expressive attitudes have the function of allowing individuals to reveal their true nature to others and to themselves, ego-defensive attitudes serve to conceal and defend the self-image. Prejudicial attitudes are often ego-defensive. Persons who cannot admit to deep feelings of inferiority can bolster their egos by attitudes of superiority toward convenient minority groups. Such people are often unaware of their defense mechanisms. However, when provided with insight into the underlying reasons for holding an ego-defensive attitude, some people exhibit remarkable and enduring change.

The Values of the Receiver

A related but somewhat different approach to designing a persuasive message focuses upon the relationship between the attitude object and the receiver's values. Rosenberg (1960) suggests that an attitude can be thought of as the product of two cognitions: (1) the importance the receiver places upon the values that might be associated with the object, and (2) the receiver's judgment of the object's potential to facilitate or hinder the attainment of these values. Thus, a strong positive attitude toward an object would consist of perceptions that the object can lead to the attainment of important values. A strong negative attitude would consist of perceptions that the object tends to block the attainment of important values.

> **4.19.** ***Attitude change may be produced by changing the receiver's judgment of the attitude object's potential to affect the attainment of relevant values, or by changing the receiver's estimate of the importance of the values.***

The application of this approach might begin with (1) determining the values that are associated with the object, (2) acquiring the receiver's ratings of the importance of each value, and (3) determining the receiver's perception of the object's potential to promote or block each value. Then you would have a guide to predicting what arguments might be most persuasive. An argument that would produce attitude change is one which enhances the receiver's perception that the object can promote a highly-rated value. Another effective argument is one that increases the importance of a value the receiver believes the object can promote (although values are usually more resistent to change). An example of an ineffective argument is one that relates the object to a value the receiver feels is unimportant.

While this technique is too involved to be practical except in rare cases, it may at least provoke insight into potentially productive and nonproductive message content in attitude change.

Introducing Opposing Arguments

There are usually at least two sides to every issue. In a debate each advocate can be expected to state the arguments that support his/her own view. Sometimes, however, a communicator will also introduce arguments that appear to favor the opposition—and then refute them. This may be a good idea in some cases, but in other cases, it only raises doubts and questions. When should a communicator introduce opposing arguments?

> *4.20. Introducing and refuting opposing arguments
>   may be facilitative when (a) the receiver is
>   already familiar with the issue, (b) the receiver
>   initially disagrees with the communicator's posi-
>   tion, (c) the receiver is highly intelligent and
>   may seek out opposing arguments before making
>   a decision, and (d) the receiver will hear the
>   opposing viewpoint later.*

The cases in which *ignoring* opposing arguments are advisable are the obverse of the above, namely, when the receiver (a) is not familiar with the issue, (b) initially agrees with the communicator, (c) is not highly intelligent and inquisitive about the issue, and (d) will not hear the opposing viewpoint later. Although some empirical support exists for each of these factors, the most study has been devoted to the final factor—the question of what to do when it is likely that the opposing viewpoint will be heard later. Also, the question has been altered from the perspective of attitude change to the question of what tactic to take to strengthen an existing attitude against future counter-attacks.

> *4.21. To strengthen an existing attitude against future
>   counter-communications, it is better to intro-
>   duce the receiver to weak forms of opposing
>   arguments rather than only present agruments in
>   favor of your position.*

McGuire (1964) suggests that building up a resistance to counter-communications is analogous to building up biological resistance to disease. Just as innoculating individuals with a mild dose of a virus will allow their systems to build up resistance to the disease, presenting mild counter-arguments will allow for a build up of resistance to a full scale attack later on.

To test this "innoculation and immunization theory," McGuire conducted a series of studies using non-controversial cultural truisms as issues (e.g., brushing your teeth is a good idea). These truisms, beliefs which have essentially no opposition in our society, were found to be very susceptible to change. People have no occasion to defend these beliefs, and are consequently easily swayed. McGuire presented subjects with messages which (1) simply supported the truisms (everybody does it, dentists approve, etc.) or which (2) included mild counter-arguments (too much brushing may harm the gums, etc). The message containing the counter-arguments produced more resistance to a later counter-communication.

Another kind of message content that may help produce resistence to later counter-communications is to warn the receiver about the impending attempt to influence him/her.

> *4.22.   The impact of subsequent counter-communications may be lessened by warning the receiver not to be swayed by opposing propaganda from another source.*

Freedman and Sears (1965) observe that the effects of forewarning may be due to (1) increasing the receiver's suspiciousness of the second communicator, (2) causing the receiver to be less attentive to the second message, or (3) leading the receiver to rehearse the arguments supporting the first message prior to hearing the counter-communication. Their data offer the most support for the third explanation.

Stating vs. Not Stating the Conclusion

Is it more effective to let an audience come to its own conclusion or to make the conclusion of your arguments explicit? It has been suggested that people do not like to be told what to think and are usually more persuaded by their own conclusions. Most research fails to support this impression.

> *4.23.   It is almost always advisable to state the*

conclusion explicitly rather than to allow receivers to draw their own conclusions.

The main problem with leaving the conclusion implicit is that receivers may not come to the "right" conclusion. In fact, they may not come to any conclusion at all. When the issue is the least bit complicated or when receivers have low motivation or low intelligence, explicitly stating the conclusion is safer and better. Exceptions to this rule are cases, such as in psychotherapy, in which "long-term persuasion" is involved. In such cases, it may be that people who arrive at their own conclusions are more convinced than those who are explicitly told what to think and do.

The Extremity of the Position Advocated

Those who have ever haggled with a vendor in Mexico or a real estate agent in the United States know that the seller begins with an inflated price and that the buyer initially understates the price s/he is willing to pay. In persuasion should you state your conclusion in extreme form—actually expecting a smaller, but still substantial, change—or will that tactic result in no change because the receiver rejects your message in total? Is it better to advocate a more modest position? The answer is: It depends.

4.24.   *When the receiver has low involvement in the issue, advocating an extreme position on the issue will result in the greatest attitude change. When the receiver has high involvement, advocating a position only moderately different from the receiver's initial position will result in more attitude change than advocating an extreme position.*

If the issue has low salience with your audience, ask for more than you expect to get. For uncommitted receivers, the amount of attitude change is usually a compromise between the receiver's initial position on the issue and the position advocated in the communication. So, to bring the receiver to the position you desire, you must argue in favor of a position that is even more extreme than you actually desire. However, this tactic may boomerang for receivers who are highly involved in the issue.

Sherif, Sherif, and Nebergall (1965) found that when highly ego-involved individuals were presented with a persuasive message that differed substantially from their position, no attitude change occurred. Such people are firmly committed to their position on the issue and are very resistant to persuasion. If any change can be produced, it will occur by advocating a very small shift in the direction wanted. Producing significant change involves a long-term campaign in which the receiver is brought along little by little in a series of messages. Generally, however, a person who is highly ego-involved cannot be expected to change his/her position through persuasive communication alone.

Message Structure—HOW to Say It

This section reports some of the variables and techniques researchers have studied in connection with structuring persuasive messages. First, principles for sequencing message content are presented. Second, research dealing with types of emotional and rational appeals is considered. Next, techniques for changing attitudes by directly manipulating the receiver's behavior are presented. Finally, a set of miscellaneous, flamboyant, attitude change techniques is reviewed.

Sequencing Variables

A major area of persuasion research concerns the order of presenting message elements. Three aspects of the area are: (1) order of debate, (2) sequencing elements in a single communication, and (3) message repetition.

Order of debate. In a debate, which side has the advantage—the side that goes first or the side that goes second? Or, given that two opposing communications are separated in time, for example, as in successive issues of a magazine, is there a primacy effect (an advantage for the first communication) or a recency effect (an advantage for the second communication)? Research dealing with impression formation demonstrates the importance of first impressions in producing a "set" for interpreting later information; leading to the prediction of a primacy effect. However, research in learning demonstrates both primacy and recency effects; although in actual practice content covered at the end of a course is recalled better on the final exam than content covered early in the course. The evidence from persuasion research is also complex. Several factors interact to produce primacy-recency effects.

> *4.25. In successive communications neither the first nor the second message is always favored. A primacy effect will be more likely when the receiver (a) is unfamiliar with the issue, (b) is unaware that the other side of the issue will be presented later, and (c) makes a public commitment following the first communication. A recency effect is augmented by (a) lengthening the delay between the first and second messages, and by (b) shortening the delay between the second message and the attitude measurement.*

Primacy-recency effects in persuasion are difficult to predict not only because there are several intervening factors, but also because in reality communicators can take advantage of factors that researchers have not considered. For example, the second communicator can take advantage of weaknesses in the first message. On the other hand, the first communicator may be able to "defuse" some of the second communicator's arguments by debunking them before they are presented. Both presenters have advantages which they may, or may not, employ. Also, it is usually the case that there are not just two communications in a controversial situation, but rather there are many. So, in practice, the order of presenting two messages is normally not so important as a variety of context variables.

Sequencing elements in a single message. Research has been done on the most effective ordering of different kinds of message content. Generally, the evidence is that these sequencing effects are dependent upon a sizable number of variables and interactions. Consequently, the principles offered below oversimplify each relationship and should be viewed only as very tentative guides.*

The problem of primacy-recency effects in debating order can also be raised in relation to the most effective order of sequencing "pro" and "con" arguments in a single message.

> *4.26.* *When a communicator wishes to reveal some "con" arguments, they should be presented after the "pro" arguments if the receiver is not familiar with the "con" arguments. When the receiver is familiar with the "con" arguments, present and refute them before presenting the "pro" arguments.*

When the receiver is unfamiliar with the controversy, it may often be best not to raise any "con" arguments at all. But when it does appear advisable (see principle #4.20), introduce and refute them only after the naive receiver clearly understands the "pro" arguments. However, when faced with a hostile audience which is familiar with the issue, it is better to acknowledge and attempt to refute the "con" before presenting the "pro" arguments.

Should you present your "pro" arguments followed by your conclusion, or should you present your conclusion first and then

---

*For research and elaboration of these issues, see Hovland, Janis, and Kelley (1953) and McGuire (1969).

offer your supporting arguments? A similar question can be asked about the order of presenting your arguments in terms of their persuasiveness. Should you begin with your weakest arguments and lead up to your most convincing arguments (climactic order) or should you begin with you strongest argument and present weaker arguments later (anticlimactic order)? In both cases the answer depends upon the receiver's initial stand and interest in the issue.

> *4.27.   When the receiver has relatively little interest in the issue but may be favorable to your viewpoint, present your conclusion first and use an anticlimactic order in presenting your arguments. When the receiver is involved in the issue and is initially opposed to your viewpoint, present your arguments in a climactic order and then present your conclusion.*

When people are not interested in a topic, holding their attention presents a major problem. Disinterested receivers, if they attend to the message at all, may stop attending before you have presented your entire case. Hence, it is advisable to get your most critical information across in the early parts of the message. On the other hand, when full attention is likely, a presentation that "builds" may be preferred, particularly when the receiver is antagonistic. Approaching an antagonistic receiver with a mild threat to his/her belief is less likely to produce hostile reactions and total rejection of the message than using a strong initial attack.

> *4.28.   Present information which leads to pleasant contingencies first.*

Begin by presenting content that is pleasant and rewarding to the receiver. Beginning with rewarding information will reinforce the receiver's efforts to attend and to learn, and may facilitate the acceptance of less rewarding information presented later in the message.

4.29. Present need-arousing information prior to need-satisfying information.

Begin by telling the receiver why s/he should pay attention to your message and how s/he could stand to profit from accepting your conclusion. If the need is not apparent, need-arousing content may be required. For example, Cohen (1957) presented a message to college students arguing that grading on the curve is the best method. When preceded by anxiety-arousing information (the possibility that grading standards might be toughened) the arguments that grading on the curve is the best and fairest method were more effective than when the need-arousal followed the message.

When it is possible to conceal the source of information until the most strategic moment, is it better to reveal the identity of the source before or after presenting the information? Some evidence is available concerning low credibility sources.

4.30. The adverse effects of a low credibility source can be lessened if the source is identified after rather than before the message.

When a low credibility source is identified prior to a message, the receiver may tend to discount the information. When the receiver is persuaded by message content prior to learning that it originated from a low credibility source, considerable attitude change may still persist. This generalization is consistent with other evidence showing that the tactic of denigrating the opposing source is more effective if the attack is made prior to the opponent's presentation rather than after the other source has presented his/her message. The retroactive effects of low source credibility are often minimal.

Message repetition. Learning research shows that repetition of information aids retention. Does the repetition of a persuasive message help in persuasion?

4.31. Repetition helps.

Repetition helps. But only up to a certain point. Laboratory experiments in persuasion, and field studies of advertising in mass media, demonstrate the positive effects of repetition. However, it appears that the gain achieved reaches an asymptote rather rapidly. For a given receiver little gain is likely after one or two repetitions, although as McGuire (1973) notes, a greater number of repetitions in mass media channels may be productive if different members of a changing audience are exposed to the different repetitions of the message. It is logical to believe this, or why would television advertisers spend so much money on the incessent repetition of a single commercial? In fact, it is tempting to believe that advertising professionals, given their high-paid talent and access to enormous funds, have special and "secret" knowledge about human motivation and persuasion. Informed observers think otherwise. For example, Britt (1969) claims that advertising agencies virtually never state the objectives for campaigns in quantitative terms and that their "proofs of success" are only rarely related to campaign objectives. He concludes that, in general, advertising agencies really do not know whether their campaigns are successful or not. There is no compelling reason to believe that advertising executives are wiser, or more ignorant, than social psychologists.

Appeals to Emotions or Reason

Is human behavior a product of deep-rooted inner urges, tensions, and drives of which we are largely unaware, or are we the masters of our fate, studying, understanding, and finally manipulating our environment by rational procedures? Which are more effective—emotional appeals or rational appeals?

Early researchers who attempted experimentally to test this question failed to add to knowledge about persuasion. The concepts of "emotional appeal" and "rational appeal" are too broad and ill-defined to be useful. Recent research has focused upon a limited number of more precisely defined appeals. The most attention has been devoted to fear appeals, although humor has also received some study. In general, rational appeals, while the subject of considerable interest by scholars in speech and rhetoric, have received very little experimental study.

Fear appeals. Fear appeals stress the punishing consequences of failing to follow the communicator's recommendations. The rationale is that the anxiety produced by informing receivers of their vulnerability will motivate them to take the actions necessary to avoid the fearful occurrence.

4.32. Fear appeals can be effectively used to change attitudes and behavior.

Fear appeals have been shown to be effective in a variety of contexts. In education, Griffeth and Rogers (1976) demonstrated that students in a driver education course who had been exposed to a fear appeal about auto accidents improved their driving performance and greatly reduced error rates on driving simulators.

Health-related issues have been the most popular topic for fear appeal research. In a classic study, Janis and Feshbach (1953) compared the effects of three levels of fear appeal on motivating people to practice good dental hygiene. A low-fear appeal presented factual information about the causes of tooth decay and made recommendations concerning dental care. A moderate-fear appeal added mild, impersonal descriptions of the dangers of tooth decay and gum disease. A high-fear appeal presented the painful and damaging consequences of dental neglect, used repulsive pictures, and personalized the threat ("this can happen to you"). Increasing the level of fear appeal was successful in producing worry and anxiety. However, effects upon attitudes and actual behavior were inversely related to the strength of threat. The low-fear appeal produced considerable conformity to recommendations, whereas the high-fear subjects showed essentially no change in dental care behavior. The effect of fear appeals was shown to be a tricky issue.

4.33.   *The effectiveness of fear appeals is related to the receiver's final level of anxiety, a moderate anxiety level being more effective than either very high or very low levels of anxiety.*

Janis (1970) describes the relationship between the receiver's final level of anxiety and message effectiveness as taking the form of an inverted U (see Figure 4.4). A very low level of anxiety is ineffective simply because receivers are not given motivation to change. As anxiety rises, change occurs until an optimum level is

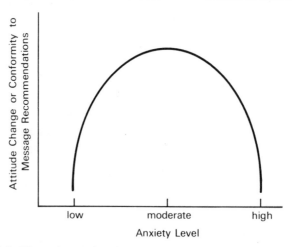

Figure 4.4. The relationship between attitude change resulting from a fear-arousing message (or the degree of conformity to the recommendations set forth in the message) and the receiver's final level of anxiety about the issue.

reached. Further increases in anxiety cause defensive-avoidance of the entire topic, finally resulting in total denial.

The question of how much threat a fear appeal should apply is a function of the receiver's initial level of anxiety about the issue. For receivers with very little anxiety a relatively strong threat will be needed to bring them to the optimal level of anxiety. Receivers who exhibit more initial concern should be threatened less. In some cases, anxiety reduction would be appropriate.

The problem of what information is threatening is difficult to determine because what frightens one person may not frighten another. However, Rogers (1975) suggests two components of fear appeals in the health area: (1) the depicted severity of the fearful consequence (e.g., the extent of bodily harm), and (2) the depicted likelihood that the receiver could fall victim to the consequence. If one of these two factors is known to be weak in the belief of the receiver, the fearfulness of the other must be stressed, and an apparently strong fear appeal will be required. For example, in one study a very strong fear appeal was required to persuade people about the dangers of looking directly at the sun during solar eclipses.

This inverted U-shaped relationship has also been observed when learning or test performance is plotted on the vertical axis. Test performance tends to be poor at low anxiety levels, when the student is presumably unmotivated, but performance improves as motivation increases. After a point, further increases in anxiety are debilitating, until a state of total inability to perform is reached. This relationship between learning and anxiety is suggestive of research findings about the strength of threat in fear appeals and message complexity.

4.34. The level of threat in fear appeals should be moderated when the message is complex and places demands upon comprehension.

When the issue is complex, arousing a high level of anxiety may be defeating because anxiety interferes with the ability to concentrate and learn message content. If the behavior necessary to escape the adverse situation is hard to learn, a high-fear appeal is not recommended, since receivers may conclude that they can reduce their psychological tension more easily by avoidance rather than by learning and performing the complicated procedure of the message. This brings us to another critical component of fear appeal messages—the specificity of the preventive practices recommended.

4.35.   Fear appeals should include specific and effective recommendations for preventive action.

The purpose of arousing anxiety is to motivate people to engage in behaviors which will reduce their noxious drive states. If the recommendations are not clear or appear to be ineffective, anxiety reduction through avoidance and repression may result. It may not be sufficient simply to inform the receiver that s/he can avoid a disease by getting innoculated. It may also be necessary to include information such as where to call and how to schedule an appointment. The receiver must also be convinced that the recommendations will be effective. Rogers and Mewborn (1976) showed that for appeals dealing with cigarette smoking, safe driving, and venereal disease, subjects' perceptions of their lack of ability to avoid the danger strengthened their intentions to adopt the recommended preventive measures.

There are several other factors that may influence the effectiveness of fear appeals. For example, research has been conducted on interactions with individual variables, such as self-esteem and "coping" versus "avoiding" tendencies (see Cronkhite, 1969). In general, while persuading through the use of fear appeals presents complex problems, this approach also holds considerable potential for dealing effectively with significant issues.

Humor. In view of the widespread use of humor in persuasive messages, practice-oriented people are surprised at the apparent lack of scientific interest in the area. Researchers know why. The area is difficult to treat experimentally. For example, how should humor be defined—by the intent of the source, by the receiver's reactions, by the arousal of certain psychological states, or by the presence of certain message elements such as incongruity? Humor is one of the most difficult human expressions to study.

The scant research that has sought to determine whether a humorous message is more or less persuasive than a serious version of the same communication leads to one generalization:

4.36.   The effects of humor on persuasion are generally unpredictable.

Besides the general inconclusiveness of the research, the most salient observation is the possibility that humor may backfire. For example, a message intended to argue against the practice of censorship through the satirical device of asserting that nursery rhymes are obscene and should be censored was interpreted as being a straightforward and reasonable message by people who were themselves in favor of censorship (Gruner, 1965). If you do not get the point of a joke, you misunderstand the sender's real message.

Those who have attempted reviews of the literature about humor in persuasion have come to varying conclusions. Mendelsohn (1964) suggests that humor be used sparingly and warns against boomerangs and allowing the receiver to identify with the butt of the joke. Sternthal and Craig (1973), reviewing humor in advertising, feel that while humor does not offer clearcut advantages and may interfere with comprehension, it may help through attracting attention, enhancing source credibility, creating a positive mood, acting as a reinforcer, and reducing the effect of counter-argument action by distracting the receiver. Markiewicz (1974), reviewing attitude change research, concludes that the effects of humor on comprehension and source evaluation are inconsistent and the effects on retention and persuasion are not significant.

Rational appeals. Aristole distinguished between *ethos,* persuasive appeals that focus upon characteristics of the source, *pathos,* appeals to the emotions, and *logos,* appeals to reason. Some critics of contemporary research have charged that the modern attitude change literature is little more than an updating of Aristole. Actually, classical Greek rhetoric of logos went far beyond the issues that have been studied scientifically. Some of these ideas are fundamental to modern logic (e.g., the genetic fallacy, syllogistic reasoning, argument by analogy, etc; see Salmon, 1963). While these principles are true *a priori,* that is, they can be neither substantiated nor refuted by experimentation, the relative persuasiveness of these arguments for different purposes could be studied. Some research has been done on the ease with which people can follow different logical arguments. For example, linear syllogisms (since A is better than B, and B is better than C, A is better than C) are easier to solve than nonlinear syllogisms (since A is better than B, and C is worse than B, A is better than C). But the matter of selecting arguments on the basis of persuasive effectiveness has not been researched. Nevertheless, practicing communicators should find the "rules of logic" useful, particularly in terms of analyzing the opponent's message for logical fallacies and signs of misuse.

Attitude Change via Behavioral Change

Most approaches to persuasion focus upon changing attitudes so that changes in behavior will follow. A different approach focuses upon changing behavior so that changes in attitudes will follow. By far the most influential statement of this approach is Leon Festinger's (1957) theory of cognitive dissonance.

Cognitive dissonance. Festinger's theory of cognitive dissonance deals with pairs of cognitions: (1) an individual's cognition that s/he has behaved in a certain way, and (2) his/her attitude about that behavioral act. When there is a conflict between such cognitions as "I smoke" and "Smoking causes cancer," an uncomfortable psychological tension is aroused. This tension, or cognitive dissonance, can be resolved in a number of ways (see Figure 4.5).

What does the theory of cognitive dissonance predict will happen to a person's attitude if s/he can be induced to engage in behavior that is inconsistent with a privately held attitude?

4.37. ***If a person can be induced to perform an important act that is counter to the person's own private attitude, attitude change may result.***

Suppose that an education student who has a negative attitude toward the use of media in instruction is induced by the instructor to make a speech about the positive aspects of using media in instruction. What will happen to the student's attitude? The student is faced with two cognitions: (1) I have just publically announced that media are useful in instruction, and (2) my private attitude is that media are *not* useful in instruction. To the degree that this inconsistency arouses dissonance within the student, some change will occur. Since it would be difficult to deny the behavioral act, the student's attitude may change to be congruent with the behavioral cognition.

This technique was in fact tried by Simonson (1977). Some students entering a large media methods course were randomly assigned to a treatment in which they were asked by a person claiming to be a member of the College of Education Instructional Improvement Needs Assessment Committee to give a talk about the positive aspects of media. The talk was videotaped so that "the entire committee can get together and observe all the videotapes made by students." The results were that students who made the videotaped statements showed more positive attitudes than students who were not induced to make the public commitment. Also, the former group learned somewhat more course content during the subsequent semester.

But perhaps a student might think something like this: "I know

a. Dissonance arousal because of the conflict between
a behavior and a cognition.

b. Dissonance elimination by changing a behavior.

c. Dissonance elimination by changing a cognition.

d. Dissonance reduction by modifying a behavior and
bolstering a cognition.

Figure 4.5. Modes of dissonance arousal and reduction.

I just made a speech arguing in favor of something I don't personally believe, but I really had no choice in the matter. I did it only to obtain rewards and avoid punishments from that more powerful person." What would happen to the student's attitude then?

> *4.38.* *When a person is induced to perform an attitudinally-discrepant act because of promise of reward or punishment, attitude change will occur only to the degree that the person feels the magnitude of the reward or punishment was insufficient to justify the attitudinally-discrepant behavior.*

Cognitive dissonance can be thought of as a theory of rationalization. When a person can rationalize his/her behavior by an appeal to external forces, attitude change is not likely. For example, students in Simonson's study could protect their anti-media attitudes by rationalizing that they were coerced into making the pro-media videotape. However, students who felt some measure of free will in engaging in the act probably experienced some dissonance.

Ideally, a change agent would like to offer the minimum inducement that will produce the attitude-discrepant behavior. The dilemma, as Calder and Ross (1976) note, is that the very conditions that are most likely to produce the desired behavior (large rewards and severe punishments) work against the internalization of the desired attitude. A sufficient level of reward or punishment to induce the behavior must be applied, but it should be the minimum amount necessary to achieve this end. A delicate balance is required.

Suppose that a person has worked hard to achieve a goal only to discover that the goal is not as desirable as previously believed. What will be the person's attitude toward this goal?

4.39. People value things they have worked hard to achieve, even when the things turn out to have little manifest value.

If a person holds the cognitions (1) I have worked hard to acquire X, and (2) X is worthless—dissonace will be aroused. A mode of dissonance reduction is to evaluate X more positively, thus providing the person with a means of justifying his/her effort. Consequently, dissonance theory implies that if you want to make a person value something—say, membership in an organization—make it a difficult goal to achieve.

This principle bears a resemblance to recent research on the attribution theory approach to motivation. Attribution theory predicts that when people attribute the rewards they acquire to their own efforts, they will be motivated to work further. For example, Dweck and Reppucci (1973) found that when children attributed their successes to their own hard work they were more likely to persist under adverse reward conditions than children who failed to relate their level of achievement to the outcome of their own efforts.

Role-playing. In role-playing, participants are asked to behave as they think a certain kind of person would behave in particular situations. Can engaging in this kind of make-believe behavior affect attitudes?

4.40. Role-playing can have powerful persuasvie impact.

Janis and Mann (1965) told subjects that they were studying certain aspects of human behavior which are difficult to observe in real life, and that they were consequently using role-playing as a technique for observing how people might behave. Subjects were asked to imagine that they were visiting their doctor who had been treating them for a persistent cough. The role-playing session proceeded something like this:

Doctor: "Well, last time you were here you asked for the whole truth, so I'm going to give it to you. This X-ray (pointing to it) shows there is a small malignant mass on your right lung. Moreover, results of the sputum test confirm this diagnosis."

Role player: "What you're saying, doctor, is that I have lung cancer, right?"

"Unfortunately, the tests leave no doubt about the diagnosis."

"What next?"

"Immediate surgery is necessary. I've arranged for you to report to the hospital tomorrow morning. Plan on spending at least six weeks there, because chest surgery requires a long convalescence."

"I dread asking this question, but how are my chances?"

"I wish I could be totally encouraging; however, frankness dictates that I tell you there is only a moderate chance for a successful outcome from surgery for this condition."

"Is there anything I can do to improve my chances?"

"We've discussed this before, but I'd like you to refresh my memory on your smoking habits."*

The session continued with a discussion of cigarette smoking and its consequences. The role-playing subjects showed marked attitude changes and reduced their cigarette smoking much more than a control group who merely listened to a recording of one of the role-playing sessions. Even 18 months after the experiment, the role-players continued to smoke fewer cigarettes than control subjects. Since the control subjects were exposed to the same information as the role-players, it must have been something about the active involvement that was so effective.

4.41. *Active participation produces more attitude change than passive reception of information.*

Several researchers have found that participants in role-playing are affected more than observers. In related research, subjects who participated in group discussions about an issue changed attitudes more than subjects who just listened. The active participant is

*From Miller and Burgoon (1973), p. 45.

apparently more aroused, more involved, and more able to experience the emotions that might occur in reality.

Providing a model. Much of our behavior is learned by imitating someone else's behavior. Psychologists have shown that people will do a wide variety of things simply because they have observed other people doing them—leave large or small tips at restaurants, walk under ladders, reveal or hide their feelings, and so forth.

4.42.   Attitudes can be changed when the receiver becomes involved with a human model.

Emotional responses as well as overt behavior can be learned by observing others. For example, Zimbardo and Ebbesen (1970) reviewed studies in which subjects learned emotional responses and behaviors to stimuli (e.g., feeling and behaving non-fearfully to snakes) by observing a live model (who handled snakes without showing signs of fear). Classroom teachers should give thoughtful consideration to the kind of model they are providing to their students. The previous discussion of observational learning in the memory chapter and the up-coming discussion of the effects of televised violence upon children are relevant to the topic of modeling.

Miscellaneous Flamboyant Techniques

Largely because they do not fit easily elsewhere, five additional interesting techniques are now presented. While these techniques have generally been the subjects of less empirical study than most of the other issues discussed in this chapter, they are not necessarily any the less valid.

The effectiveness of "overheard" messages. Resistance to persuasion may be reduced if the receiver feels that s/he is not the direct object of manipulation. One technique for disguising persuasive intent is to arrange a situation where the receiver is allowed to overhear a persuasive communication.

4.43. *Persuasion may be more effective if the receiver overhears the message rather than receives it directly, particularly when the conclusion is agreeable to the receiver.*

Researchers have devised situations in which subjects hear persuasive messages, on the one hand, from a source who apparently did not know that he was being overheard and, on the other hand, from a source who was obviously aware of the subject's presence. Attitude change was greater in the "overheard" condition. Brock and Becker (1965) found that this effect occurred only when the message advocated a conclusion which was acceptable to the receiver. When college students "overheard" a message arguing for a disagreeable conclusion (raising tuition), no persuasion resulted. Some television advertisers appear to be attempting to use a form of this technique in commercials showing "candid camera" scenes of ordinary people "caught in the act" of praising the sponsor's product.

The foot-in-the-door technique. How can you get a person to do something s/he would probably rather not do? The foot-in-the-door technique involves approaching the person in stages.

4.44. *Persuading a person to comply with a small request increases the likelihood that the person will later comply with a more important request in the same area.*

Freedman and Fraser (1966) sought to persuade home owners to place a large sign saying "Drive Safely" or "Keep California Beautiful" in their front yards. People who had previously agreed to put a small sign in a window or in their car were more likely to comply than a control group. In another experiment, these researchers found that the rather preposterous request to allow a team of five or six men to come into a home and spend two hours searching through closets and cupboards to make a list of all the products in use, was agreed to much more frequently if the person had previously answered a few questions over the phone about household soaps. Thus, it is not only easier to persuade people to perform an easy-to-do task than a hard-to-do task, but once they have performed the easy-to-do task it is more likely that they can be persuaded to perform the hard-to-do task.

Distraction. Forewarning receivers that a communicator will attempt to influence them usually creates resistance to attitude change. One explanation of this is that forewarning increases the likelihood that receivers will engage in covert counter-argumentation. The technique of distraction is intended to reduce the receiver's counter-argumentation.

> *4.45.   Reducing covert counter-argumentation by presenting distracting stimuli along with the message may enhance persuasion when the message is easy to comprehend.*

In distraction research, subjects are exposed to a persuasive message and simultaneously are exposed to irrelevant sensory stimulation (e.g., irrelevant pictures or sound effects) or are asked to engage in irrelevant activity (e.g., adding or a copying task). In most studies, these subjects showed more attitude change than subjects who heard the message without distraction. In other studies, distraction inhibited persuasion. One difference appears to relate to message comprehension. If the message is complex, distractions can interfere with learning and inhibit attitude change. Distraction seems to work only when the message is easy to understand. (See Miller, 1973, for a review.) Often the effects are not very large, and distraction may be difficult to engineer in mass media situations. However, distraction may be a useful technique in controlled cases when a specific behavior is sought.

Creating a positive atmosphere. Some researchers dealing with the distraction technique suggest that a pleasant distraction is more effective than an unpleasant distraction.

4.46. *In general, it is probable that persuasion will be enhanced if the receiver is in a "positive frame of mind" or is engaging in an enjoyable activity.*

Several researchers have found that people are more persuasible when they are being treated to refreshments. The pleasantness of the environment (e.g., temperature, comfort) appears to have a similar effect, as do various techniques to put the receiver in a "positive frame of mind." For example, Veitch and Griffitt (1976) found that subjects who reported feeling a positive affect after hearing a news broadcast featuring "good news" reacted more positively to strangers than subjects who heard "bad news."

Inducing self-dissatisfaction with attitude-value inconsistency. It was mentioned earlier that some individuals who hold prejudicial attitudes for ego-defensive reasons show considerable attitude change when their reason for holding the attitude is pointed out to them. A similar technique involves showing people inconsistencies in their attitude-value system.

4.47. *Confronting people with inconsistencies in their own attitude-value system may lead to self-dissatisfaction that produces changes in attitudes and long-term behavior.*

Milton Rokeach (1973) asked university students to rank the importance they placed on 18 values: A comfortable life, an exciting life, a sense of accomplishment, a world at peace, a world of beauty, equality, family security, freedom, happiness, inner harmony, mature love, national security, pleasure, salvation, social recognition, self-respect, true friendship, and wisdom. Overall, students ranked *freedom* first and *equality* eleventh. By various means. Rokeach suggested to students that their relative ranking of these two values was indicative of a high concern with one's own freedom but of a low concern with other people's freedom. He then asked students to relate this to their liberal positions on civil rights. When faced with these contradictions, many students expressed considerable self-dissatisfaction with their apparent hypocrisy. The procedure not only resulted in attitude and value changes, but in long-term behavioral changes as well. Students in the treatment were much more likely than control students to respond positively to a membership drive by the National Association for the Advancement of Colored People and to enroll in courses dealing with problems of prejudice and race relations. Such self-confrontation procedures may have many applications, even including the potential for personality change.

The Channel

The term "channel" can be used in several ways:

1. Channel can refer to the type of medium used: film, television, radio, and so forth. Questions can be raised about the relative effectiveness of these channels. For example, is persuasion more effective if television rather than radio is used? Are some media more credible than others? Is face-to-face communication more persuasive than mediated communication? These questions are dealt with under the heading *Media Types*.

2. Channel can refer to human sensory capabilities, such as vision, hearing, and touch. These human information processing channels correspond to attributes that are present in media—the potential of presenting visual information, auditory information, and so forth. Under the heading *Media Attributes* the topics of visual persuasion and the use of language are discussed.

3. Channel can also refer to objects. Thus, attitude change and formation through *Direct Experience with Attitude Objects* is considered very briefly in this section.

Media Types

When the term "channel" is used in the literature on attitude change, authors are usually referring to some media type, such as film, television, radio, or a print medium. Sometimes the author is implicitly coupling a medium with its distribution-reception system. That is, when the term "television" is used, the author may be thinking of network broadcast television in which millions of people are simultaneously exposed to the same message in the context of their home viewing environments. That conception is quite different from closed-circuit instructional television. Also, there are vast differences between programs presented over any given television system. For example, if, in attempting to assess the "persuasive impact of television," television is taken to include the Nightly News, the Lawrence Welk Show, Sesame Street, deodorant commercials, and televised Presidential debates, the results may be of little or no descriptive or predictive value.

Even so, terms such as "television," "newspapers," and "radio" are frequently used in the literature, and many people have rather definite ideas about the relative effectiveness of these media types in attitude change. Film has frequently been mentioned as a particularly persuasive medium. Lenin, for example, extolled the virtues of film as a powerful tool to engineer social change, and the Nazis used film in World War II as an effective propaganda instrument. Even those dealing with instruction are impressed with the persuasive possibilities of film: "The motion picture seems to be a powerful medium for attitudinal communication because it can so realistically dramatize phenomena and events" (Haney and Ullmer, 1975, p. 39).

What does the *research* say about the differential persuasive effectiveness of different types of media?

4.48. *No one media type has been explicitly shown to have greater persuasive effectiveness than any other media type.*

While there has not been much research comparing the persuasive effectiveness of media types, the majority of the published studies fail to show differences among media. It appears

that persuasion is equally effective via any of several media; that
is, no specific medium can assure either success or failure.
However, any medium can be well or poorly used. Different media
possess different properties which allow for different communications possibilities. So, approaching the question of media effectiveness from the viewpoint of media *type* is not satisfactory;
approaching the question from the viewpoint of media *attributes*
may be more revealing. This approach is discussed shortly. First,
though, let us compare face-to-face communication with mediated
communication.

4.49.   *Face-to-face communication is more effective in promoting acceptance than mediated communi- cation, particularly in difficult cases.*

While the evidence emerging from the experimental laboratory
is somewhat equivocal on this issue, the results of field studies are
conclusive. Studies of political campaigns and research in the
diffusion of innovations show that when attitudes were changed
on important issues, it was usually the influence of another person
rather than of the media that was primarily responsible. While
media may be more effective in bringing an issue to the attention
of the public, personal influence is often needed to obtain
commitment.

The effectiveness of face-to-face communication has little to do
with the type of information presented, but rather appears to be
the result of factors associated with the physical presence of the
source. For example, the live source can apply "social pressure,"
relying upon the receiver's reluctance to directly contradict a
person. After all, it is harder to say "No" to a person standing
right in front of you than it is to refuse impersonal requests. Also,
face-to-face communication may be more effective because the
source can tailor his/her message to each receiver and alter it
on-the-spot if necessary. So comprehension may be better. Finally,
face-to-face communication has the advantage of increasing the

likelihood that the message will be attended to. With regard to this last point, one of the main reasons that media campaigns fail is that the target audience does not attend to the message.

4.50. *Persuasion via media may be ineffective under conditions that permit selective exposure.*

"Selective exposure," as the term is used in attitude change, refers to the tendency of people to expose themselves to communications that agree with their predispositions and to avoid those which disagree with their positions. In other words, people may use media to reinforce the ideas they already have. It should be noted, however, that while the phenomenon of selective exposure was an established "law" of communications behavior until the late 1960's, more recently social scientists have noted that people do sometimes expose themselves to discrepant information, but only if they think that new information will not give rise to cognitive dissonance. When a person is certain about a belief, or views an issue to be of little importance, s/he will not engage in selective avoidance, because the new information does not have the potential for psychological threat.

In any event, for whatever reason, it is often the case that media messages do go unattended by the target audience. In fact, the people the communicator most desperately wishes to reach may be the very ones who are least likely to expose themselves to the message.

Media credibility, a concept analogous to source credibility, is a topic that has received attention from practitioners and re-searchers concerned with mass communication.

4.51. *In mass communication, television is currently most often judged to be the most credible medium, although for some purposes and audiences, newspapers, radio, or magazines are more credible.*

Media credibility has usually been studied in terms of a news source. Since the early 1960s, television has replaced newspapers as the most believable source of news. However, newspapers may have higher advertising credibility, and, in one study dealing with health issues, magazines were rated higher than newspapers. So media credibility depends upon a number of variables, including receiver characteristics, such as age, sex, and education (see for example, Becker, Martino, and Towers, 1976). Also, different sources within a medium (different television spokesmen, different newspapers, etc.) differ in credibility, making the effect of the medium *per se* inconsequential as compared to the total impact of other factors in the persuasion situation. Additionally, although the relationship is widely assumed to exist, it is yet to be demonstrated that media credibility has an impact on attitude change.

The social effects of mass communication: Television and children. How have contemporary mass media shaped society—and vice-versa? This panoramic question is beyond the scope of this book. However, one aspect of the question that is of particular concern to educators will be treated briefly: What is television doing to our children?

In a typical piece, the January 23, 1977, Sunday newspaper supplement called *Family Weekly* asked "Is There Too Much Violence on Television?" "No" answered Herbert Schlosser, President of NBC, arguing that frequency counts do not meaningfully index viewer effect. "Yes" answered George Gerbner, Dean of the Annenberg School of Communications, expressing fear that our children may "grow up mean and terrorized by vivid images of meanness around them."

Not all social scientists are as clear on the issue as Gerbner. George Comstock (1975), who led a team at the Rand Corporation in an extensive review of research on television and human behavior, notes the "cacophony" of conclusions about the effects of violence on children's antisocial behavior. While laboratory experiments have often linked aggressive behavior with seeing violent acts on television, the relationship has not been clearly demonstrated in the "real world." Several scientists take the position that television is only one of many influences in the lives of children, and it most likely serves to reinforce whatever predispositions exist in the individual. It has even been suggested that television violence may occasionally have a cathartic effect— reducing aggressive drives. Other scientists disagree, observing that television may show violence-prone individuals "how-to-do-it," and that the long-run manifestations of extensive exposure to violence have not yet been expressed.

Part of the reason the answer is not clear is that the issue is complicated. However, Comstock (1975) does place some confidence in a few emerging generalizations:

The amount of time spent viewing television varies considerably among children, but usually averages at least two hours a day and is often as much as five to six hours a day, although much of this time children are simultaneously or intermittently engaged in other activities. Among the very young, some of this activity involves imitating what they have just seen on the screen. Viewing time is greater for those lower in IQ, academic achievement, and socio-economic status. These children also more frequently perceive television drama as accurately portraying reality. Attitudes and information may be readily accepted when children have no contradictory firsthand experience on the topic from their environment. While young children cannot distinguish commercials from program content, children soon learn to distrust commercials and find them generally disagreeable. Children rate television as a credible news source.

Regarding the relationship between violence on television and violent behavior in children Comstock sides with those who feel that television probably increases the likelihood of subsequent aggressive behavior. However, he notes that a number of mediating factors intervene, such as:

...the degree to which the observed behavior is perceived as rewarded or effective, the viewer's state of excitation or arousal,

> the degree of similarity between the observed environment and the actual environment, the availability of a target perceived as appropriate for the act, and the perceived lack of sanctions against the act (1975, p. 28).

Comstock emphasizes that his conclusion is tentative and refers only to the direction of the effect, not its magnitude or consequences on society.

Almost lost in the concern about the feared antisocial effects of television is the possibility of fostering prosocial behavior. Several investigators have demonstrated that socially desirable acts can also be learned from television (e.g., Sprafkin, Liebert, and Poulos, 1975). Those who control commercial television have not been accused of being overzealous in exploiting this possibility.

Media Attributes

Under the section titled Media Types, questions were raised, such as "Is persuasion via television more effective than persuasion via radio?" Obviously, this question is very similar to "Is *learning* via television more effective than *learning* via radio?" Both questions represent hypotheses for what have been called "media comparison studies." While there are only a few published media comparison studies dealing with persuasion, there are hundreds of them dealing with learning. However, in both cases the overwhelmingly predominant finding has been the same: No significant difference.

This repeated research finding has puzzled many people. Intuitively, it would seem that the choice of medium should be an important factor in communicating successfully. Yet over and over researchers have found that medium A is no better or worse than medium B in facilitating the attainment of a variety of objectives.

The problem lies in the statement of the research question. The aspect of a channel that determines its effectiveness for achieving communication objectives is not the media type, but the media attributes employed. A media attribute is the potential of a given message vehicle to present information of a certain kind. If you wanted to know what the media attributes of a communication channel are, you would ask questions like: Is it possible to show pictures? Can the pictures be in color? Can motion be shown? Can sound be presented? Is the pace of the presentation flexible or fixed? In what ways is the channel responsive to receiver differences?

When channel variables are specified in terms of media attributes rather than media types, differences are often found in learning effectiveness. Words are found to be more effective than pictures for some kinds of learning, while pictures are better in other cases. The attributes of color and motion aid learning in particular cases and neither facilitate nor interfere with learning for other objectives. While research on the persuasive effectiveness of media attributes is very skimpy as compared to learning, a few observations on the topic are appropriate.

Visual persuasion. Over 80 percent of all the information we take in is through the eyes! We live in a visually-oriented society. The popular conception is that pictures have almost mystical power. What is the research evidence?

4.52. *While messages including pictures are preferred and attract attention, the addition of pictures does not necessarily enhance persuasion.*

Pictures do attract attention. But the question is, attention to what? Advertisers have found that while inserting a picture of a pretty girl in a male-oriented advertisement produces more notices of the ad, there are often no corresponding increases in message comprehension or purchasing behavior. Similarly, while researchers have found that people generally like and prefer messages containing pictures, this preference is often not transferred to the subject matter. For example, researchers usually find that adding illustrations to textual material fails to enhance attitude change. But a few researchers have found a positive effect for pictures. Results depend on *how* pictures are used.

One clue to the effective use of pictures is provided by Culbertson (1974), who found that while news photographs were generally not rated as having any more emotional impact than "equivalent" verbal descriptions, pictures did seem to be at an advantage when the subject matter was concrete—referring to actual objects—whereas words seemed to be at an advantage when the topic was an abstract idea or concept. This impression is in agreement with the better established generalization that in learning, pictures are better for concrete information and words are better for abstract information. Accordingly, it is not unreasonable to assert that:

> *4.53.   Pictures may contribute to persuasion when they are used in a way that communicates evaluative information about the attitude object.*

We sometimes overlook the fact that in addition to providing simple stimulation, pictures can present information. When the pictorial information about an attitude object is positive, persuasion may be enhanced. That is, pictures work just like words in this respect. A difference is that communicators are usually more skillful in designing verbal messages than pictorial ones, and receivers are better at decoding verbal than nonverbal messages.

Generally, if the research on *teaching* with pictures can be generalized to *persuading* with pictures, a few broad bits of advice seem warranted:

1. Use pictures to refer to concrete subject matter. A good picture-word combination is to use pictures to provide the examples for the concepts developed verbally at a more abstract level.

2. Emphasize the relevant evaluative-persuasive cues by (a) keeping the pictorial design simple; (b) drawing attention to the relevant cues by techniques involving composition, color, motion, or "pointers" such as arrows; and (c) reducing the number of distracting, irrelevant cues.

3. Be aware that pictures are not a "universal language" and may not be accurately interpreted by people poor in pictorial literacy, such as young children and those in remote developing cultures.

4. Be aware that even people with high pictorial literacy often only "see" rather than "look at" pictures, and may require special verbal prompts to learn from them.

Attempting to persuade with pictures is probably a very risky proposition, and the earlier discussion about presenting the conclusion versus allowing the receiver to draw his/her own conclusion may be particularly apt in visual persuasion; nevertheless:

4.54. *Visual persuasion may occur without awareness.*

Because people are generally less aware of what they learn from pictures as compared to words, visual persuasion may be a paricularly effective technique for disguising the intent to persuade. Still photographers and film makers can rather easily make a subject look good or look bad. Faking with statistics is made even simpler by presenting your "facts" graphically (see Figure 4.6).

The visual presentation of your own self may be a persuasive act. Good salesmen are well aware of the techniques of "body language" and eye contact. Dress is important. One researcher found that he was able to get people to do things like pick up a paper bag and give a dime to a stranger if he was wearing a uniform. Other researchers have found that males were evaluated differently depending upon whether or not they were wearing a neck tie.

A related question concerns the impact of pictures on credibility. Or, to put it colloquially, "Is seeing believing?"

4.55. *The use of pictures may affect media credibility and the credibility of media personalities.*

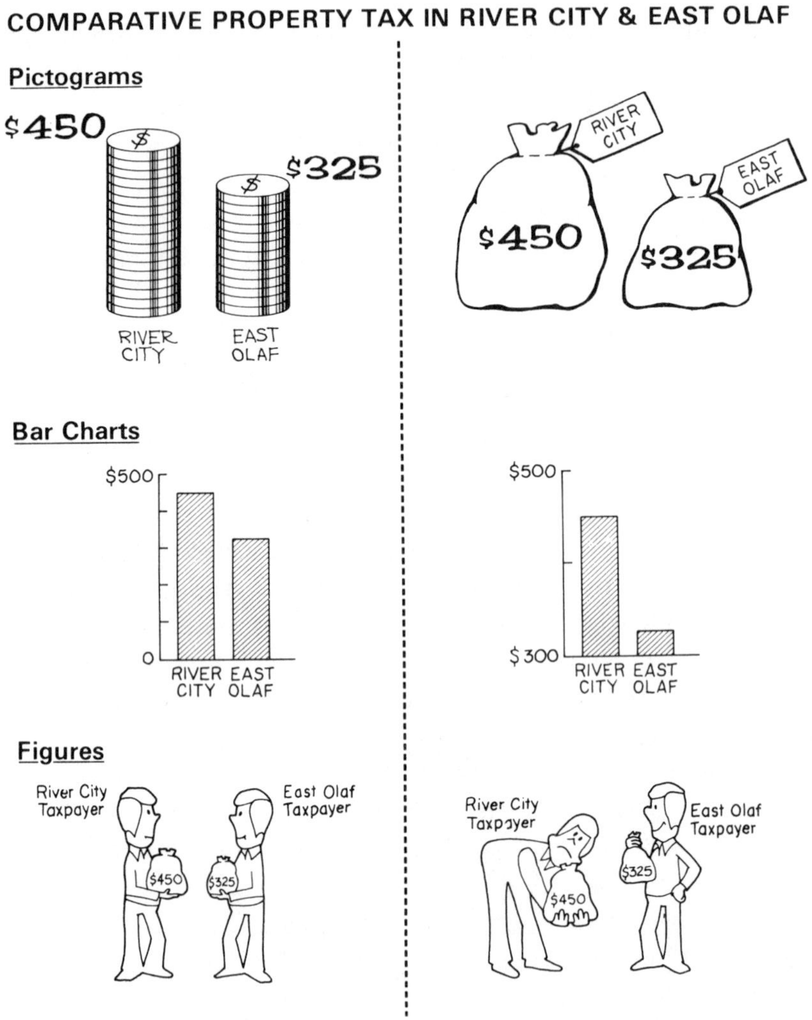

Figure 4.6. Visual persuasion. Using pictograms, bar charts, and figures, the versions on the left suggest that there is little difference between the property taxes in River City and in East Olaf. The versions on the right suggest that there is a large difference.

Ryan (1975) wondered if television's current high status as a news source is associated with the use of news film. He compared credibility ratings of newspaper accounts of events with television accounts that (a) included news film or (b) did not include news film. Film often made a significant positive contribution. Duck and Baggaley (1975) showed how ratings of a televised speaker's expertise could be manipulated by inserting cut-aways of the audience, portraying them to be either attentive or bored. Thus, unethical media producers may be able to engage in "hidden persuasion" through the manipulation of techniques of which the lay person is unaware.

Clearly, people have unknowingly learned many of their attitudes about social objects from mass media. For example, public attitudes about sex roles in business and love making have been influenced by the mass media. Often these attitudes are learned from stereotypes presented incidentally to the main purpose of a media dramatization. Ferreting out these "unintended side effects" would require a high level of social responsibility on the part of those who control our media.

One particularly frightening possibility of the unscrupulous use of visual persuasion drew a great deal of attention when in 1956 a motivational research firm claimed that they had been successful in increasing sales of popcorn and Coke in a New Jersey movie theater by flashing the commands to "Eat" and "Drink" on the screen at speeds of 1/3000 of a second. A Congressional investigation resulted, and the technique was banned. The legislation was, however, needless.

4.56. *Persuasion via the presentation of subliminal stimuli does not appear to be a practical possibility.*

The idea of subliminal persuasion is that a stimulus presented at a level below the detection threshold takes effect at a level that is free from conscious restrictions and is thereby very effective.

Visions of being in the grip of uncontrollable desires to "Buy Fleming's Bread" or "Vote for Levie" fascinated the public. Early research which appeared to lend credibility to the technique has now been seriously questioned. Recent experimental attempts to influence behavior by subliminal visual stimuli have failed (see George and Jennings, 1975). This is not to deny that the phenomenon may exist under very carefully controlled conditions for specific types of behaviors, but the possibility that the technique may be successful in practical contexts for the kinds of purposes originally envisioned now seems very unlikely.

The use of language. World War II was, at least in retrospect, a war of words.

> I know that one is able to win people far more by the spoken than by the written word, and that every great movement on this globe owes its rise to the great speakers and not to the great writers.
>
> > Adolf Hitler
> > *Mein Kampf,* Preface

> Let us therefore brace ouselves to our duties and so bear ourselves that, if the British Empire and its Commonwealth last for a thousand years, men will still say: "This was their finest hour."
>
> > Sir Winston Churchill
> > Speech, House of Commons
> > June 18, 1940

In addition to Hitler and Churchill, Roosevelt, de Gaulle, MacArthur, Tokyo Rose, Axis Sally, and the Voice of America also used words as weapons. Psychological warfare was practiced by both sides and gullible Americans were warned not to be deceived by propaganda techniques such as "card stacking" and the use of "glittering generalities." But wartime leaders and propagandists are not the only ones dependent upon words. The effective use of words is also a matter of considerable concern to salesmen, lawyers, preachers, businessmen, educators, and peacetime politicians. In fact, to everyone, it might seem, except social psychologists. Curiously, they have done very little research in the area. About the best that can be said is:

> *4.57.   While it is not clear how, or if, eloquence enhances persuasive effectiveness, poor delivery may detract from source credibility.*

A few researchers have shown that unskillful use of language, such as mispronunciations, hesitancy, and disorganization, can result in low evaluations of source credibility—usually in regard to competence. On the other hand, slickness, high intonation, and enthusiasm may reveal a blatant intent to persuade and hence lower trustworthiness (see McGuire, 1969). Generally, style of delivery has been an unimportant and confusing issue to experimenters.

Even less research has been done on the related matter of selecting words and syntax. For example, while slogans are widely used in public issues, no basic research exists on their effective construction. However, in a symposium on traffic safety campaigns, Mendelsohn (1964) observed that slogans such as "Drive Carefully" are probably meaningless, since they do not offer an action mechanism. "Make the last 'one-for-the-road' coffee" may be more likely to have some effect. Finally, culminating a unique and provocative set of studies, Kanouse and Abelson (1967) found that when a persuasive argument is stated as a concrete, positive verb (an observable action that implies approval; e.g., buy, produce), then it is most effective to support the argument with concrete evidence, whereas if the argument is stated as an abstract, negative verb (an unobservable action which implies disapproval; e.g., ignore, resent), then it is most effective to support the argument with abstractly stated evidence.

Direct Experience with Attitude Objects

While most attitude research has focused upon persuasion

through communication, a few investigators have studied the attitudinal effects of direct experience with attitude objects. One approach is derived from theories of learning. Since attitudes are learned, and since people can learn from their experience with objects, it follows that certain learning principles might apply to attitude formation and change resulting from direct experience with attitude objects.

> *4.58.   Attitudes formed through direct contact with an attitude object will tend to be positive if the experience is rewarding or is associated with positive contingencies, and will tend to be negative if the experience is punishing or is associated with negative contingencies.*

In one of the most widely quoted studies in the literature, Staats and Staats (1958) demonstrated the operation of classical conditioning in attitude change. Stimuli such as nationalities (e.g., Dutch) and male names (e.g., Harry) were repeatedly paired with words having known attitudinal values. Pairing a stimulus with positively valued words enhanced the evaluation of the stimulus, whereas pairing it with negative words resulted in lowering the evaluation of the stimulus. Later researchers obtained similar results with electric shocks and other stimuli. When a student's contact with a subject matter (e.g., math) is repeatedly coupled with feelings of boredom, frustration, or anxiety, a negative attitude toward the subject will be formed.

Classical conditioning is not the only learning theory implicated by this principle. As noted in the chapter on memory, reinforcement has a powerful influence on learning. When experience with an object results in rewards, the approach behavior associated with a positive attitude is strengthened. When a student's contact with a subject matter results in rewarding consequences, such as feeling a sense of accomplishment or being praised and given high grades, a positive attitude toward the subject will be formed. There may also be one-trial learning in attitude formation. Just one experience of being stung by a bee or frightened by a shark may produce long-lasting attitude change.

While it is clear that people arrange their lives so that they may have repeated experiences with things they like, what about the reverse situation? That is, do people tend to like the things with which they have repeated experience, even though the object may have no inherent reward function? According to some research, yes.

4.59. Mere experience with an object may foster a positive attitude.

In a monograph titled "The Attitudinal Effects of Mere Exposure," Zajonc (1968) presented evidence that repeated exposure to a class of stimuli led to more positive attitudinal judgments about the stimuli. This relationship was demonstrated for a wide range of stimuli (such as words, symbols, art objects and music), tending to confirm the common belief that people like what they are familiar with. Another common belief, that people tend to be negative toward things they are not familiar with, has not been put to experimental tests, but would appear to be a corollary of this principle. In practice, however, it is unlikely that stimuli are repeatedly encountered in contexts which are completely free of positive or negative affect, and several researchers have found that, with increasing exposure, stimuli presented in positive contexts become more positive and stimuli presented in negative contexts become more negative.

The Receiver

The simple SOURCE→MESSAGE→CHANNEL→RECEIVER communication model encourages the impression that the receiver is an empty vessel into which the source pours the message. This model, as well as early communication research, puts the emphasis on the source. While the receiver was not wholly ignored, s/he was regarded primarily as a passive reactor to whom something was done. Receivers, however, have proved to be intractable. They are highly active in the process, altering the view of persuasion from a primarily "stimulus-bound" process to a primarily "response-bound" process.

A frustrating aspect of receivers for attitude researchers and for practicing communicators is their heterogeneity. A persuasion technique that works quite well for some individuals will have no effect on others and may even boomerang in some cases. In persuasion, different folks are in particular need of different strokes, a fact that mass communicators are well aware of but can do little about. It might seem that communicators involved in individualized persuasion situations are at an advantage as compared to mass communicators. However, obtaining accurate, relevant information from a single individual can be very difficult and, generally, it is more difficult to predict the effect of persuasion upon a particular individual than to predict the general trend of a group reaction. But even incomplete information can be superior to no information. Accordingly, this section is devoted to offering some directions which an audience analysis might take. What information about the receiver is most likely to be helpful in persuasion?

Information about the receiver's existent position on the particular attitude issue of concern is discussed first under the heading "topic-specific factors." Next, the question of persuasibility (i.e., the ease with which an individual typically yields to social influence) is discussed, first, in connection with demographic characteristics (age, sex, etc.) and, then, in connection with several individual ability and personality factors. Next, characteristics related to individual differences in the speed with which people adopt innovations are considered. Finally, some of the influences that the receiver's group memberships contribute to the persuasion situation are discussed.

Topic-Specific Factors

One of the basic tenets for the practicing communicator is "know your audience." In attitude change, the most useful things to know about the receiver are the things that bear most directly upon the attitude you are interested in modifying. Information of this type is suggested by principles presented earlier in this chapter. For example, how much does the person know about the topic, how interested in the topic is s/he, and what is his/her present stand on the issue? (See principles #4.20, #4.25, and #4.27.) Other topic-specific questions concern the needs, psychological functions, and values which are implicated by the attitude. (See principles #4.17, #4.18, and #4.19.) Another aspect of the receiver's attitude is mentioned in principle #4.24, namely, the degree of involvement the receiver has in the issue. Because this factor is so critical in terms of setting limits to the potential for attitude change, it will be elaborated upon here.

> *4.60. It is very difficult to change the attitudes of receivers who are highly committed to their positions on an issue.*

While this principle may seem obvious, some of the ramifications of the principle are not so obvious. Beyond the simple point that people who are committed to a position are hard to change, a deeper investigation of the phenomenon of involvement shows why such attitudes are so resistant to change.

Sherif, Sherif, and Nebergall (1965) propose that it is inadequate to represent an individual's attitude as simply a point on a scale from most positive to most negative. In Figure 4.7, the positions on an attitude issue held by two individuals, Frank and Ernest, are shown to be a stand of -2 on a seven-point scale. However, Frank and Ernest, while holding identical positions on the issue, have quite different attitudes in terms of their commitments to the position. Sherif, Sherif, and Nebergall have devised procedures for determining the range of positions an

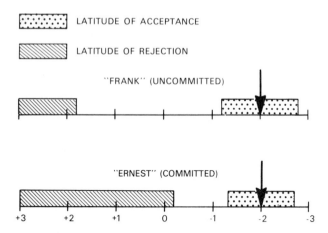

Figure 4.7. Latitude of acceptance and rejection for two individuals who hold the same position on an attitude issue, but who differ with respect to their degree of commitment on the issue.

individual is willing to accept (called the latitude of acceptance), the range of positions the individual rejects (the latitude of rejection), and the remaining positions on the issue (called the latitude of noncommitment). In Figure 4.7, Frank, who is uncommitted to his stand on the issue, has a much narrower latitude of rejection than does Ernest, who rejects a wide range of positions on the issue. In framing a persuasive message, a communicator who advocates a position that could be classified as falling at about the +1 or +1.5 position on the scale may expect to have a persuasive effect on Frank. What would be the likely effect of arguing this position with Ernest? No change. Such an argument would be ineffective with Ernest because it falls within his latitude of rejection. That is, Ernest has already decided that such an argument is wrong, and will reject it out of hand. To have any effect upon Ernest, the communicator must advocate a position of -.5 or so, a position that is actually opposed to the communicator's own position!

A more precise statement of Principle #4.60 is provided by Sherif, Kelly, Rodgers, Sarup, and Tettler (1973) as the primary conclusion of one of their experiments (Study IV): "Susceptibility to change in response to short-term exposure to communication is inversely related to degree of involvement in the issue at hand" (p. 325). This information shows why it is so difficult to change people's minds about things they really believe in. The attitude change that can be expected for such individuals is very modest. Substantial change can be obtained only after a long campaign in which the receiver is very carefully brought along little by little.

This formulation also depicts two other common observations about the attitudes of highly committed individuals. The first observation is that highly involved people tend to see the issue largely in terms of black and white: "You're either for me or you're against me." Less involved individuals who are uncommitted to a broader range of positions on the issue are able to make finer discriminations. The second observation is that committed people are generally more certain about what they are against than what they are for. The major difference between committed and uncommitted individuals lies in the widths of their latitudes of rejection. Committed people reject a broad range of positions, giving clarity to what they are against on the issue.

The degree to which a receiver is committed to a position is often related to the extremity of the stand.

4.61. People who hold extreme positions on an issue are usually more committed than people who hold moderate positions.

Sidewalk orators and campus demonstrators usually hold more extreme positions on the issues of their concern than less committed persons. That is not to imply that extreme views are necessarily invalid. As Shaw notes, "All great truths begin as blasphemies." But those who are on the extreme ends of an issue tend to espouse their causes with greater vigor than middle-of-the-road advocates. Thus, the paradoxical situation exists in which the people who hold viewpoints most discrepant from the communicator's viewpoint and who consequently have the greatest apparent potential for change in the communicator's direction are the very people who are least likely to be affected by the message.

Other information about the receiver that could be helpful includes the degree to which the attitude in question is related to other attitudes held by the receiver. Attitudes embedded in a cluster of related attitudes are more resistant to change than those that exist in isolation.

Certain situation-specific information may also be useful. For example, what is the receiver's attitude toward the source? What communication channels are preferred by the receiver? In what environment is the receiver likely to receive the message? What situations are likely to foster attentiveness or distraction? Suffice it to say that each attitude topic presents problems that are specific to that particular topic and that these questions should be raised in an audience analysis. Let us now turn our attention to questions about the receiver that may be relevant whatever the attitude topic may be.

Demographic Characteristics

Demographic characteristics are those variables that typically appear in statistical descriptions of populations: age, sex, race, socioeconomic factors, and so forth. While there are vast differences in the persuasibility of individuals within any demographic category, some general relationships between persuasibility and groups of individuals across categories have been observed.

> **4.62.   *Persuasibility increases up to a maximum somewhere between the ages of five and nine, and then declines somewhat until adolescence when it levels off.***

McGuire (1969, 1973) predicts this relationship between age

and persuasibility on the basis of certain "plausible assumptions" and from combining the results of separate studies. The increase in persuasibility from infancy is attributed to increasing ability to attend to and comprehend information, after which people apparently become somewhat less susceptible to influence. McGuire also predicts a decline in persuasibility at senility due to lessening ability to attend, and comprehend. There are also some data produced about 20 years ago suggesting that the persuasibility of males is somewhat more likely to decline with age than females (see McGuire, 1969).

4.63. According to past research, females are more persuasible than males.

If females are more persuasible, it is not due to some sex-linked genetic determinant, but is a function of socialization processes favoring submissive, dependent behavior and roles for women. It is reasonable to expect that as perceptions of appropriate feminine (and masculine) behavior change, the traditional persuasibility of women will diminish. Perhaps persuasibility among males may even increase. In any event, individual differences in persuasibility among different females and different males are, and will continue to be, sizable.

Occasional research seeking relationships between persuasibility and other demographic characteristics has appeared, but no other consistent findings have emerged.

Aptitudes and Personality Characteristics

People's personalities consist of sets of more or less stable abilities and response tendencies that direct the ways in which they interact with their environment. Some of these characteristics have been shown to be related to persuasibility. Note that the evidence of these relationships is correlational, not cause and effect. For example, Laird and Berglas (1975) found that yielding in an attitude change situation was significantly related to a measure of field dependency. This does not imply that field dependency causes persuasibility or that persuasibility causes field dependence. Correlation simply implies the mutual presence of two (or more) phenomena.

Intelligence. An intuitive expectation is that the more intelligent a person is, the less persuasible s/he will be. Numerous researchers have found just the opposite. It seems that the relationship between intelligence and attitude change is a function of two factors: comprehension and yielding.

> *4.64.   Intelligence is positively associated with persuasibility when message comprehension is paramount and is negatively associated with persuasibility when yielding is paramount.*

In the first paragraph of this chapter it was noted that before persuasion can occur, perception and comprehension must take place. The receiver must understand the message before s/he can accept it. So, to the degree that persuasion is dependent upon message comprehension, intelligence will be positively correlated with persuasibility. On the other hand, intelligent people appear to be more resistant to the "persuasive impact" of a message than less intelligent people.

A study by Eagly and Warren (1976) supports this view. They exposed high school students of differing levels of verbal intelligence to two persuasive messages: one message included a set of complex supporting arguments; the other message was unsupported. They found that opinion change was positively related to intelligence for the complex message and negatively related to intelligence for the simple message. McGuire (1973) speculates that, in general, maximum persuasibility occurs at moderate levels of intelligence. Because of failures of attention or comprehension, low-intelligent people are relatively unsusceptible, and, because of extreme resistance to being influenced, high-intelligent people are also relatively unsusceptible to persuasion.

Self-esteem. The most heavily researched personality characteristic in persuasion is self-esteem. The early conclusion was simply that persons low in self-esteem are more persuasible than persons high in self-esteem. However, as with most issues in persuasion, further research produced a more complex picture.

4.65. *Receivers who are very low or who are very high in self-esteem are less persuasible than receivers who have moderate levels of self-esteem.*

The relationship between self-esteem and persuasibility is moderated by attention and comprehension factors. Low self-esteem seems to be related to poor attention and comprehension of persuasive messages so that people low in self-esteem are relatively difficult to influence. High self-esteem is associated with confidence in one's own views; therefore, persons with high self-esteem are also relatively difficult to influence. Hence, the relationship between self-esteem and persuasibility has the form of an inverted-U. This is also the kind of relationship between intelligence and persuasibility and between anxiety level and attitude change (see Figure 4.4, page 228).

McGuire theorizes that many personality variables bear this inverted-U relationship with persuasibility, and sometimes even a double inverted-U relationship. Regarding the entire research area, McGuire (1968) comments: "If it is safe to make any simple generalization about personality-influenceability relations, it is that no simple generalizations are valid" (p. 1172).

Other personality characteristics. A sizable group of other personality characteristics have been studied in connection with persuasibility. A few of these are noted below. Ignoring the high probability that these characteristics function in interaction with other variables, only the main effects of these characteristics on persuasibility are mentioned. Hence, the following statements not only oversimplify the facts of the experimental literature, but also oversimplify the facts of life.

Reviewing the work of others, Cohen (1964) has described a number of personality factors that may affect persuasibility: *Authoritarianism,* a personality type associated with obedience to authority, toughness, and cynicism; *Other-directedness,* the tendency to conform to goals and standards of others; *Richness of fantasy,* the ability to imagine and anticipate the rewards or punishments conveyed by a communicator; *Need for cognitive clarity,* the tendency to react to ambiguous situations by seeking more information; and *Field dependence,* the extent to which an individual's perceptions are affected by the surrounding field. Cronkhite (1969) notes research relating persuasibility to *lack of aggressiveness,* and other research suggesting that *dogmatic* individuals are highly susceptible to persuasion from authoritarian sources. In more recent research, Snyder and Tanke (1976) found that attitude change following counterattitudinal behavior will be greater for individuals low in *self-monitoring.* Stone and Hoyt (1974a) found differences between people who are *source-oriented* or *message-oriented,* while Horai and Wasserman (1974) found *Machiavellianism* to be negatively related to subjects' favorableness toward others.

These are but a few of the personality variables that have been studied in connection with the "content-free" factor of persuasibility. But even this small sample of findings confirms two things we know about people: they are complex and they are different. Pondering this bewildering assortment of evidence, a communicator might dispare of ever attaining a satisfactory level of persuasive effectiveness. However, the fact that a variety of personality factors have been identified does not compel the conclusion that they will always operate in practice. The effects of personality characteristics are probably weak in many cases.

Characteristics Related to the Adoption of Innovations

The area called the "diffusion and adoption of innovations" deals with the study of how an innovation (a new idea, practice, or instrument) is communicated and accepted over time among the members of a social system. Different members adopt innovations in an ordered time sequence from its first appearance. Readiness to adopt is related to a variety of demographic and personality characteristics.

>4.66. *As compared to receivers who are slow in the adoption of innovations, earlier adopters tend to be better educated, more literate, have higher social status, and greater upward social mobility. Earlier adopters tend to be more intelligent, empathetic, venturesome, and achievement motivated, while being less dogmatic and fatalistic.*

An innovation gains acceptance and adoption throughout a social system according to a bell-shaped frequency distribution. At first, adoption occurs slowly, then accelerates, leveling off as the innovation is adopted by about half the individuals in the system, and then traces a mirror path back down as the slowest members to adopt join the others. Individuals have been grouped into "adopter categories" on the basis of where they fall in terms of relative speed of adoption. Individuals adopting at a time one standard deviation earlier than the average adopter are called the "early majority," those adopting even one standard deviation more rapidly are called "early adopters," and so forth (see Figure 4.8).

Rogers and Shoemaker (1971) have described some of the characteristics of individuals who fall within each of these categories.

"Innovators" are venturesome, lacking in close ties to their local peers, and more cosmopolite in their social relationships.

"Early adopters" are well integrated into their local social system and are often opinion leaders. Change agents often attempt to identify and influence these opinion leaders early in a diffusion campaign.

"Early majority" adopters are more deliberate and are less

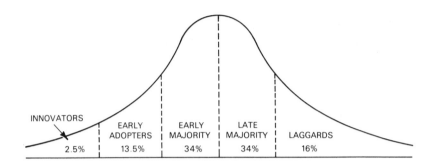

Figure 4.8. Adopter categories in the diffusion of innovations. (From Rogers and Shoemaker, 1971, p. 182.)

likely to exert opinion leadership than are early adopters.

"Late majority" individuals are skeptics, adopting only after social pressure or economic necessity is considerable.

"Laggards" are extremely traditional and suspicious of any change. Many are near-isolates.

Group Influences

Communicators should recognize that the receiver is not an isolated individual, but a person whose thoughts, actions, and attitudes are inextricably interwoven with those of the people around him/her.

> *4.67.   People are strongly influenced by the groups they belong to and by the attitudes of their reference groups.*

The classic study demonstrating the potency of group influence was done by Newcomb (1963). He studied changes in political attitudes of women in a small Eastern college during the four-year period 1935 to 1939. Most women came from wealthy, conservative families. When they were confronted with a highly liberal faculty and an involving, liberal intellectual climate at school, attitudes became dramatically and progressively more liberal during most students' college careers. In a 20-odd-year follow-up study, graduates had retained many of the attitudes they acquired in college. In fact, quite amazingly, the quartile in which a person fell on a conservatism-liberalism attitude measure taken at graduation was highly predictive of her vote some 20 years later in the 1960 Nixon-Kennedy election.

Reference groups are groups a person admires or would like to belong to. They serve as comparison points or frames of reference for evaluating a person's own ideas and status. When a message has the approval of one of the receiver's reference groups, attitude change should be facilitated. For example, Landy (1972) found that subjects were more influenced by a speech if they were led to believe that an attractive group had been attentive and receptive to the speech.

> *4.68. An individual's resistance to change from a group attitude is related to the degree with which the person values the group and to the saliency of the group norm.*

Usually, groups act as agents for resistance to change. People who do not conform to group expectations may be expelled from the group, thus enforcing conformity for those who value their group membership. While it is clear that the importance of attitude issues will vary for groups, there is some pressure for conformity even on questions not particularly relevant to the goals of the group. For example, in a study of friendship associations, it was found that attitudes having little relevance to friendship were nevertheless frequently adopted because individuals perceived their friends as exerting pressure for adoption.

A group, however, is more than just a collection of people. While one member of an aggregate of individuals will be influenced by the others in trivial ways, long-lasting influence on important issues will occur only when the individual is well-integrated into the group. Also, a group can disband and lose its influence rapidly. Bauer (1973), for example, notes that members of the German Wehrmacht became susceptible to allied propaganda in World War II after unit morale had disintegrated.

4.69.   *Group discussion and decision can facilitate attitude change.*

Occasionally, the group acts (or may be used) as an agent for change. Several studies have shown that attempts to change food preferences and eating habits can be facilitated through group discussion and decision (see McGuire, 1969). Thus, on some occasions, it may be easier to change the position of a whole group than to change the attitude of the single individual in the group. Also, once a new group norm is established, the group will act as an agent to preserve the new attitude.

Group discussion and decision can also enhance commitment. For example, when students engage in group discussion and decide to set higher achievement goals, motivation for individual students is heightened.

Final Comments

From a cursory look at this chapter, one might conclude that a great deal is known about how to modify people's attitudes and, hence, that persuasion should be an easy matter for the skillful practitioner. Alternatively, one might conclude that attitude change is an extremely complex process in which numerous factors interact and, hence, that persuasion is likely to be unpredictable in all but the simplest and most controlled laboratory situation. One might, then, legitimately ask if one of these points of view is more nearly correct than the other, or if there are, in fact, any general statements which can be made about the practical utility of the 69 principles offered in this chapter.

Generally, in free societies, persuasion on controversial issues via mass media alone is typically ineffective. Many factors—competing messages, selective exposure, group influence, and other uncontrollable aspects of the real-life situation—often cancel out a communicator's impact. The public is heterogeneous; different appeals have different effects on different individuals. Field studies of media campaigns have repeatedly demonstrated the futility of hoping to manipulate attitudes through mass communication alone.

But, what about those cases in which the communicator wishes to influence only one person or one small group of people under more controlled circumstances? Again, the bases for pessimism are impressive. People who are strongly committed to a position on an issue are remarkably resistant to change; presenting them with conflicting information has little effect on their attitudes. In fact, challenging people's values often has the reverse effect of causing them to entrench in their original positions. And, even for less committed individuals, the factors that interact to produce attitude change are difficult to discover and to control. So, despite the apparent sophistication of the scientific discoveries of regularities in how people react to persuasive messages, in practice, people remain basically unpredictable. And, even when a persuasive message does have an impact, its effects often fade rapidly.

This chapter, then, clearly does not offer magical solutions to difficult problems. Hopefully, what this chapter does do is to suggest some responses to simpler problems. Given that the receiver is not previously committed to a hostile viewpoint, given that the nature of the situation and group influences do not preclude change, and given that the communicator can engineer the perception and comprehension of the message, it is not unreasonable to expect that the use of appropriate principles offered in this chapter could contribute to persuasive effectiveness.

Of course, the question then becomes "Which principles are appropriate?" Appropriateness is explicit in some principles. For example, the circumstances in which the application of principles for enhancing source credibility and attractiveness are relatively apparent. However, the circumstances for selecting and applying other principles are not so clear and are more dependent upon the message designer's experience and ingenuity. For example, the situations in which role playing or one of the "miscellaneous flamboyant techniques" should be chosen do not automatically reveal themselves. It might never occur to a classroom teacher to use the somewhat bizarre foot-in-the-door technique to convince students to engage in a behavior which initially appears undesirable to them. Similarly, the use of effective techniques derived from cognitive dissonance theory are often counter-intuitive at first.

It should be noted that trickiness is not being advocated, nor is message design in the absence of testing and evaluation being suggested. The point is that a thoughtless, mechanistic use of attitude change principles will not suffice. While the principles may be thought to represent science, their application lies mainly within the realm of practical art. So, the answer to questions about the actual utility of these principles is dependent not only upon differences among message design situations but also upon differences among message designers themselves.

References

Aronson, E., Willerman, B., and Floyd J. The effect of a pratfall on increasing interpersonal attraction. *Psychonomic Science,* 1966, *4,* 227-228.

Bauer, R.A. The audience. In I.S. Pool (Ed.), *Handbook of communication.* Chicago: Rand McNally, 1973.

Becker, L.B., Martino, R.A., and Towers, W.M. Media advertising credibility. *Journalism Quarterly,* 1976, *53,* 216-222.

Britt, S.H. Are so-called successful advertising campaigns really successful? *Journal of Advertising Research,* 1969, *9*(June), 3-9.

Brock, T.C. and Becker, L.A. Ineffectiveness of "overheard" counterpropaganda. *Journal of Personality and Social Psychology,* 1965, *2,* 654-660.

Calder, B.J. and Ross, M. Attitudes: Theories and issues. In J.W. Thibaut, J.R. Spence, and R.C. Carson (Eds.), *Contemporary topics in social psychology.* Morristown, N.J.: General Learning Press, 1976.

Cantor, J.R., Alfonso, H., and Zillman, D. The persuasive effectiveness of the peer appeal and a communicator's first-hand experience. *Communication Research* 1976, *3,* 293-309.

Cohen, A.R. Need for cognition and order of communication as determinants of opinion change. In C.I. Hovland (Ed.), *The order of presentation in persuasion.* New Haven, Conn: Yale Univeristy Press, 1957.

Cohen, A.R. *Attitude change and social influence.* New York: Basic Books, 1964.

Comstock, G. The effects of television on children and adolescents: The evidence so far. *Journal of Communication,* 1975, Autumn, 25-34.

Cronkhite, G. *Persuasion: Speech and behavioral change.* New York: Bobbs-Merrill, 1969.

Culbertson, H.M. Words vs. pictures: Perceived impact and connotative meaning. *Journalism Quarterly,* 1974, *51,* 226-237.

Duck, S.W. and Baggaley, J. Audience reaction and its effect on perceived expertise. *Communication Research,* 1975, *2,* 79-85.

Dweck, C. and Reppucci, N. Learned helplessness and reinforcement responsibility in children. *Journal of Personality and Social Psychology,* 1973, *25,* 109-116.

Eagly, A.H. and Warren, R. Intelligence, comprehension, and opinion change. *Journal of Personality,* 1976, *44,* 226-242.

Festinger, L. *A theory of cognitive dissonance.* Stanford: Stanford University Press, 1957.

Freedman, J.L. and Fraser, S.C. Compliance without pressure: The foot-in-the-door technique. *Journal of Personality and Social Psychology,* 1966, *4,* 195-202.

Freedman, J.L. and Sears, D.O. Warning, distraction, and resistance to influence. *Journal of Personality and Social Psychology,* 1965, *1,* 262-266.

George, S.G. and Jennings, L.B. Effect of subliminal stimuli on consumer behavior: Negative evidence. *Perceptual and Motor Skills,* 1975, *41,* 847-854.

Griffeth, R.W. and Rogers, R.W. Effects of fear-arousing components of driver education of students' safety attitudes and simulator performance. *Journal of Educational Psychology,* 1976, *68,* 501-506.

Gruner, C.R. An experimental study of satire as persuasion. *Speech Monographs,* 1965, *32,* 149-153.

Haney, J.B. and Ullmer, E.J. *Educational communications and technology* (2nd ed.). Dubuque, Iowa: Wm. C. Brown, 1975.

Heider, F. Attitudes and cognitive organization. *Journal of Psychology,* 1946, *21,* 107-112.

Horai, J. and Wasserman, L. Machiavellianism and attitude similarity-dissimilarity as antecedents of interpersonal attraction. *Personality and Social Psychology Bulletin,* 1974, *1*(1), 81-82.

Hovland, C.I., Janis, I.L., and Kelley, H.H. *Communication and persuasion.* New Haven, Conn.: Yale University Press, 1953.

Insko, C.A., Lind, E.A., and LaTour, S. Persuasion, recall, and thoughts. *Representative Research in Social Psychology,* 1976, *7,* 66-78.

Janis, I.L. Effects of fear arousal on attitude change. In L. Berkowitz (Ed.), *Advances in experimental social psychology,* Vol. 3. New York: Academic Press, 1970.

Janis, I.L. and Feshbach, S. Effects of fear-arousing communications. *Journal of Abnormal and Social Psychology,* 1953, *48,* 78-92.

Janis, I.L. and Mann, L. Effectiveness of emotional role-playing in modifying smoking habits and attitudes. *Journal of Experimental Research in Personality,* 1965, *1,* 84-90.

Kanouse, D.E. and Abelson, R.P. Language variables affecting the persuasiveness of simple communications. *Journal of Personality and Social Psychology*, 1967, *7*, 158-163.

Katz, D. The functional approach to the study of attitudes. *Public Opinion Quarterly*, 1960, *24*, 163-204.

Katz, S. and Bernstein, E. Is an out-of-role act credible to biased observers and does it affect the credibility of neutral acts? *Journal of Personality*, 1975, *43*, 215-230.

Kelman, H.C. Three processes of social influence. *Public Opinion Quarterly*, 1961, *25*, 57-78.

Kelman, H.C. and Hovland, C.I. "Reinstatement" of the communicator in delayed measurement of opinion change. *Journal of Abnormal and Social Psychology*, 1953, *48*, 327-335.

Liesler, C.A. and Munson, P.A. Attitudes and opinions. In M.R. Rosenzweig and L.W. Porter (Ed.), *Annual Review of Psychology*, (Vol. 26). Palo Alto: Annual Reviews, Inc., 1975.

Laird, J.D., and Berglas, S. Individual differences in the effects of engaging in counter-attitudinal behavior. *Journal of Personality*, 1975, *43*, 286-304.

Landy, D. The effects of an overheard audience's reaction and attractiveness on opinion change. *Journal of Experimental Social Psychology*, 1972, *8*, 276-288.

Markiewicz, D. Effects of humor on persuasion. *Sociometry*, 1974, *37*, 407-422.

Mendelsohn, H.A. *The Denver symposium on mass communications research for satefy.* Chicago: National Safety Council, 1964.

Miller, A.G. Constraint and target effects in the attribution of attitudes. *Journal of Experimental Social Psychology*, 1976, *12*, 325-339.

Miller, G.R. and Burgoon, M. *New techniques of persuasion.* New York: Harper and Row, 1973.

Miller, N. The relationship between distraction and persuasion. *Psychological Bulletin*, 1973, *80*, 310-323.

McGuire, W.J. Inducing resistance to persuasion: Some contemporary approaches. In L. Berkowitz (Ed.), *Advances in experimental social psychology*, Vol. 1. New York: Academic Press, 1964.

McGuire, W.J. Personality and susceptibility to social influence. In
E.F. Borgatta and W.W. Lambert (Eds.), *Handbook of Personality Theory and Research.* Chicago: Rand McNally, 1968.

McGuire, W.J. Nature of attitudes and attitude change. In G.
Lindzey and E. Aronson (Eds.), *Handbook of Social Psychology*
(2nd ed., Vol 3). Reading, Mass.: Addison-Wesley, 1969.

McGuire, W.J. Persuasion, resistance, and attitude change. In I.S.
Pool (Ed.), *Handbook of Communication.* Chicago: Rand
McNally, 1973.

Newcomb, T.M. Persistence and regression of changed attitudes:
Long-range studies. *Journal of Social Issues,* 1963, *19*(4), 3-14.

Norman, R. When what is said is important: A comparison of
expert and attractive sources. *Journal of Experimental Social
Psychology,* 1976, *12,* 294-300.

Rogers, E.M. and Shoemaker, F.F. *Communication of Innovations.* New York: The Free Press, 1971.

Rogers, R.W. A protection motivation theory of fear appeals and
attitude change. *Journal of Psychology,* 1975, *91,* 93-114.

Rogers, R.W. and Mewborn, C.R. Fear appeals and attitude
change: Effects of a threat's noxiousness, probability of
occurrence, and the efficacy of coping responses. *Journal of
Personality and Social Psychology,* 1976, *34,* 54-61.

Rokeach, M. *The nature of human values.* New York: The Free
Press, 1973.

Rosenberg, M.J. An analysis of affective-cognitive consistency. In
C.I. Hovland and M.J. Rosenberg (Eds.), *Attitude organization
and change.* New Haven, Conn.: Yale University Press, 1960.

Ryan, M. The impact of television news film on perceived media
credibility. *Journal of Applied Communications Research,*
1975, *3,* 69-75.

Salmon, W.C. *Logic.* Englewood Cliffs, N.J.: Prentice-Hall, 1963.

Sherif, C.W., Sherif, M., and Nebergall, R.E. *Attitude and attitude
change.* Philadelphia: W.B. Saunders, 1965.

Sherif, C.W., Kelly, M., Rogers, H.L., Sarup, G., and Tittler, B.I.
Personal involvement, social judgment, and action. *Journal of*

Personality and Social Psychology, 1973, *27,* 311-327.

Shrigley, R.L. Credibility of the elementary science methods course instructor as perceived by students: A model for attitude modification. *Journal of Research in Science Teaching,* 1976, *13,* 449-453.

Simonson, M.R. Attitude change and achievement: Dissonance theory in education. *The Journal of Educational Research,* 1977, *70,* 163-169.

Singletary, M.W. Components of credibility of a favorable news source. *Journalism Quarterly,* 1976, *53,* 316-319.

Snyder, M. and Tanke, E.D. Behavior and attitude: Some people are more consistent than others. *Journal of Personality,* 1976, *44,* 501-516.

Sprafkin, J.N., Liebert, R.M., and Poulos, R.W. Effects of a prosocial televised example on children's helping. *Journal of Experimental Child Psychology,* 1975, *20,* 119-126.

Staats, A.W. and Staats, C.K. Attitudes established by classical conditioning. *Journal of Abnormal and Social Psychology,* 1958, *57,* 37-40.

Stone, V.A. and Hoyt, J.L. Effect of likability and relevance of expertness. *Journalism Quarterly,* 1974 (a), *51,* 314-317.

Stone, V.A. and Hoyt, J.L. The emergence of source-message orientation as a communication variable. *Communication Research,* 1974(b), *1,* 89-109.

Sternthal, B. and Craig, C.S. Humor in advertising. *Journal of Marketing,* 1973, *37,* (October), 12-18.

Triandis, H.C. *Attitude and attitude change.* New York: John Wiley and Sons, Inc., 1971.

Veitch, R. and Griffitt, W. Good news—bad news: Affective and interpersonal effects. *Journal of Applied Social Psychology,* 1976, *6,* 69-75.

Walster, E., Aronson, E., and Abrahams, D. On increasing the persuasiveness of a low prestige communicator. *Journal of Experimental Social Psychology,* 1966, *2,* 325-342.

Worchel, S., Andreoli, V., and Eason, J. Is the medium the

message? A study of the effects of media, communicator, and message characteristics on attitude change. *Journal of Applied Social Psychology,* 1975, *5,* 157-172.

Zajonc, R.B. The attitudinal effects of mere exposure. Journal of *Personality and Social Psychology Monograph Supplement,* 1968, *9,* 1014-1025.

Zimbardo, P. and Ebbesen, E.B. *Influencing attitudes and changing behavior.* Reading, Mass.: Addison-Wesley, 1970.

Sources for Principles

The reader may have noticed a few stylistic differences between this chapter and the three preceding ones. As noted in the Preface, the first author was primarily responsible for the earlier chapters, while the second author was primarily responsible for the attitude change chapter. Secondary sources were the major basis for principles offered in the first three chapters, and representative sources related to specific principles are cited at the end of each chapter. The second author relied more upon primary sources. Also, references, whether primary or secondary, are usually given in the text. The few princples for which a reference is not cited are principles which are so widely recognized that they can be found in any of several surveys of the attitude change literature. For example, the reader may want to consult McGuire (1969), which is the most complete and authoritative review available at this time. Other good reviews include those by Cohen (1964), Cronkhite (1969), Triandis (1971), Zimbardo and Ebbesen (1970), and Liesler and Munson (1975). Reviews of sub-topics are cited within the chapter at appropriate places.

AUTHOR INDEX

Numbers in *italics* are pages on which bibliographic references appear.

SUBJECT INDEX